Core Anthroposophy

Teaching Essays of Ernst Katz

Core Anthroposophy

Teaching Essays of Ernst Katz

Introduction by Donald Melcer

2011
SteinerBooks

SteinerBooks
610 Main Street, Great Barrington, MA 01230
www.steinerbooks.org

With grateful acknowledgment to the Katz Family Trust and the Anthroposophical Society in America for permission to reprint the following essays: *The Mission of Rudolf Steiner; About Your Relation to Rudolf Steiner; Meditation– An Introduction; Meditation According to Rudolf Steiner; Cosmic Secrets in Rudolf Steiner's Health Verses: A Meditative Tale; Thoughts about the Foundation Stone* © 2010 by the Anthroposophical Society in America; and to the Anthroposophical Society in The Netherlands for permission to reprint *Contemplations about the Holy Spirit*, originally published in Dutch, translated by Jannebeth Röell © 2010 by the Anthroposophical Society in The Netherlands. *Essays on Rudolf Steiner's* PHILOSOPHY OF SPIRITUAL ACTIVITY was originally published as "Essays on the *Philosophy of Freedom*" in *Free Deeds,* May 1962-July 1963, by Garber Communications, Blauvelt, NY. Used with the permission of the publisher.

Library of Congress Cataloguing-in-Publications Data is available.

ISBN: 978-0-88010-722-8

All rights reserved, No part of this publication
may be reproduced in any form or by any means without
the prior written permission of the publisher.

Printed in the United States

Contents

Introduction	VII
1. The Mission of Rudolf Steiner (2004)	1
2. Essays on Rudolf Steiner's *Philosophy of Spiritual Activity* (1962-1963)	23
3. About Your Relation to Rudolf Steiner (1985)	82
4. Meditation — An Introduction (1975)	115
5. Meditation According to Rudolf Steiner (1993)	131
6. Cosmic Secrets in Rudolf Steiner's Health Verses: A Meditative Tale (1992)	155
7. Thoughts about the Foundation Stone (1997)	175
8. Contemplations about the Holy Spirit (1963)	192
9. About Rudolf Steiner's Concept of Four Types of Etheric Forces (1989)	206
Notes	227

ERNST KATZ
July 23, 1913 – September 2, 2009

Introduction

Ernst Katz (1913-2009) was a warm and caring person who, with his radiant wife, Katherine, dedicated their lives to bringing anthroposophy to the Great Lakes area of the United States, ultimately enriching the spiritual lives of many people from coast to coast. They were two of the principal anthroposophists in America during the second half of the Twentieth century. This book is intended to be an extension of their work, making Ernst's carefully written teaching essays available to present and future students of anthroposophy.

Anthroposophy, originated by Rudolf Steiner, is a freshly evolved path for spiritual development that satisfies the longings of many people of this era who have been searching for a path of personal and community development—one that embodies an integrated spiritual and material understanding of humanity, earth, and cosmos.

Ernst, when a teenager, was one such seeker. He and a close friend systematically attended the churches of their hometown in the Netherlands, seeking a source for understanding the essential spiritual questions of life: where do we come from, what is our purpose, and what is our future? They were unable to find anything meaningful for their youthful, searching minds. A short while later, Ernst attended a lecture about anthroposophy by Dr. F. W. Zeylmans van Emmichoven. There he found what he had been looking for: a clear path—though complex and challenging—for understanding all of life and its spiritual meaning. At age sixteen he became a student of anthroposophy under the guidance of Zeylmans, who himself was one of Rudolf Steiner's foremost pupils and who had introduced anthroposophy to Holland.

While still a teenager Ernst decided to pursue a career in science. He later completed his doctoral studies in physics at the University of

Utrecht during the extremely difficult years of the German occupation of Holland during World War II. After the war, in 1947, he was invited to join the Physics Department of the University of Michigan, and continued as Professor of Physics until his retirement. During his tenure at the university, he became one of the foremost teachers of anthroposophy in America, and was quite likely the only professor in the country who taught courses in both natural science and "science of the spirit" (anthroposophy) at the university level. His courses in anthroposophy were taught in the "free offerings" of the university, which were elective courses for credit. Ernst also led anthroposophical study groups that attracted people from all of southern lower Michigan.

In the early 1960s, Ernst began writing essays to help students comprehend the profound wisdom contained in Rudolf Steiner's major works. He had the ability to explain complicated esoteric ideas in clear analogies that most any educated person could understand. Never did he invoke the language of science to explain a difficult idea, but was able to explain it with examples from everyday life. You will appreciate his marvelous way of writing throughout this book. Rudolf Steiner wanted anthroposophy to be presented in a form understandable to anyone willing to work through the many radical ideas upon which it was based, and Ernst became a master at writing explanatory guides for some of the most important anthroposophical concepts.

The Mission of Rudolf Steiner: The first essay in the book was the last one published. In it Ernst explains the importance of maintaining the connection between Rudolf Steiner and the anthroposophical movement. He always began any teaching of anthroposophy with a recognition that anthroposophy was the life-work of Rudolf Steiner and his gift to humanity. Ernst's essay embodies all he had learned about anthroposophy in his almost 80 years of study and practice. It is one of the clearest expositions of the mission of Rudolf Steiner ever written.

Essays on Rudolf Steiner's "Philosophy of Spiritual Activity": Following the opening essay comes a series of teaching guides for the book that Steiner said would outlast everything else he produced: *The Philosophy of Spiritual Activity*. It contains the whole of anthroposophy in a form that requires rigorous thinking by the student for any level of comprehension. As all who have studied this book know, there are many, many levels attainable. Ernst takes the student through every major avenue of exposition slowly and carefully without supplying his own interpretation, but pointing out what the student must consider through his own effort.

This approach preserves the personal freedom of the student, which is a cornerstone of anthroposophy.

About Your Relation to Rudolf Steiner: This series of essays addresses the question, "how can a person interested in anthroposophy develop a personal connection with its long dead founder?" Is it even possible to do so? From a materialistic point of view it is, of course, impossible. However, if one is open to the possibility that we humans continue a life of consciousness after death, then the possibility of a spiritual connection exists. Ernst introduces this forward-looking presentation this way: "This booklet is written out of a concern for the spiritual well-being of man in the future, out of a sense of responsibility toward future generations. It is intended as a conversation, reaching out across future times. Contemporaries are welcome to participate."

Meditation — An Introduction: Early in the study of anthroposophy, one learns that the three stages of higher cognition that can be attained at this time in the course of evolution depend on the ability to incorporate meditation into one's daily life. How, though, does one begin meditating, since it is an unfamiliar practice to many in our culture. This essay presents six forms of meditation that strengthen the capacities for thinking, feeling, taking action (willing), tolerance, receptivity, and perseverance. These are often referred to as "the six basic exercises" of anthroposophical meditation.

Meditation According to Rudolf Steiner: These essays offer the student a deeper understanding of meditative practice. From the back cover of the original booklet we read: "This short study ... intends to show the special place which Rudolf Steiner occupies as a guide for meditative development in the Western world. His unique emphasis on freedom of the individual combined with his wise advice on some frequently asked questions, forms the gist of this booklet."

Cosmic Secrets in Rudolf Steiner's Health Verse: A Meditative Tale: The Health Verses seem beautiful and simple upon first reading. So simple in fact, that it leaves one wondering about their health bestowing value. However, when they are practiced individually and with others, their power is immediately revealed. Ernst shows how cosmic forces are activated through one mantric poem that can strengthen daily life. Many have noticed also that it facilitates peaceful, restful sleep that brings increased vitality upon awakening.

Thoughts about the Foundation Stone: The Foundation Stone meditation is a difficult but complete image of our current and immanent stages of development. It is a meditation for the rest of our lives. Ernst says this about the inner nature of the verses: "Born out of fire, through pain and suffering, that magical formula, the Foundation Stone, is destined to guide the souls of seeking human beings, in the present time and in centuries to come, toward solutions of the great riddles of existence, toward overcoming the great scourges of our time—deep loneliness, desperate anxiety, and tragic confusion—by touching the timeless, ever-flowing wellsprings of spirit-life, spirit-love, and spirit-light, behind which the mystery of Christ holds sway."

Contemplations about the Holy Spirit: This set of essays addresses one of the deeper mysteries expressed in anthroposophy, a mystery that must be understood to fully recognize what Rudolf Steiner needed to accomplish through anthroposophy. The question is, "What is the sin against the Holy Spirit and why can this sin not be forgiven?" The impulse of the Holy Spirit is to join all people in brotherhood and is reflected in the celebration of the festival of Pentecost. Those who reach a high level of understanding the necessity for every person to learn to forsake self-needs and interests for the needs of humankind will have a choice of working for the good of humanity or turning back and pursuing self-aggrandizement. The latter is the sin against the Holy Spirit. It is not an abstract speculation, but one that all individuals will face sometime in the future.

About Rudolf Steiner's Concept of Four Types of Etheric Forces: Students of anthroposophy often wonder, "how is spiritual energy transformed into inorganic and living substances?" Ernst provides an introduction to this essential question by careful analysis and explanation of the four "etheric forces" Rudolf Steiner often mentions. These are not forces in the usual mechanical sense, but represent transitional stages of the origin and development of material substance and life. In this essay Ernst, the physicist, is writing to science teachers. By necessity he must incorporate the language of mathematics for some of his explanations. This essay provides a link between the thinking of natural science and spiritual science. If you are not versed in math, much can be learned by studying the conclusions presented in this essay. The domain of etheric formative forces involves substance, uniformity, transformation, and individuality. Two of Steiner's lecture series, *The Warmth Course* and *The Light Course*, are helpful resources for understanding this essay.

Above all else, Ernst was a teacher. He had mastered the art of listening, the hallmark of all great teachers. Without judging, he listened to the questions people brought him. These essays are his thoughtful responses to questions asked by many people over many years. We hope you will find a caring companion who can answer some of your questions about life and destiny as you conduct your own studies of anthroposophy. Let Ernst be one of your teachers. You will not be disappointed.

Donald Melcer

RUDOLF STEINER
February 25, 1861 – March 30, 1925

I

The Mission of Rudolf Steiner

IN THIS ESSAY I want to give a personal description, not very scholarly, of the mission of Rudolf Steiner. What was this mission? We have no direct mission statement from his own hand. We have of course all that found external expression of his mission, all the practical applications of anthroposophy in education, in medicine, in agriculture, in the arts, in the architecture of the Goetheanum and of many other buildings, in poetry and in drama, in jewelry making, and especially in eurythmy, but also in philosophy and in the guidance of inner development, and more. But to find what his mission actually was we should realize that it was a spiritual mission, an esoteric mission, which we can only find by contemplating what may be called his "esoteric biography." There one finds revealed how Rudolf Steiner's life was guided and inspired by a lofty spiritual being, the world encompassing spirit of our time. In Western esotericism this being bears the name Saint Michael. Rudolf Steiner can be seen as the human, earthly, Ambassador of Saint Michael, who is the spiritual Ambassador of the divine Christ Being.

Significant markers of the guidance and inspiration by Saint Michael can be clearly discerned in the circumstances surrounding Rudolf Steiner's life at its very beginning as well as at its untimely end.

At the beginning we note the following unusual circumstances: Rudolf Steiner was born shortly before midnight on February 25, 1861, in the tiny village of Kraljevec.[1] Owing to negligence of the midwife, the child was bleeding almost to death. It was questionable how long he would survive. If this birth had been normal he would have been baptized a few days later in the church of Kraljevec, but now an emergency baptism was called for. However, the schedule of the church of

Kraljevec could not accommodate this emergency. So the child was carried two miles through wintry February cold and snow to the church of Draskovec, a neighboring village, and was baptized there on February 27, and named:

Rudolfus Josephus Laurentius Steiner

or, as we would say:

Rudolf Joseph Laurence Steiner.

It is significant that the church of Draskovec was dedicated to Saint Michael. It was a Saint Michael Church! Apparently destiny had arranged circumstances so that Saint Michael would stand guard, as it were, like a god-parent, at this human being's entry into physical life on earth.

Toward the end of Rudolf Steiner's life, from Christmas 1923 to March 30, 1925, Saint Michael is in evidence like the final chords of a great symphony. The esoteric lectures of the School for Spiritual Science, which Rudolf Steiner gave in 1924, were a direct inspiration of Michael. The closing sentence of the last of these lectures reads: "Thus may be confirmed the content of the present Michael communication." And the last words of the very last lecture that Rudolf Steiner was able to give, known as "The Last Address," on September 28, 1924, describe in imaginative poetic words Saint Michael as the Messenger of Christ.[2] In addition, the essays that Rudolf Steiner wrote weekly for the newsletter *Das Goetheanum*, during the last months of his life, from his sickbed, are known as *The Michael Mystery*.[3] They are his Michael legacy.

In this way Rudolf Steiner's life was bracketed by a relationship to Saint Michael, by his baptism and by his last lectures. To understand more concretely how this relationship became his mission in the course of his life we need to outline two basic themes. First, the place of Saint Michael in the hierarchy of spiritual beings. Second, how spiritual beings guide human life.

About Angels and Archangels

Associated with each human being is an Angel who accompanies the same individual soul through all successive incarnations, and leads it to circumstances of destiny that give it opportunities to compensate imbalances from previous incarnations. On the other hand, the angel evolves through our deeds.

Likewise, an Archangel is associated with each cohesive group of human beings. This may be a large group, such as a country or a city; it may be a church congregation or a business corporation, even a very small group such as a family. Not all Archangels are of the same rank. The Archangel of a family is of course of a lower rank than the Archangel of a city. There are seven leading Archangels. They take turns in guiding the evolution of humanity by leading a particular civilization to prominence.

According to a treatise, written in 1508 A.D. by Johannes Trithemius, a learned abbot in Sponheim, Germany, each leading Archangel in turn guides human evolution for 354 years and four months. His timetable sets the autumn of the year 1879 A.D. as the beginning of a Michael age. It is remarkable that this was known already in the early sixteenth century. Rudolf Steiner confirms that this indeed happened in late November of that year.[4] And he added that the Archangel Saint Michael, one of the original seven leading Archangels, received at that time what one may call a promotion. He was to lead a civilization that would, for the first time ever, encompass all of humanity. Therefore, in 1879 Saint Michael became the supreme being whose rank towers above all other Archangels. This rank is often referred to as "time spirit." This exalted, illustrious being, Saint Michael, the guiding spirit of our time for all of humanity, the Ambassador of the Christ Being, is of primary importance in the life and mission of Rudolf Steiner.

How Archangels Exert Their Guidance

The way Archangels exert their influence is subject to evolution. In ancient times it differed from the way it is today. For the Archangels of lower ranks the difference is not very great. They inspire their influence into the feeling life of human beings subconsciously while they sleep, as feelings of belonging to their group. But in ancient times the higher Archangels interacted with human beings in a more conscious way. This took place at the Mystery Centers. There spiritual beings, usually Archangels, gave guidance to specially developed human beings, the "Initiates," the teachers. The initiates would then guide the population for which they were responsible, in accordance with the inspirations they received from the beings of the spiritual world. In that way, influences from the spiritual world could penetrate into the human environment. And vice versa, things of the human world could be observed, and in a way digested by spiritual beings. Through their contact with the spiritual world the initiates of the Mystery Centers exerted absolute power over their population.

It is important to realize that the Mystery Centers worked always behind closed walls. One could not apply for admission to become an initiate, like one applies today for admission to a university. Candidates were chosen, and then had to undergo years of cloistered training, secluded from the outside world by confining walls. In such a setting the student would become very dependent on the teacher. The initiation wisdom of the teachers was strictly secret. Its betrayal drew the death penalty. That system functioned for long ages. There were Mystery Centers in many, many places. They were of different ranks, and were led by initiates of different ranks. There were what I would call little Initiates and Great Initiates. Initiates of a certain rank would receive guidance from Archangels of a corresponding rank, so their guidance affected smaller or larger groups of people. There were seven leading Initiates. Each of these exalted individualities in turn gave guidance to an entire civilization. One of the greatest among these seven was Zarathustra, who guided the ancient Persian civilization. Other ones did likewise at different times for other civilizations.

It is difficult to convey an adequate impression when one speaks of these Great Initiates. They excel in insight, goodness, and creativity. The noted French author Edouard Schuré wrote a wonderful book, *The Great Initiates*, with beautiful, sensitive descriptions of their lives and works. Though written almost a century ago, this book is still a classic, and highly recommended reading.

In the course of time, the Initiates in the Mystery Centers found that gradually it became more and more difficult to maintain the contact with the spiritual world. The Mystery Centers started gradually to peter out, to degenerate. A number of them actually closed. Why did this happen? It was the result of the evolution of human consciousness. At the time when the Mysteries flourished, people's consciousness differed markedly from ours. They possessed an ancient kind of dreamlike clairvoyance. We are much more awake in the sense world. They were more dreamy, but that did not prevent them from doing their work. This kind of dreaminess with the associated spontaneous clairvoyance was a condition for the Initiates in the Mysteries.

Gradually the consciousness of people around the world started to change. They became more and more awake. Not right away as much as we are today. If one reads the Greek literature, one can see that they were still far removed from what we have today, not only regarding the content, but the whole way of looking at the world. A milestone in this gradual awakening process is the work of Aristotle (c. 350 B.C.). Then, in the Roman time, the consciousness became more similar to what we have today. At present we are more awake in the sense world than even the Romans were, and this process of awakening is likely to continue further into the future. But our awake consciousness is *incompatible* with the ancient form of clairvoyance. As people's consciousness became more awake, the contact with the spiritual world became more and more tenuous. There was a real danger that the contact with the spiritual world would cease completely. We should recognize that this evolution was necessary in order to introduce the possibility of human spiritual freedom. But the complete loss of contact with the spiritual world would have meant a horrible future for mankind and for the earth.

At this season of spiritual darkness a turning point of time occurred. A new cosmic spirit-light entered into the earthly stream of evolution: the Mystery of Golgotha—the life, death, and resurrection of the divine Christ Being. This is the greatest of all Mysteries, for its impulses were offered not only for one civilization, but for all of humanity. Thus the Mystery of Golgotha obviated the ancient Mysteries, which were concerned with one civilization only. Moreover, unlike the ancient Mysteries, which took place in seclusion and secrecy, the Mystery of Golgotha took place in public. It opened the possibility of a new kind of contact of human beings with the spiritual world, by a new kind of Initiates. This kind of contact is entirely *compatible* with fully awake human consciousness, such as we have at present, and may expect to have even more in the future. This is a completely new impulse. While the ancient Mysteries were disappearing, this new kind of connection with the spiritual world was born. In this new Mystery stream a new kind of Initiate arose, again with seven leading Initiates, sometimes referred to as "Masters of Wisdom and of Harmony of Feelings" or simply as the "Masters." Though in essence all Masters keep in touch with each other in a spiritual way and always act in concert with each other, as a rule only one of them steps forward into the public domain and then speaks and acts for all of them. They each have been assigned a particular task.

Two of these Masters are of primary importance for the guidance of the spiritual life of the entire Western world. Modern esoteric schooling requires by its very nature no seclusion nor secrecy. However, in some cases external circumstances may make one or the other a practical necessity: In any case, such schooling must bear an intimate relationship to the Mystery of Golgotha, the Mystery of the divine Christ Being.

Who are these two Great Initiates, whose task is to guide the spiritual life of the Western World? They do not appear in history as leaders of popular masses. They guide in a subtle unobtrusive way that is nevertheless most effective.

About the Leading Initiates of the Western World

One of the two Great Initiates who are the guides of the spiritual life of the Western world is fairly well known. His name is Christian Rosenkreutz.[5] He lived in the Middle Ages, and according to Rudolf Steiner, he has reincarnated several times since. And he felt it to be his mission to make it possible for every human being, no matter of what standing in modern life, to rise to spiritual heights. His Rosicrucian teachings were given in the form of alchemical imaginative imagery, a form that was appropriate for medieval consciousness. Rosicrucian students could continue with their professional work in the outer world in the daytime, but then in special meetings, at special moments they could work at achieving contact with the spiritual world. In that time, secrecy still had to be required, though this was not due to intrinsic values, but served as protection against the vicious attacks of the Inquisition, which persecuted with most cruel punishments all who deviated from the precisely prescribed Roman Catholic faith.

Rudolf Steiner describes the work of Christian Rosenkreutz as being in harmony with the will of Saint Michael, and as a precursor of anthroposophy. He builds on this past. His first encounter with the Rosicrucian stream may have been through Goethe's unfinished tale *Die Geheimnisse* (The Secrets) where Goethe poses the question: "Who put the roses onto the cross?" Rudolf Steiner labels his first two *Mystery Plays* as Rosicrucian Mysteries, and in his major work *An Outline of Esoteric Science*, the only explicit description of how one can meditate centers on the Rose Cross. He mentions Christian Rosenkreutz and the Rosicrucian stream in numerous lectures and states that Christian Rosenkreutz is an active spiritual helper also in present times.[6]

The second modern leading Great Initiate who guides the spiritual life of the Western world is called the "Master Jesus." It is said that he incarnates in every century A.D. His task is to further humanity's understanding of the Mystery of Golgotha. This is a continuing task, because, as John the Evangelist writes, this Mystery is so rich, profound, and inexhaustible that if all its wisdom were written out the whole earth would not have enough room to contain these writings. It follows that more and more of the Christ Mystery will gradually become known in the course of time. The "Master Jesus" is the unobtrusive inspirer of this growing knowledge. Who is this "Master Jesus?"

Understanding the answer to this question requires a subtle appreciation of one of the most profound riddles of Christianity, onto which Rudolf Steiner was able to shed considerable light. One has to work one's way up to understand that the *human* "I" or ego of Jesus of Nazareth worked up to age twenty-nine on his body in a preparatory way, so as to make it a worthy receptacle for the *divine* "I" of Christ. Then this human "I" of Jesus left this body prior to the baptism in the river Jordan, in order to make room for the divine "I" of Christ to enter into this body, and use it for three years as His instrument. The physical life of the divine Christ Being was a unique occurrence that accomplished its entire mission in the physical world in one incarnation. It was a life complete in itself, after which, therefore, no reincarnation is to follow.

But what happened to the human "I" of Jesus, which had left the body, to make room for the divine "I" of Christ? According to Rudolf Steiner this human "I" of Jesus was one of the most advanced human individualities. This is the very "I" of the "Master Jesus." As a human being this "I" reincarnates. In other words, the body of Jesus was inhabited in succession by two different beings: before the baptism by Jesus, after the baptism by Christ. The "I" of Jesus reincarnates as a human being; the "I" of Christ does not reincarnate, being a divine entity. If one considers what Rudolf Steiner achieved in his Christological work as new insights into the Mystery of Golgotha, then one can realize that this aspect of his mission was greatly helped by inspirations from the "Master Jesus."

However, the guidance of the spiritual life of the Western world by these two Great Initiates required an adjustment when the Archangel Saint Michael, the spiritual Ambassador of Christ, was promoted to become the time spirit, the leading spiritual guide for all of humanity, in 1879 A.D. A third leading Great Initiate was needed as special earthly Ambassador of

Saint Michael. His rank would have to be above all regional Initiates, in conformity with the supreme rank of Saint Michael. We shall see that it was the destiny of Rudolf Steiner to be able to accept the mission of being this Michaelic Initiate.

Three Aspects of Rudolf Steiner's Esoteric Biography before 1900

Rudolf Steiner's ability to accept the mission of being the Ambassador of Saint Michael developed gradually, starting with certain experiences in his childhood and in his maturing years. Three such experiences stand out as important markers in this development. A first such marker or aspect in his esoteric biography refers to his childhood. It is substantiated by his autobiography.[7] From age two to age eight young Rudolf lived in the small town of Pottschach, south of Vienna. There he lived close to nature. He often enjoyed walks through beautiful meadows and forests. In the distance loomed the impressive sight of majestic mountains. But Rudolf saw more than what the eye perceives. Of this time he writes: "I distinguished things and beings which are 'seen' and those which are 'not seen.'" Clearly, he possessed a spontaneous nature-clairvoyance. One finds a precipitate of this faculty in the fairy tale that Felicia Balde tells in Rudolf Steiner's second Rosicrucian Mystery Play: *"The Soul's Probation."* There Felicia tells poetically of a delicate boy, who lives close to forests and fields, and whose description matches closely what we know of Rudolf Steiner's childhood in Pottschach. Of this fairy tale a few telling lines are:

> The spirit-weaving of his little world
> Took hold of him so fully
> That it was no less strange to him
> Than were his body and his limbs.
> The trees and flowers of the woods
> Were all his friends.
> There spoke to him, from crown and calyx
> And from the lofty tree tops, spirit beings,
> And what they whispered he could understand.
> Such wondrous things of worlds unknown
> Revealed themselves unto the boy
> Whenev'r his soul conversed
> With what most people would regard as lifeless.

We have here the seed of what became Rudolf Steiner's awareness of the spirituality that lives behind the sense-perceptible world. But soon he became aware that other people had no understanding for his spiritual perceptions, so he became silent about them. In his autobiography, referring to that time, he writes: "That the spiritual world is a reality was as certain to me as the reality of the physical." It would become an important part of his mission to draw people's attention to this world of elemental spirituality of *nature*.

A second aspect of Rudolf Steiner's esoteric biography relates to an event that happened when he was about six years old, indicating a clairvoyance at the level of the human soul. One day he sat alone in the waiting room of the small Pottschach railway station where his father was employed. It was a rather bare room, with merely a few benches and a potbelly stove to warm the room. Young Rudolf saw a woman enter whom he did not know, but he noticed that her features looked somewhat similar to his mother's. The woman approached him with very strange gestures and spoke to him, imploring him to help her now, and later. Having thus spoken and gestured, she moved to the potbelly stove and the boy saw her vanish into it. This was a visionary experience that puzzled him. The next day at home he noticed a strange silence. After a while he learned that the news had just come in that a distant relative had committed suicide the day before. It was then clear to him that the soul of this relative had sought him out for help. This was Rudolf Steiner's first experience with a departed soul. The experience was important for the boy, but it is also important to realize that this soul in need of help came to young Rudolf Steiner, knowing apparently that here was a human being who was in a position to help now and in the future.

We have here the seed of Rudolf Steiner's awareness of the world of departed souls. This seed developed not only into his insights of what one has to go through in the life between death and a new birth; it also showed the need of departed souls to receive help from the living. In his autobiography, referring to the time when he was about eighteen years old, we find the sentence: "When someone died I followed him further into the spiritual world.... No one was interested to hear about it." It became an important part of his mission to draw people's attention to the possibility of communicating with the so-called dead.

A third aspect of Rudolf Steiner's esoteric biography relates to a most important event that happened in 1879, when he was eighteen and three-quarters years old. He had graduated from high school with high marks and was accepted as a student at the Technical University in Vienna. To make his study possible his family moved to Inzersdorf, a suburb of Vienna, where his father was again station master of the Austrian railway station. From there Rudolf was to commute daily by train to Vienna for his studies at the University.

In the same train, weekly, rode a strange man. He was a licensed herb gatherer who went to pharmacies in Vienna to sell the medicinal herbs he had collected.[8] This man had profound insights into the spirituality in nature, related to the sun and the moon. For Rudolf Steiner it was a blessing of destiny that he could share with this man some of his own experiences. In his *Mystery Plays* Rudolf Steiner pictures this man in the role of Felix Balde.[9] However, Rudolf Steiner had questions that went far beyond the grasp of Felix, so Felix brought him in contact with another man in Vienna, whose identity has never been revealed.[10] Rudolf Steiner refers to him as a "Master" and states that he taught him what one needs to know in order to work effectively out of the spiritual world into this materialistic age. To conquer the "dragon" of materialism you have to get into its skin. It seems to me that Rudolf Steiner may have stayed with this man for a long weekend. When they parted the Master said: "You know now who you are! Act accordingly, and remain always true to yourself." How many people can say that they know who they really are? We should recognize this as an initiation. It is an answer to the call of all ancient Mystery Schools, which is engraved in stone above the entrance of the Greek temple in Delphi:

GNOTHI SAFTON
Translated: "Know Yourself"

To the challenge: O man, know yourself! here the answer was achieved: You know now who you are. This happened in November of 1879! Precisely at the beginning of the Michael age, in the autumn, the Michael season, when Saint Michael became the supreme leading Archangel (time spirit) for all of humanity. This initiation event connected Rudolf Steiner most intimately with Saint Michael. From that moment on one can say that Rudolf Steiner is the Ambassador of Michael, the leading Great Initiate of our Michael age. This was an event of world historic importance that took place completely unnoticed by the outer world.

However, Rudolf Steiner did not immediately step forward as an esoteric teacher. For twenty-one years he was silent. Why was this so?

For two important reasons. First, because there is a spiritual law that states that an initiate must not step forward and teach before he is forty years old. With very few exceptions, esoteric teachings given out by persons before they have reached the age of forty, and the concomitant maturity, are suspect and unreliable. Second, Rudolf Steiner used the twenty-one years from his initiation in 1879 to his fortieth year in 1901 to prepare himself for his task by absorbing what was alive in the culture around him, by entering "into the skin of the dragon." Through his studies at the Technical University he became proficient in mathematics, the natural sciences, philosophy, history, literature, many languages, architecture, and more. Through the cultural life of Vienna he became at home in all the arts and crafts, but also in politics and social questions. Through his tutoring activities he learned much in psychology and education. Later, through his work at the Goethe archives in Weimar, publishing Goethe's scientific output, he came in contact with many top scholars of that time, as well as with a large variety of avant-garde cultural circles and individualities. At age thirty he obtained a doctorate degree in philosophy. You would have a hard time finding another initiate who holds such a university degree. After finishing his assignment in Weimar (which resulted in the publication of several volumes of Goethe's original scientific writings, with extensive editorial comments by Steiner), he lived for many years in Berlin, making his living as a literary writer for various magazines, and at times as a co-owner of such magazines, as a teacher at a workman's college, et cetera—a remarkably diverse spectrum of experiences that made him proof against the dragon, as we learn from Felicia Balde's fairy tale in poetic imaginative language: When the boy in the fairy tale had grown to manhood and lived in a large city, he had a dream:

> A savage dragon prowled
> In circles round about him, —
> And yet could not come near him.
> He was protected from the dragon by
> The beings he had seen beside the rock-born spring
> And who with him had left his home
> For this far distant place.

That happened twenty-one years after he left home, as tells Felicia's Balde's tale. So Rudolf Steiner had to wait this amount of time, which was, moreover, still the last part of the dark period (Kali Yuga) that ended in 1899. In those years he met many people from all walks of life, quite a few of them we might call somewhat oddballs, who had ideas they felt were necessary to get civilization, which had crystallized into rather strict forms, out of its immobile way of life and into a new kind of spirituality: mostly poets, painters, artists. Through all of these experiences, which were often hard to bear, he became able to give his spiritual insights a form compatible with the scientific attitude of our time.

The Birth of Spiritual Science, Anthroposophy

When he reached the age of forty, Rudolf Steiner made a few attempts to awaken Michaelic spirituality among befriended circles, but met with severe lack of understanding and at times even with very strong and vicious hostility. Why did he not stop? What motivated him to develop anthroposophy? This was a great sacrifice that was his response to an esoteric experience about which we are informed through a letter he wrote to his intimate coworker, Marie von Sivers, later his wife. This letter was written when he was almost forty-four years old, and is preserved in the archives in Dornach.[11] There he wrote in a complaining way how difficult it was to find understanding for what he was offering. He could have gone on as a writer, as a literary critic, as an author of philosophical literature, and so on, what he had been doing so far. But for days on end he was visited every night by the "Masters," the Initiates. Of course he was not visited by them in the flesh; he was visited spiritually. They urged him, saying: You have this equipment now; you have what it takes to get into the skin of the dragon. We cannot do this, and it has to be done. It is a task that is needed for the further evolution of humanity. Of course he hesitated. But then, through their urging, he decided to accept this mission, which now we can say was to make available to mankind this new way of connecting with the spiritual world, to speak into this materialistic age of the spiritual world in a way that is fully compatible with modern, fully awake consciousness; that is, in a Michaelic way, to bring anthroposophy into the world. That was a task the two leading Initiates of the Western world mentioned earlier could not fulfill because they could not go into the skin of the dragon themselves. In accepting this mission Steiner was well aware how little understanding he would meet. And, of course, he was also aware that he could not carry this mission out alone. He needed the help of the other two Great Initiates, as well as the help of many people, but this help would often come too little and too late.

We should realize that it is not at all self evident that at age forty he started to talk about esoteric matters. It was a great sacrifice for which we should be deeply grateful. It was a Michaelic urgency that he accepted. And then it became, of course, something that was a part of himself. That is how anthroposophy was born.

I will not dwell on his incredible output in the years that followed. I assume that you are familiar with his basic books, some of which have been translated into twenty languages; with his wonderful gift of more than six thousand lectures that touch on practically all aspects of human life with new insights; with his artistic creativity in poetry, drama, architecture, sculpture, painting, jewelry design, and especially with the creation of the new art of eurythmy; with his deep insights into social questions and into religious issues; and above all, the guidance for inner development toward a consciousness of the spiritual world in a truly Michaelic way, with new ways in medicine, in pharmacology, in agriculture, and especially in education, and more. All of this is impressive, but one can ask—and one should ask—Why did he consider it necessary in 1923 to re-found the Anthroposophical Society that had been founded in 1913? Why?

There may have been several reasons, but I believe there was one common denominator to all of the reasons: The Society of 1913 was unable to make itself representative of the impulses of Saint Michael, an outlook that encompassed all of humanity, not as a uniform mass, but as a living, differentiated organism. The old Society showed its lack of understanding by a proliferation of special interest groups, where certain individuals used the Society as a springboard for their own idiosyncrasies. This is, of course, a real danger for a free society such as the Anthroposophical Society. People enter and gather around some person and become his or her adherents, and start doing their own thing. This had taken on such proportions that this first Anthroposophical Society was beyond repair. It had to be re-founded in an entirely new way. The Anthroposophical Society newly formed at Christmas 1923 has a strongly Michaelic stamp. In this connection I should like to draw your attention to three outstanding esoteric characteristics of Rudolf Steiner's heritage.

Three Outstanding Esoteric Characteristics of Anthroposophy

Rudolf Steiner stated that if anthroposophy in the future became disassociated from his individuality, then it would become a mere theory, and as such a worse theory than some other theories in the world. Moreover, it would then become a tool of Ahriman. This is a first characteristic of anthroposophy. It should be rightly understood. It certainly does not mean that one should approach anthroposophy with blind belief in Rudolf Steiner's words. On the other hand, I know of anthroposophic institutions—I will not mention names—where an attitude prevails of a belief in anthroposophy, but where the name of Rudolf Steiner is not welcome. One may surmise various reasons for this attitude: a fear of becoming dependent, a feeling that times have changed in these eighty years, a wish to place other persons in the center of attention, and more.

I think that one can understand the formulation of this first characteristic of anthroposophy in a positive way through the following consideration. Rudolf Steiner's favorite professor was the Goethean scholar Karl Julius Schröer. According to Rudolf Steiner, Schröer was so involved in Goethe's work that with everything he thought or did he would ask himself: What would Goethe think or do in these circumstances? Of course, Goethe had died fifty years earlier, and Schröer certainly did not expect to find answers to all his questions in Goethe's works. But he felt that the spirit-individuality of Goethe could offer a mental framework that could be helpful in meeting the challenges of life. As an aside, many present-day marriages would run a much happier course if both partners would adopt the habit of asking themselves what their partner would think or do under the circumstances and challenges that life presents. One does not become dependent on the other person by such practice, but rather rises above one's own one-sidedness. One can take a similar attitude with respect to Rudolf Steiner on the basis of one's study of anthroposophy. One loses nothing of one's independence thereby. For he stated explicitly that a truly modern Initiate does not want to dominate, but rather wishes to be considered as a counselor or a friend. Indeed there are no greater respecters of human freedom than the modern Initiates, says he.

If one avoids treating anthroposophy as a rigid body of information, and approaches it as Schröer did with respect to Goethe, then anthroposophy becomes something alive that remains connected with the spirit-individuality of Rudolf Steiner. One can say all of this in yet another way. The statements one finds in the anthroposophical literature have to be understood in context. Part of the context is the audience to which a statement was made, but a major part of the context is the individuality of Rudolf Steiner. He was very, very serious about the danger of fabricating anthroposophy into a tool of Ahriman.

A second characteristic that permeates all of anthroposophy can be found by observing one's own reaction of feelings when one is exposed to any aspect of it. To understand what I mean here requires subtle self-observation. One can then feel in all of Rudolf Steiner's works—whether they be philosophical, esoteric, or artistic; whether they be buildings, sculptures, or paintings; or discourses about history, science, medicine, agriculture, education, or what have you; in short, in everything that he placed into the world—a slight inner pull that tends to loosen one's being from one's physical body. This effect is particularly pronounced when one watches a good performance of classical eurythmy. This characteristic is typical for the work of a Great Initiate.

Some people are unconscious of this feeling, but they feel an inner fear, as their bond to their physical body is their only source of feeling secure in life. When these people encounter anthroposophy, they will react with all sorts of intelligent reasons why this is not for them. They may even become antagonists, or enemies of anthroposophy, usually without knowing that this fear is the true reason for their opposition.

By the same kind of subtle self-observation, one can notice that our culture provides a very large number of stimuli that pull one's inner being into a closer bond to one's physical body, and therewith to one's natural instincts. Many modern works of art, and also certain forms of esotericism on the present-day esoteric supermarket, produce this second kind of feeling. The first kind of feeling, of loosening your consciousness ever so slightly from your physical body, is a subtle assist towards an awareness of the reality of the spiritual world.

There is a third kind of feeling for which our civilization provides stimuli. It pulls the unguarded mind in the direction of illusions, which are liked by many.

Our culture abounds with products that produce feelings of the second or third kind. The feelings of true spiritual science are the beginning of esoteric understanding of oneself and the world. It is remarkable that these feelings are not only related to anthroposophic art forms, but to everything that Rudolf Steiner produced. One could also say everything that he produced was not only meant as a source of information, but was, in addition, a work of art.

Sometimes statements, or entire paragraphs, or verses, are circulated, purportedly of Rudolf Steiner's origin, without giving precise references. It may then be difficult to decide for oneself whether to consider such a communication genuine or a falsification, a fake. I find that the feeling which such a communication evokes with respect to loosening one's being from the physical body, or binding one to it, can be a valuable hint as to whether the communication is genuine or false. One can test things in this way. I want to point to this characteristic because everything that a Great Initiate does has the stamp of his initiation, the stamp of his connection with the spiritual world.

The third outstanding characteristic of anthroposophy is its relationship to departed souls, to the so-called dead, and to the process of reincarnation. Here Rudolf Steiner made a very strong statement, saying that our civilization is on a downward course and this trend can only be reversed in a healthy way if we are able to build bridges across the gap that separates our sense-perceptible world, the world in which we live consciously, from the world of the departed souls and the souls that are on their way to reincarnation. Without this, our civilization cannot become healthy. And he gave extensive instructions how such bridges can be built. There are mainly two topics in the work of Rudolf Steiner that relate to this bridge building between the living and the so-called dead.

One bridge is to read to those discarnate souls whom one has known in life, or with whom one had a significant relationship. Read to them material that can help them orient themselves in the world they are in. That world is often painful to them on account of the materialistic mindset of the living. Read esoteric anthroposophic literature, or the Gospels, or other spiritually inspired literature. This is the greatest gift one can give to departed souls, says Rudolf Steiner. Especially in this materialistic age there is a great deal of hunger for this among the dead, because materialistic thoughts cannot travel into the spiritual world, and so there is a kind of starvation through lack of contact with people who are living, whom the departed soul still loves. There are a few people in this country who practice reading to the dead, some in small groups, others alone by themselves. Personally I have the impression that this sort of work is best done alone. Sometimes, when one has been reading to a particular soul or souls, it happens that the thought wells up: Do I really reach them? How can I know? I find that if one creates after the reading a pause of inner quiet and loving silence, one can sometimes receive a clear signal that says "Thank you." This can be helpful in giving a sense of certainty that one has actually reached through.

I have been asked whether one should read aloud or silently. What matters to the departed soul is what goes on in your conscious mind. He or she picks up the thoughts and feelings of what is being read. Many people can hold a thought clearly in their mind only when they read aloud slowly. So that is what they should do. When such people read silently they skip through the pages and do not dwell with sufficient intensity on the thoughts they are reading. Other people do not know what they are reading when they read aloud. All their energy goes into pronouncing the words. For them it is better to read silently and try to understand every sentence. At first one should read in the language that was closest to the departed soul in life, usually the mother tongue. After a few years, one can read in any language, as long as one understands the thoughts and meaning of the words one is reading—Rudolf Steiner speaks here of five years.

A second bridge between the living and the dead is based on the possibility of asking questions of a departed soul and receiving answers. The questions must be of a soul-spiritual nature, not of a materialistic kind. It is best to entertain the question when one goes to sleep, but it can also be done during the day. The answer comes into one's heart upon awaking the next day, or a few days later. To be effective, this process requires a mental procedure that is not easy, but can be learned by practice. Rudolf Steiner describes this in a most remarkable lecture he gave in Bern, Switzerland, on November 9, 1916 (GA 168). To ask a question, one has to imagine the dead person as one knew him or her in life, and one has to imagine that he or she speaks the question to us. This is the reverse of what one would naturally be inclined to do. One would be inclined to imagine that one asks the question oneself by addressing the image of the departed person's soul. That would be completely ineffective. One has to imagine that the image of the dead person speaks the question to us, and then let it go. Then the next morning, or one of the mornings following, one feels the answer rising up out of one's own heart upon awaking. This is where the dead person has planted the answer, as it were.

Of course, knowing just a little psychology will tell you that a lot of ideas and impulses can rise up out of a person's heart that are mostly merely products of our own wishful thinking. One has to learn to recognize the qualitative difference between such personal messages from one's own heart and the answers that come from a departed soul. In the process of learning to recognize this difference, one is likely at first to make mistakes. But by practice and sensitive inner observation one can gain certainty in this field. I don't write this as a theory. It is my experience that it works and can bring significant enrichment to one's life and to the life of the departed soul.

This being so, I am surprised that hardly any friends ask questions of Rudolf Steiner in this way. One objection may be the belief that he is again in incarnation, hence no longer among the dead to receive one's questions. However, one should consider that an Initiate of his high stature is conscious of the world of the dead, regardless of whether he is incarnated or not. Therefore I consider this objection invalid. Another objection may be that he stated that one can ask questions only of dead persons one has known in life, and most living persons, including myself, have not known him personally. However, he also stated that the equivalent of a personal connection can be established by getting to know some very personal aspects of the dead person's life, for example the handwriting. By reading Rudolf Steiner's autobiography as well as accounts of many people who have met him and have worked with him, and by studying his literary and artistic output, one can actually achieve a degree of acquaintance with him that goes deeper than what one would have acquired by meeting him personally in life. Given this deeper acquaintance, this second objection is invalidated. There remains the possibility of a third objection. One may fear that one may become dependent on Rudolf Steiner in a way that encroaches upon one's freedom because his answers would be planted in one's heart rather than being placed before one like a book. This objection is based on a misconception that sprouts from unjustified fear. One should remember his statements that modern Initiates are the greatest respecters of a person's freedom and independence, and that he never wants to dominate, but rather be a counselor and a friend. That means that his answers are always in the form of suggestions of possibilities and clarifying insights. If one gives proper weight to these statements the third objection appears to be groundless.

If someone says that he or she has consulted with Rudolf Steiner and he said that this or that must be done, one can right away discard such a message, for it violates the conditions just mentioned. Any advice that rises up from the heart as an answer from the dead is never compulsive. Therefore, any objection like the third one mentioned is invalid.

In this way, and possibly in other ways, the work of this great leading Michaelic Initiate extends and continues beyond his death. If you have read one sentence in a book of Rudolf Steiner, you have access to his being, but any question you will ask must be worthy, and any answer that comes back should be treated as wisdom for personal use and not for directing others.

The entire topic of contact with the dead has to be approached with a sound, even somewhat scientific mind. If one wants to put aside what this Michaelic period offers in clarity of thought and insight, then one gets into a woozy world of distortions and falsehoods. If you look at the whole literature of Rudolf Steiner, especially at what appeared after World War I, you will find that it is all given with the notion: Do with it whatever you can. There is no domination intended. But his mission is not finished. As a Michael mission it will last at least through the Michael period, at least till about 2250 A.D. There is a story which I heard Walter Johannes Stein, one of Rudolf Steiner's brightest pupils, tell. As a young man, Stein went up to Rudolf Steiner and said: "Dr. Steiner, in time all books become obsolete. Which of your books will last the longest, and how long will that be?" You have to be rather brash to address a great teacher in this way, but Rudolf Steiner did not blink an eye, because he saw that Stein was serious, and answered: "My *Philosophy of Spiritual Activity* will last the longest, and it will last for 300 years." That means, in effect, that it will last throughout the Michael age. This is just one indication that the mission of Rudolf Steiner, as Ambassador of Saint Michael, is still continuing today. And that implies that Rudolf Steiner must be accessible. But as a friend, he will only act if we ask. And such asking may be justified because even a complete knowledge of his published works cannot answer all the questions that present themselves today, where new situations have developed. So, what I want to say is: It is important with regard to Rudolf Steiner, not to disassociate anthroposophy from his person, but to connect with his person, as a wise and helpful friend, in as living a way as possible.

Final Considerations

One's view of Rudolf Steiner influences one's understanding of one's membership in the Anthroposophical Society. Unlike membership in many other societies, it is inappropriate to ask: What do I get from the Society in exchange for paying my membership dues?

There are organizations in the world to which people donate money, not hoping to get anything in return, for example the Red Cross. They feel that it is highly unlikely that one will be hit by a catastrophe that will require Red Cross help. They support this organization because they feel that it is worthwhile to have such an organization in our civilization. Likewise, I submit that membership in the Anthroposophical Society is a support action for an organization that works towards healing spiritualization of our civilization. To me the future health and well-being of the Anthroposophical Society requires that this view of its worldwide Michaelic mission takes root in the hearts of its members and supporters.

In the last ten years of the life of the Anthroposophical Society, one often came across the word "Outreach." But this has not been very effective. Why? Because there has to be a balance between "Outreach" and what I would call "Inreach," the education and assistance of the membership regarding those faculties and understandings that need to be cultivated to serve the mission of the Society, which is the mission of Rudolf Steiner. I believe that a great step forward has been achieved at present by appointing two general secretaries, one for international affairs and one for national affairs, whose task will lean heavily on "Inreach" work.

So what was and is the mission of Rudolf Steiner? I want to answer this question by means of a picture that I ask you to imagine and by a poem that Rudolf Steiner wrote. I hope that the picture will tell more than a thousand words can tell. With this picture I try to summarize the various aspects of the mission of Rudolf Steiner. It is my picture. Do not try to paint it. Rather keep it fluid in imagination. I could present it especially well because I spoke from the stage of the Detroit Waldorf School. It is a large stage, brightly illumined, backed by a white wall on which is painted a great mural of Saint Michael subduing the dragon.

Imagine in the front of this stage stands Rudolf Steiner, in his black suit as we know him from many pictures. About five feet behind him stand two figures, one somewhat to the right and the other somewhat to the left. The one on the right appears in red regalia. It is Christian Rosenkreutz, who renewed the Mysteries for the Western world in such ways that his students could remain engaged in worldly pursuits. The one on the left appears almost transparent, of a bluish hue. It is the Initiate who is most closely associated with the Christ Mystery, the

"Master Jesus." About fifteen feet behind these two, on a slight elevation, stands Saint Michael, and on a somewhat higher elevation about fifteen feet behind Saint Michael stands the radiant figure of Christ, surrounded behind Him by a semicircle of angelic beings of the various hierarchies.

From Christ streams forward a rose-pink stream of divine love towards the smaller hill where Saint Michael, the Ambassador of Christ, stands. He adds brilliant cosmic light to the stream of divine love. Now this stream of light-permeated divine love streams farther forward, spreading slightly, reaching the two Great Initiates of the Western world. They focus the stream onto Rudolf Steiner in front of them.

As Rudolf Steiner receives this stream from the spiritual world behind him, he transforms it so that it becomes a power that fills the entire space in front of him—the Ambassador of Saint Michael, with a living three-dimensional mosaic of constantly moving little luminous cells of the most variegated colors and brightness, a spectacle that tells, in a secret language of light and love, how the human being can find who he or she really is, and what the mission of each one is, in being active, always true to oneself. Thus Rudolf Steiner, the Ambassador of Saint Michael, who is the Ambassador of Christ, brings to humankind, in a form appropriate for our consciousness, the inspiration of cosmic light-permeated divine love. That is (as well as I can say it) the mission of Rudolf Steiner, which he accepted and carried out.

However, one can ask: Did Rudolf Steiner ever actually state what he considered to be his mission?

In his autobiography he describes eloquently and sensitively all the people he met and what they felt as their mission, but nothing about his own mission. Of course, his autobiography covers the period only up to 1907, and most of his esoteric work came later. But once, on his sickbed, only a couple of weeks before he died, he wrote a poem that tells what he felt as his mission.

Unlike many other poems he wrote during his creative life (which start typically with "The light of the sun," or "The sphere of spirit is the soul's true home") this last verse is a declaration of his Will, what he wanted to accomplish against the odds of the forces that want to degrade the human being to the level of being merely a thing, a thing that can be fashioned to specifications, that is bound by external rules, and can be discarded after being used. The human thing. This verse starts with the words "I want ..." (Ich möchte ...):

I want with cosmic spirit
To enthuse each human being
That a flame they may become
And fiery will unfold
The essence of their being.

The other ones, they strive
To take from cosmic waters
What will extinguish flames
And pour paralysis
Into all inner being.

O joy, when human being's flame
Is blazing, even when at rest.
O bitter pain, when the human thing
Is put in bonds, when it wants to stir.

Ich möchte jeden Menschen
Aus des Kosmos Geist entzünden
Daß er Flamme werde
Und feurig seines Wesens Wesen
Entfalte.

Die Anderen, sie möchten
Aus des Kosmos Wasser nehmen
Was die Flammen verlöscht,
Und wässrig alles Wesen
Im Innern lähmt.

O Freude, wenn die Menschenflamme
Lodert, auch da wo sie ruht.
O Bitternis, wenn das Menschending
Gebunden wird, da wo es regsam sein möchte.

2

Essays on Rudolf Steiner's *Philosophy of Spiritual Activity*

I

Later this year (1962) Rudolf Steiner Publications intends to bring out Rudolf Steiner's *Philosophy of Spiritual Activity*. This book occupies a focal position among Steiner's works. The present article wishes to place the importance of this work in a proper perspective. Subsequent articles will comment more in detail on its contents. But let me first assure the reader about my motivation in writing these articles. I have no financial interest in the publication or sale of this book. My writing is a free deed. The book has meant and still means a great deal to me. It is one of those works that one can reread at different periods in one's life; and with every reading one can gain fundamental new insights. It has taught me methods of thinking I was in search of but was unable to find alone. I know that many of my contemporaries struggle with the same problems as I did, and my hope is that they will find the same satisfactions through the study of this book.

The Philosophy of Spiritual Activity was first published in 1894. What interest can a modern person, living in the nineteen sixties, have in a book that is some seventy years old? New books attract many readers who wish to be informed about the latest ideas and fashions. Really old books have a classic value; for example, Aristotle still attracts a rather wide circle of readers, although his ideas are not generally accepted today. On the other hand, they serve an educational purpose. What once was the highest in human knowledge and philosophy is still useful as a stage to be passed through quickly during the development of the Western mind. Thus we can look with delight upon how much farther we think we have progressed in our exploration of the unknown than did men of classic times. But *The Philosophy of Spiritual Activity* has neither the sensational value of the brand new nor the tradition-honored value of the classic. Then what value does it have?

It is a curious fact that a remarkable number of discoveries, fundamental to our present civilization and our way of life, were made in a certain period some sixty to seventy years ago. Our civilization does not grow according to a smooth curve. There are short periods when many new discoveries of great importance are made, and there are longer periods when the consequences of the new impulses are worked out gradually. The period from approximately 1892 to 1906 was a time of such an unusually strong influx of new ideas and inventions. We can note a few typical examples without which our culture in its present form would be impossible:

1895 (Germany) Roentgen discovers X-rays.
1895 (Vienna) Freud and Breuer publish the first comprehensive studies on hysteria, thereby laying the foundation for knowledge of the driving forces in man's subconscious mind. This was the basis of what developed later into psychoanalysis.
1896 (Italy) Marconi takes out patents for wireless telegraphy, the forerunner of radio, TV, and radar.
1896 (Paris) Becquerel discovers radioactivity, the basis of atomic science and technology in peace and war.
1899 (Berlin) Planck discovers the basis of all modern understanding of the atom: the quantization of energy.
1901 (Holland) Eyckman and Grijns discover the first Vitamin (B).
1903 (U.S.A.) The Wright brothers make the first flight with an engine-powered aircraft.
1905 (Switzerland) Einstein publishes the first paper on the theory of relativity.

Many more examples could be added, but these few must suffice. The point is: It would be difficult to find any other period of fourteen years in which so much originated that is absolutely essential for our modern, completely new way of life. Of course this does not imply that these innovations were made independently of what went on in the time before 1892, or that no important progress was made after 1906. But there is this qualitative difference between a new departure and further elaboration.

The new ideas of that period of sixty to seventy years ago were not restricted to any particular country. They flashed up like a shower of meteorites over the entire territory of modern civilization; their incidence was so abundant that some were not brought to full use until much later. In the light of these historical facts, much that appeared in that fourteen-year period from 1892 to 1906 merits very careful study. Personally, I suspect that the key ideas for the solution of most major problems of our present day can be found among works of that period. And problems our time certainly has. They are of unprecedented weight. We may well ask: Is perhaps this *Philosophy of Spiritual Activity* of 1894 also a new departure, a key to the solution of some basic modern problems?

It is of interest to ask what Rudolf Steiner himself thought of his *Philosophy of Spiritual Activity*. During his life he wrote many books, delivered thousands of lectures and reached millions of people. He knew his time objectively as did very few people; he was personally acquainted with many leading figures in the arts and sciences. His opinions carry weight, even if they concern his own works.

Once, toward the end of his life Rudolf Steiner was approached by one of his most gifted and brilliant students, Dr. Walter Johannes Stein, who raised a question in his usual direct way. Asked Dr. Stein, "In the long run all books become antiquated, but which of your writings, Dr. Steiner, will, in your opinion live the longest?" Without a moment's hesitation Rudolf Steiner replied, "*The Philosophy of Spiritual Activity* will outlive all my other works; it is good for several centuries at least." (This episode was reported by Dr. Stein in the early thirties to a group of students in Holland, among whom was the writer of this present article.)

In several other places Rudolf Steiner writes about the importance he attributes to this book. In essence, his remarks can be expressed thus: There are many roads leading to knowledge, to the spirit, but one point they all have in common: one cannot really attain one's goal unless at some stage one works one's way through to a new mode of thinking. This new mode of thinking imparts full certainty to one's thoughts, feelings, and actions. To attain this, one requires what is given in the *Philosophy of Spiritual Activity*. Its significance is like that of a focal point through which light rays from different directions have to pass. This is just as true for exoteric as it is for esoteric paths of study.

We have noted that the book was written at a time of great significance for our modern civilization, and we have seen that its author rated it highly. However, the question still remains: What good is this work to us, here and now? What problems does it solve or illuminate? As I see it today there are three problem-areas whose questions haunt every person with uncanny intensity. Many young people rebel because these problems are not brought into the full light of consciousness, while the old, in despair, become bored or depressed. Those in the middle years of life often try to repress the problems by the most varied means. If one reduces these problem-areas to their most concise form one arrives at the following queries, each of which is typical of a whole complex of questions:

1. Who am I?
2. What set of values shall I accept in my relations to other people? (and do I really have a choice?)
3. What certainty can I find in answering these three questions?

The problem-areas indicated by these three questions are not new to mankind. In fact, so much has been written about these problem-areas through the ages that one wonders how anything more can be advanced concerning them. People often derive verbal answers from such writings of the past. Some say that their aim in life is to make money; and others say that they want to have a good time; again, others say that these questions are futile and need not, or rather cannot, really be answered. But one can observe in the behavior of all such people that their answers are not genuine, not consistent with their own lives. Meanwhile, the questions continue to ferment subconsciously; they are prevented from being resolved consciously through a lack of adequate concepts.

Some religious minds offer dogmatic, absolute answers. However, through modern means of communication people come in contact with so may sides of all issues of life that they gradually free themselves from the notion that a question has merely one answer, which, once found, can be recorded for all future time in a dogmatic, absolute way.

There is also something else in our age that constantly stimulates these questions in men's minds. The progress of modern science and technology has made everyone aware of the fact that some things can be known with a degree of real certainty that was undreamt of in previous times. The feeling of certainty with which, for example, a skilled auto mechanic can grind the valves of your automobile is a comparatively new element in the history of the human mind. Other new feelings of certainty similar to this are becoming very widespread, and they renew with instinctive compulsion man's quest for a similar degree of certainty where his deeper questions are concerned. On the other hand, it is true that science as currently conceived, considers such questions as out of bounds. There is little agreement in detail today as to what precisely is the "scientific method." But there is wide agreement that the scientific method precludes answering questions of this type.

It is Rudolf Steiner's great discovery—following in the preparatory footsteps of Goethe and many others—that the usually accepted limitation of the domain to which the scientific method can be applied is inconsistent with that method itself. A proper understanding of what we call scientific knowledge leads to an extension of the fields of inquiry, and includes the basic questions mentioned above. That this wider range can be included, where one is able to deal appropriately with these inner questions, is the consequence of Steiner's new method of thinking and valuing our concepts. This is why Steiner gives his book the startling motto: "Results of introspective observations according to the method of natural science." For the average contemporary reader it seems as if this motto contains a flagrant contradiction. In reality, however, it puts a finger directly on the sore spot of our time.

A reader who is not trained in the intricacies of the scientific method, or who has a "mental block against science," may fear that this book is too difficult. But the basis for such fear is not justified. For, as I tried to point out with the example of the auto mechanic, through the technological facts of life everyone today is familiar with the scientific method in a very concrete way.

The style in which the book is written is neither high-brow nor stilted. It is remarkably relaxed. However, there is no denying that the book is not easy reading, but for an entirely different reason. No really rewarding book is easy reading. What is difficult in this book is its new way of thinking, the active thinking-participation to which the reader is called, the new approach to seemingly familiar problems, the holding back with conclusions until all sides of a problem have really been explored, instead of rushing hastily into the first solution that happens to present itself. In our hurried lives we are not accustomed to such careful consideration as is necessary for the basic issues with which the book deals.

All in all, the book is so rich that students who make its ways of thinking their own are rewarded in proportion to their efforts. In future articles I hope to comment in more detail on the actual substance of *The Philosophy of Spiritual Activity*.

II

The present article continues the series of comments on Rudolf Steiner's *Philosophy of Spiritual Activity*, started in the previous issue of *Free Deeds*, which is to be published later this year (1962) by Rudolf Steiner Publications. This article deals mainly with the first chapter of the book, and the comments are intended for those who have not read Steiner's work, as well as for those who have.

In the course of time a good deal of criticism has been leveled at this first chapter in particular. Some readers object to the fact that the views of a number of different philosophers are presented here with no other apparent purpose than to knock them over. Others feel that it is a waste of time for a modern reader to have to plough through quotations from thinkers whose names in many cases have all but vanished from history and philosophy books today. Moreover, the question that is raised at the outset finds no answer in this chapter; it is merely transformed into another question, which could more profitably have been taken as a starting point at the outset.

Such criticism is of course inconsequential if the critic is not aware of what the author really tries to accomplish. In what follows we hope to provide some background, against which the first chapter can be seen in better perspective.

It was stated in the previous article that today as in Rudolf Steiner's time we are concerned with three problem areas of human life, characterized by these representative questions:

1. Who am I?
2. What set of values shall I accept in my relations with other people —and do I really have a choice?
3. What certainty can I find for answering these questions?

The first two questions can actually be combined into one, which is the one Rudolf Steiner begins with. It is the question whether man is inwardly free or whether everything that he thinks, feels, and does, is fully determined by compelling causal factors outside of the "I." Indeed, if man were fully determined by such compelling causes, his "I" would merely be an unimportant appendage. The question, "Who am I?" loses all interest if the "I" is not free to manifest itself in any way. Likewise, if the moral values are fully determined by factors outside the "I" then it is futile for the individual to worry about their choice. But, no matter in what form we look at our first and second questions, we always find ourselves driven back to the third question: "How can we know for sure?"

The usual modes of thought are not capable of shedding enough light on problems such as these. Solutions cannot be given in a form suitable for the ordinary type of reading ("reading for information"). What the book intends in the first place is not information, but the awakening of an inner activity for each reader. It is a book of exercises, designed to awaken the reader so that he learns to find his own way among basic questions such as these. Only by conscientiously building his own answers within himself can these answers acquire for each reader the deep meaning for which he is searching.

The exercises of the first chapter are given in the form of discussions of historical examples of certain points of view regarding the question of man's free nature. These points of view are still widely held today. They are all based on open or hidden hypotheses. Through a careful study of these examples the reader should gain the experience that the usual approaches to the question of man's free nature fall to pieces when one examines the general validity of the underlying hypotheses, when one asks "How do you know for sure?" This experience is one of the basic ingredients out of which the further development of the book is built.

Only after this experience is it really evident that one cannot take up the question of man's free nature first. There is a certain order in which one has to deal with problems if one is to make any real progress. The first chapter helps one to experience what this order is. One must first deal with the question of how one can know anything for sure. The next several chapters work on this question successfully.

There is still another aspect to the first chapter. Rudolf Steiner always addresses himself to the full human being. This requires that each question must be approached from various sides, namely, as many sides as correspond to essentially different aspects of human nature. Steiner had a profound and intimate knowledge of human nature, which he considers as made up of nine basic components or strata, often called sheaths, which contain the true "I" as a kernel. Therefore it follows that any complete approach to the human being must explore nine avenues. It is like peeling an onion with nine skins.

The nine approaches to the question as to whether or not man is inwardly free, form a complete spectrum. Their value is not derived from the fact that it was Spinoza who said this or Spencer who said that.

These and other authors are quoted only as representatives of certain typical modes of thought, particular kinds of one-sidedness, caused by the dominance of one of the nine factors of human nature. The meaning of our term, "a complete spectrum," can be explained thus: If today a thousand people of high intelligence were asked to write about their own thoughts concerning the question whether man is inwardly free, practically all of them would write according to one or another of the nine views cited by Steiner. The spectrum of the thousand essays would not differ essentially from that given by Steiner. The thousand would fall into nine classes. This is what we mean by a complete spectrum.

The student is to gain experience from this complete spectrum of typical kinds of one-sided thinking. Only after all sides have been explored and found in error, can one really feel satisfied with the conclusion that one must search in a fundamentally different direction. The vista of this new direction opens before the reader because of the lessons learned from these nine approaches.

Thus, the first chapter fulfills an important pedagogical function. Viewed in this context, the stature of the first chapter is established in its full dignity.

Let us characterize Steiner's complete spectrum of nine approaches. The first component of human nature is the physical. Anything said about moral values from the standpoint of the physical alone is inadequate, and the quotation from David Friedrich Strauss shows it. Strauss (1808-1874), an erstwhile widely read German theologian-philosopher is of minor importance today. In his writings, he tried to be a materialist and an idealist at the same time. The resulting inconsistencies in his ideas are very widespread today.

The second of Steiner's components of human nature is the biological-evolutionary. For the problem as to whether or not man is inwardly free, the biological viewpoint cannot make valid contributions. What happens when this is nevertheless attempted is shown through the quotations from the famous English Darwinist, Herbert Spencer (1820-1903). Spencer was very influential in shaping modern biological thinking, through his book *Principles of Biology* in which he tends to show that things do not develop by arbitrary choice, but are caused. Spencer also tried to expand his mode of thinking to psychology, sociology, and morality. The resulting "synthetic philosophy" sets pleasure as the supreme cause and purpose. In regard to the question of man's free inner nature, the quotes from Spencer serve the purpose of awakening us to an awareness of an all too common error. The reader should learn to know the difference between being inwardly free and being able to make arbitrary choices.

The third component of human nature is man's world of desires. The great Dutch philosopher, Baruch de Spinoza (1632-1677), expresses himself with great clarity and strength about the nature of our needs and desires. He asserts that desires are illusions accompanying processes in our organism that are necessitated by laws of nature. Consequently, freedom is excluded. Steiner leads the reader to see the partial truth of Spinoza's view, but also points to a domain of actions that cannot properly be described in Spinoza's way, namely, those actions for which we are cognizant of all causes.

The fourth component of man's nature is one where the world of outer stimuli becomes a world of inner sensations, and where inner impulses become outer activities. At this level the problem of man's free inner nature is discussed by the German philosopher Eduard von Hartmann (1842-1906), whom Steiner knew personally and esteemed as an important contemporary philosopher, without, however, agreeing with his ideas. Von Hartmann tries to decide to what extent man's actions are determined by outer causes and to what extent by inner ones. He calls the inner causes "free." Steiner alerts the student to see that free or unfree does not mean the same thing as inner or outer causation.

The fifth component of man is his ability to reason and to direct his actions with purpose. Without quoting any particular author, Steiner points out that it would be an error if free were equated with reasonable or purposeful and unfree with unreasonable or purposeless.

The sixth component of man is the force with which he directs his thoughts, judging them true or false. Truth sometimes conflicts with our wishes, yet we can know the truth. Can man also direct his will arbitrarily, even against his wishes, asks the witty Austrian poet-philosopher Robert Hamerling (1830-1889); but soon he sees the inner contradiction involved in such an idea. The purpose of this exercise is to enable the reader to learn how to discern between the concept of inner freedom and an (impossible) ability to will as you please.

The seventh component of man is his own self as an inner, self-sustaining entity. Man's actions are never free; they are never an absolute, self-sustaining beginning, asserts the German positivist philosopher and Nietzsche-editor Paul Ree (1849-1901) in an asinine argument. There are always visible and invisible causes. By now, the reader should have no difficulty in recognizing that the issue is not whether there are causes, but whether all causes are compelling.

The student who has read carefully has come to understand that causes whose nature one knows are not in the same sense compelling as those whose nature one does not know. True knowledge is based on our thinking life, which forms the eighth component of human nature. It is the special nature of man's thinking activity that puts its stamp on human actions. Steiner agrees with the great German philosopher George W. F. Hegel (1770-1831) that this human thinking activity is of the life essence of the human spirit; it raises the mind, which man shares with the animals, to the level of the spirit.

It would of course be an error to see in abstract thought the only mark of man's humanness. The reader is cautioned to distinguish between abstraction and true knowledge.

Through the ninth component of human nature, man's spirit is able to unite with the world. It is the source of his power of love in the spiritual sense. True knowledge is always associated with this force of love. Those who say that love makes one blind, are in error.

Through the first seven approaches, the reader grows by overcoming errors, at first rather obvious ones, and then more and more subtle ones. The importance of the last two approaches, where the efforts are merely mentioned, is that they clearly point in a new direction in which our problem demands to be taken for its clarification. The question as to whether or not man is inwardly free presupposes knowledge of the nature and inner origin of this thinking activity. We phrased this question earlier in the form of "how do you know anything for sure?" This is worked out, starting from the eighth approach, in the remainder of the first half of the book. The second half of the book works out the ninth approach by illuminating the part that spiritual love plays when man becomes inwardly free.

With the care of an experienced teacher, the author has taken the reader by the hand and has guided him carefully along a path beset with many pitfalls. Starting at the level with which everyone is familiar through life, he has penetrated step by step through deeper and deeper layers of human nature, asking at every stage: Is man here inwardly free? Seven times the answer is "No," and two times the answer will turn out to be a conditional "Yes." For man's inner freedom is wisdom-permeated love.

The nine components of human nature to which this article refers are not mentioned explicitly in the *Philosophy of Spiritual Activity*. Only many years later did Steiner mention his nine-fold concept of human nature in his books and lectures. But for the present reader it can be helpful to keep this concept in mind as a guiding principle in the reading of Steiner.

It is hoped that by these very brief remarks perhaps one or another reader may be stimulated to experience the new world of understanding that can open up through a study of this first chapter of Steiner's book. In it, by examples of outstanding thinkers, one observes how humanity struggles to come to grips with an inner problem, following the most diverse paths. Finally, a synthesis of all the seemingly vain efforts paves the way to a new and deeper insight. Today more than ever before, such insight is necessary for the conduct of life in a truly human way. It fell to Steiner to live at a time when such a synthesis was just becoming possible, and to accomplish it as a free deed, out of wisdom-permeated love.

III

The previous article, dealing with the first chapter of the *Philosophy of Spiritual Activity*, described a "complete spectrum" of nine approaches to the question whether man is inwardly free or not. Nine basic pitfalls were identified. Of the basic ideas that came to the fore, we remind the reader especially of the following two.

First, there are two very different ways in which causes can operate in man. There are compelling causes and there are causes which, when fully known, do not compel. Mainly through the influence of Kant's rigid concept of causality and the success that natural science achieved in the nineteenth century by applying it, today very little understanding prevails for Steiner's concept of non-compelling causes. This latter concept should be stressed as a very essential extension of customary thought.

In the last analysis, all human responsibility as well as all creative activity in the arts is possible only as a result of the existence of non-compelling causes. This line of thought will be pursued in a later article.

Second, there is a certain order in which problems are to be attacked successfully. The problem of man's inner freedom requires first a discussion of the inner nature and meaning of our thinking activity, especially in regard to knowledge. The present article is concerned mainly with this.

The aim of the present discussion is to shed some light on the nature and certainty of our knowledge. Therefore, we should set out from a clearly understood starting point. It is not consistent to begin with some axiom or dogma that falls out of a clear sky, as some philosophers have attempted to do. Rather we should first explore in a tentative way what later can be sharpened into a firm starting point. In this tentative way, and in non-technical language, one can perhaps sum up the purpose and meaning of all philosophic activity thus: I want to think about the observed world.

Each of these words contains a whole world of conceptual mysteries, which have to be clarified step by step.

Naturally, the "observed world" designates much more than what the five senses perceive. It includes all that we observe outwardly and inwardly, in waking or dreaming, or in any manner. In pure observing, we perceive what is "given" to our consciousness, without asking questions about its truth, its worth, or its reality. This perceiving may be passive, but it may also be a willed and directed activity. Our language expresses these two possibilities by means of word-pairs such as hearing and listening, seeing and watching, etc.

Except for small children, very few people are able to observe in a pure way. Most grownups observe through a conceptual screen. Pure observation, devoid of all relations, which our thinking activity has discovered or can discover, is what the Greeks called "Chaos." This chaos of observation is a first given ingredient of all philosophy. It includes not only things but also processes and activities.

Today many popularizers of science try to sell the idea that modern science is based on nothing but pure, unbiased observation. If this were true, science would be nothing but chaos. In reality, science is based on the recognition of laws of nature which thought-free observation could never find. In order to arrive at knowledge we must bring our thinking activity to bear on the observed chaos. Thus, we establish order and organization in our perceptual world. Rudolf Steiner describes this process that leads from chaos to order with great clarity in his Ph.D. thesis, *Truth and Science*, which forms a preliminary to the *Philosophy of Spiritual Activity*.

Thus, we are led to recognize two simple facts as our points of departure:

1. It is our purpose to deal with the observed world, to gain knowledge about it. But by observing alone we cannot accomplish this goal. A second ingredient is needed.

2. This second ingredient is our thinking activity.

In ordinary life, we generally use our thinking activity without paying much attention to it. We think about the things we observe, but rarely do we observe our own thinking. Unless a special effort is made, our thinking activity is completely overlooked in the background of our consciousness.

I wish to insert here a few remarks which, though not present in the *Philosophy of Spiritual Activity*, are in agreement with Steiner's general mode of thinking. Especially today, under the influence of various forms of existentialism, one can hear more and more statements to the effect that the scientific pursuit of truth blinds us to the "fact" that life is irrational and that truth is not known, but felt. I have met people with such an antipathy against thinking that they believe their knowledge is based on completely thoughtless feelings and instinct. They consider such knowledge much more intimate and reliable. Nobody is to deny that people have feelings, and that feelings are sometimes guided by irrational, subconscious, useful life instincts. One cannot ignore this approach to truth. It is, after all, a way that was used by many in ancient times. But Western man will have to find out for himself that by surrendering to his instincts today he cannot advance very far in modern life. Time and evolution have played their part. The world and man are both transformed. The strength and reliability of the life instincts for truth are incomparably weaker today than in the distant past. Man is on his way to reach the greatest clarity of consciousness. This means that the future belongs to those who know the truth, not to those who merely feel it. Why is this so? Because only at the level of knowledge can man's inner freedom be achieved. In this connection it is significant that Christ did not say, "You shall feel the truth and the truth shall make you free." He said, "You shall know the truth...," and this implies emphasis on those activities which lead to such knowledge, namely, observation and thinking. Moreover, the judgment, "My feelings have guided me properly in many past situations, therefore I shall trust them again this time," is not a feeling but a thought. With this thought the person applies (rightly or wrongly) a concept (namely the concept of the concordance between his feelings and the truth) to his observations. Whether this application is justified in any given instance can be ascertained only by observation and thinking. From the standpoint of Steiner's philosophy, feelings are inner percepts. They may lead to useful action, but they are not knowledge.

For various reasons a person may refuse to admit to others or to himself that he relies on thinking. He may even corrupt the language and say, "I feel," when he means, "I think." In actual life today he does think!

Before proceeding further from the starting points of observation and thinking one must study their mutual relationship. It is typical for Steiner's conscientiousness that he examines very carefully what these relationships are.

Here we should pause and examine what other philosophers have done regarding their points of departure. Each has taken as his point of departure some statement which seemed to him "obvious" and "self evident." If this choice had limited validity, so had the entire philosophy that was built on it. It is a remarkable fact that all such "obvious" statements can only be judged by means of our thinking activity, which is brought in unobserved and unaccounted for. Philosophers have used it as a yardstick without first ascertaining that it was properly calibrated. Many conflicts and contradictions have resulted from the presence of this hidden element in most philosophies. The history of philosophy represents a variegated spectrum of philosophies in which the novice can easily lose his way because of the lack of agreement in the results. One may even come to doubt the usefulness of this type of pursuit altogether.

However, thinking as an inner activity has become so complex that successful living becomes more and more dependent on right thinking. But also the right and healthy functioning of the mind, of the inner life, is dependent on right thinking. Thus there are weighty reasons for disavowing those who equate all thinking with the idle spinning of useless thoughts. The fruit of thinking, rightly applied, is true knowledge, which we can make part of our own self, of our "I."

Steiner's philosophy is set apart from all others in that the thinking activity, which other philosophers introduce implicitly, is taken into account explicitly right from the start.

A further characteristic of Steiner's philosophy is the manner in which this thinking activity is introduced. This is not done by making all sorts of assumptions about it, but in the only possible consistent way: by observing one's own thinking activity introspectively, and then thinking about what has been observed.

The motto which Steiner gave to his book can now be understood on the basis of the following consideration. Most philosophers and also most mathematicians start from axiomatic statements that are accepted as true. By means of logic one can then derive a system of "truths" out of these. But the relation to reality is damaged by this procedure. Thinking is used here without observation. On the other hand, customary natural science starts from observation, but rejects all introspective observation. Thus thinking is used unobserved. Steiner admits the introspective observation of our thinking activity. Thereby he augments the domain of natural science by one additional observed element, the thinking activity. At the same time, this element is also introduced into the domain of his philosophy. The two domains unite. Thus philosophical results can be obtained by means of this introspective observation according to the augmented method of natural science.

How on this basis Steiner develops further concepts, and relates them to observation and thinking, will be described in a following article.

IV

Traditionally philosophers have been divided into two classes: dualists and monists. The dualists feel intensely the contrast between self and world, spirit and matter, subject and object, thought and appearance, concept and percept, etc. This contrast is felt so strongly by the dualists that it is impossible for them to find a bridge between the opposites. A typical example of a dualistic approach is Kant's idea of the "thing in itself." Suppose we receive from an object in the world a sense-message that passes through various stages of transformation on its way through the sense organ, the nerves, the brain, to the mind, where it becomes conscious to us as observation. We cannot doubt that there is some cause for our observation, but by the time the message has reached our mind it is so transformed that we never really observe the "thing in itself" in its true state of being. Thus the universe divides into two worlds; the "things in themselves," forever unknown, and my known subjective experiences of the things. The subject is locked up within the confines of one's own self, and at the same time is locked out of the world. Ideas such as these are widely taught today. They make for loneliness of the individual.

The monists, on the other hand, feel strongly that we are part of one single universe, and this feeling of unity leads them to ignore or slur over essential differences between opposites. A typical example of a monistic view is materialism. By starting with the idea that everything real is necessarily a property of matter, one arrives at a unified world view which must, however, according to the famous dictum of Du Bois-Reymond, forever leave unanswered the question: "How does it come about that this matter starts to think and asks questions about its own nature?" Materialism can exist only by ignoring basic questions about the spiritual activity of thinking.

So much has been written, on very good grounds, in favor of as well as against both dualism and monism, that it must be clear to the unprejudiced observer that both represent partial truths. In the second chapter of his book Steiner takes the reader through a spectrum of various customary types of dualistic and monistic philosophies. He goes on to show how all the difficulties arise from neglecting to pay proper attention to the thinking activity as a basic ingredient. Having recognized the cause of the difficulties, he is in a position to remedy the situation.

Is Steiner's philosophy dualistic or monistic? In the customary sense, it is neither. It stands in a new class by itself. But if the usual meaning of the terms is slightly broadened, it can be termed monistic. The required broadening is this: A philosophy is dualistic if it leads to a part of the universe that can be known and a part that is forever unknowable. A philosophy is monistic if it does not lead to absolute limits of cognition. Steiner's philosophy recognizes at every stage of observation boundaries of cognition, but sees in the activity of thinking the means of expanding these boundaries beyond all fixed limits.

If one wishes a pictorial analogy, one may look at the stars in the night sky. There one finds the self-luminous "fixed stars" and the "planets," which change their relative positions and are known to us only by the sunlight which they reflect. Then one can ask: Is the sun a planetary body or a fixed star? Judging by its changing position as seen from the earth, one might naively count it among the planetary bodies, as did the ancients, but judging by its size and light it is more sensible to say that it is in one class with the fixed stars. In many ways one may liken the monistic philosophies to fixed stars, the dualistic philosophies to planets, and Steiner's philosophy to the sun.

Acquiring knowledge is a process, an activity. As we perform this activity we start out with something given to us by observation: a percept. In observing we place ourselves outside that which is being observed. The universe thus is divided into subject and object, into "I" and world. At this initial perceiving stage of knowledge our view of the world is therefore dualistic.

But this dualism does not have an absolute character. As we go to work with our thinking activity and proceed to an understanding of what is perceived, we link concepts with our percepts. This process leads to a bridging of the division. Our thinking activity is definitely our own, on the one hand, yet it brings to light the laws, the constitution, and the relationships inherent in the perceived objects of the world. As a result, as knowledge is gained we end up with a monistic view of the particular section of the world that has been permeated by our thinking insight.

Thus, in actual life we alternate between a dualistic and a monistic view. The acquiring of knowledge is a transformation of a bit of dualism into a bit of monism. This new and very remarkable position of Steiner's philosophy in the dualism–monism issue is a direct consequence of the special position that the thinking activity occupies in it.

When it was said that Steiner's philosophy is neither dualistic nor monistic in the usual sense with respect to all objects, one must allow for one exception, namely, the thinking activity. With respect to this latter, the philosophy is definitely monistic. It can be labeled as "monism of the thinking activity."

By observing our thinking activity we know how it comes about, for the activity is our own. This knowledge forms the starting point on which all other knowledge is built. It leads at once to the meaning of the word "I," the agent whose activity is observed as it is performed.

Because of the possibility of this inner observation of one's own thinking activity, the cleavage of the universe into "I" and world, subject and object, is not complete. The thinking activity reaches both parts and can pull them together. This is a very basic and original apercu [insight] of Steiner. It means that the thinking activity cannot be classified as subjective or as objective. It lies beyond this division. The universe contains not two but three qualities. Some things are to be labeled subjective, others objective, but the thinking activity is of the third quality. Steiner calls it "spiritual." It is essential that the reader should grasp the meaning of the word "spiritual" in this connotation. This word occurs in most of Steiner's works and often has been misunderstood.

The prototype of spiritual experience in the anthroposophic sense lies in the absolutely clear inner observation of one's own thinking activity with this special quality that places it beyond the subjective-objective division. The understanding of all the other spiritual experiences described by Steiner in anthroposophic literature should be checked against this fully clear and fully awake quality of the spiritual experience of our own thinking activity. The title of Steiner's book *Philosophy of Spiritual Activity* is to be understood in this same sense.

What have we gained from all these arguments? If one really makes the thoughts in the first half of the book one's own, one has gained a foundation for real and certain knowledge. One has answered the question, "How do you know anything for certain?"

We say that we know something, that we understand something, if by means of our thinking activity we are able to add to any given observation fitting concepts with which we can weave ourselves conceptually into the observations. Knowledge arises within one if his "I" is linked through observation to the object(s) and through thinking to the corresponding concept(s), It is well known that one cannot define in words what concepts are, though one can point to their presence. They are the "things" on which our philosophic activity operates. Steiner also calls them "spiritual contents."

The particular thinking activity through which we grasp a concept is called "intuition." As we grow up and acquire new concepts we do so by means of this "intuition" activity. Again we can find this term in much of the anthroposophical literature. It should be kept in mind that the term "intuition" is used by Steiner consistently with this connotation: Intuition is a spiritual activity through which we make a spiritual content our own.

What has all this thinking to do with reality? According to Steiner we have only two knowledge-producing connections with reality: observation and thinking. Through these two we can understand reality, really and fully. When one has observed what can be observed and conceived all conceptual relations that can be recognized in the observations, one knows reality. Any hypothesized something that is not accessible to man in such a way that it leads to a union of percept and concept, is not real. The following scheme sums up these remarks:

$$\text{Knowledge} \begin{cases} \text{Thinking} \longrightarrow \text{Concept} \\ \text{"I"} \qquad\qquad\qquad \text{World} \\ \text{Observation} \longrightarrow \text{Object} \end{cases} \text{Reality}$$

The conclusions of the *Philosophy of Spiritual Activity* do not appeal to customary feelings, mainly because many readers are used to different, more inconsistent views. At each stage of his argument Steiner takes great pains to consider a complete spectrum of objections. Each objection is dismissed only after the insight is achieved as to why it is not valid. One particular objection could be raised in connection with what was stated earlier concerning the role of feeling relative to that of knowledge. It is certainly one correct side of the picture that the truth is to be known through thinking. However, there is no reason why feeling and thinking cannot be present simultaneously. In fact, Steiner's concept of a true individual is a person who reaches up with his feelings as far as possible into the realm of ideas. Such people put a characteristic individual stamp upon all ideas with which they operate. At the opposite end of the scale are other people who think their concepts in such a general, impersonal (hence unfeeling) manner that they appear almost as inhuman. Steiner rates the former highly, and hence agrees with a full development of the feeling life, interwoven with the thinking activity. However, one should be clear as to the functions of both in the process of acquiring knowledge. Observation and thinking lead to knowledge. The feelings that go with it lead to what one has recently come to call "personal knowledge."

Where then is the practical value of the *Philosophy of Spiritual Activity*? In two fields: knowledge (science) and morality (ethics).

In the field of knowledge Steiner's philosophy leads to two specific requirements for all philosophy and science: (1) Percepts must be perceivable. (2) Concepts must be conceivable.

Hypothesized percepts, which are forever not perceivable, such as the "thing in itself" that is supposed to lie beyond the boundaries of what can be known, are not admissible. One may hope that in future a good deal of what passes as science today will assume a different form in which the above two simple, self consistent rules have been taken more seriously than they are today.

It is remarkable that Steiner's philosophy permits a straightforward extension into the field of morality. Its contributions in that field will be discussed in one of the next articles.

V

When Rudolf Steiner had written *The Philosophy of Spiritual Activity* he raised the thought life of humankind one full step on the ladder of progress.

What is the essential nature of this step? It consists of drawing attention to the possibility of an inner awareness of the thinking activity!

When a person thinks about something his attention is directed toward that something, not toward the thinking activity itself. It is possible, however, to direct one's attention to one's own thinking activity, to observe it introspectively, to think about what is thus observed, and thus to experience its nature knowingly. Any person can experience this by a proper focusing of his attention. Those who are familiar with the creative side of thinking, for example in geometry, are particularly close to this experience. Steiner was the first to recognize the fundamental importance of the experience of thinking for the entire philosophic outlook of modern man.

Why is this experience so important? Because it is the only truly spiritual experience that is accessible to present-day normal consciousness!

All of our other experiences in normal consciousness are not truly spiritual: they are subjective. They are to a greater or lesser degree determined by our physical organism. In the vast world of our experiences we can distinguish one domain comprising all experiences that are mediated by our physical organism, by the senses, by the brain, etc. These constitute normal consciousness. Then there is another domain of experiences comprising those that are independent of the physical organism. They require the higher consciousness of which Steiner speaks in other anthroposophic works. The experience of one's own thinking activity is at the boundary between these two domains.

How is such a boundary to be understood? An analogy may help to make this clear.

Consider the freezing point of water. Under normal atmospheric pressure the freezing point (also called the melting point) is at a definite temperature, 32 degrees Fahrenheit. This temperature lies at the boundary between two temperature ranges. In the lower of these temperature ranges water exists only as solid ice. In the higher one it exists only as fluid. At the temperature of the freezing point itself, and only at that temperature, the two phases, solid ice and fluid water, can exist together in equilibrium. Thus the freezing temperature is the boundary between two temperature ranges, the range of solid ice and the range of fluid water.

Likewise experiences mediated by our senses and bodily organs are part of the domain we have learned to consider as "solid" observed facts. On the other hand, there exist purely spiritual experiences, not mediated by bodily organs. Of these we are normally not conscious; they are too "fluid." The process of grasping a new concept is of this kind. In a previous article this process was called "intuition." Then there is a domain in our inner life where observation and concept can exist together. It is the domain of our thinking activity. In this sense the domain of our thinking activity forms the boundary between the other two domains.

In order to experience this boundary domain we must direct our activity of observation toward our own thinking activity. The two activities meet and merge here. The result can be described as an experience of the freest possible inner activity and of the greatest possible certainty.

A person who has once been fully aware of this experience knows thereby that man exists as an entity in a spiritual world, while a person who has not had this experience consciously must always be in greater or lesser doubt about this fact. Through this experience one knows not only about the existence of a spiritual world but also about a few of its characteristics.

But is our thinking not determined by our physical organism? Is not the brain the organ for our thoughts? A thornier question can hardly be raised today.

Steiner observes approximately as follows: The brain is the organ for the consciousness of man at his present state of evolution. This consciousness can be likened to a theater stage. The stage does not determine the actions of the players. Likewise we observe our thoughts on the stage of our consciousness, supported by the brain. But the laws and connections of the thoughts are not caused or determined by the brain or by other bodily organs. Just as the stage does not cause the players to appear and to act as they do, so our consciousness and the bodily organization that supports it does not cause our concepts to appear and to connect themselves as they do. Thus our thoughts require a brain, yet in their content and order are independent of it. Our thoughts are caused by our spiritual thinking activity.

In the process of making one's own thinking activity the object of observation, the two sources of knowledge, namely, observation and thinking, become one. The support which is usually derived from the mutual penetration of observation by suitable thoughts and of thought (theory) by suitable observation (experiment) results here in a quality of self-supportedness. This quality is a first characteristic of the spiritual world. Symbolically it is often pictured by the ancient image of the snake that forms a perfect circle by biting its own tail.

The fact that this self supporting experience was not taken into account by other philosophers has been a major cause of their diverse limitations and errors. In his *Philosophy of Spiritual Activity* Steiner confronts his conclusions with a few of the major types of philosophy, and shows how the latter can be brought into harmony with one another and with experience by introducing the modifications resulting from the observation of thinking.

After reading *The Philosophy of Spiritual Activity* one can feel how the lives of all these philosophers are part of a great spiritual struggle of humanity toward the light of truth, and how each one fell short at some point. This is not said to deny their positive contributions. But after death each of these philosophers must have felt as a great burden the shortcoming which he had imparted to mankind. By straightening this out, Rudolf Steiner has not only made a significant contribution to the world of the living, he has redeemed this burden from those who dwell in the spiritual worlds.

In this connection one is reminded of one of the Grimms' fairy tales. In order to redeem a bewitched princess a young hero has to overcome all sorts of tests. Many before him have failed. His last task is to walk a cobblestone path without looking back, although behind him the most horrible and the most enticing sounds rise up and tempt him. As he reaches the end of the path successfully, he is joyfully greeted by the freed princess. As king and queen the happy couple is now surrounded by a host of noble heroes who thank their new king with tears of joy. They had successfully passed all tests except this last one. As they had looked back they had been turned into a cobblestone, and were condemned to make the tempting noises for each new candidate who came along. But now they are alive and happy again, ready to serve the king. Thus our young hero became at once king and a ruler over all-these noblemen.

Our brain is often like the dead cobblestones. But we must pursue thinking as a spiritual activity. As we pursue our path we can redeem in us what is symbolized by the princess. To this end we must strengthen our thinking to the point where external sense impressions are no longer all-powerful in determining its course. We must move in thought according to its spiritual nature. This spiritual nature can only be known by observing one's thinking activity in the self-sustaining manner described. Thus one can envisage at the end of the road, traversed by *The Philosophy of Spiritual Activity*, how new life is enkindled not only for our own thought world but also for the philosophies of Plato, Descartes, Hegel, Schelling, Spencer, Berkeley, Fichte, von Hartmann, Kant, Schopenhauer, and many others.

A detailed description, a complete spectrum, of the various philosophies as seen from this new standpoint, taking account of their place in history, would lead beyond the scope of *The Philosophy of Spiritual Activity*. Even with the most concise mode of expression at one's command it would be a voluminous work. But one can sense at this point of *The Philosophy of Spiritual Activity* why it became an inner moral necessity for Rudolf Steiner to write a separate work of this nature around the turn of the century. It appeared in two volumes under the title: *Die Rätsel der Philosophie (The Riddles of Philosophy)*[1] and in a way forms a continuation of *The Philosophy of Spiritual Activity*.

We do not intend to follow this line of development further. In our next articles we shall return to other aspects of *The Philosophy of Spiritual Activity*.

VI

Man's Free Activity

The most important contribution that Rudolf Steiner's *Philosophy of Spiritual Activity* makes to our present culture lies in its treatment of the problem of morality. However, the concepts that Steiner develops and brings to bear on this problem are for most people so new, unusual, and difficult, that it is hardly possible to discuss this contribution without first working one's way through careful preparatory labors. We must first grasp the new concepts, their meanings and interrelations. We must learn step by step to think them and apply them to life.

Central among these new concepts is the concept of a free activity. Just as a circle is an ideal concept that, strictly speaking, is realized nowhere in the perceptible world, so no human activities are fully free. But in both instances the ideal can be approximated to a very high degree.

Steiner looks at man's activities in the context of the universe. In this context a free activity must satisfy several criteria. In the first place, it has to "fit" into the universe without causing a conflict that would hinder the development of other beings. In the second place, it has to be fully known and understood by the acting person. The current phrase, "he knows what he is doing" must be applicable to a free action in the fullest sense. In the third place, an activity is free only if the acting person loves to perform this activity for the sake of the activity itself. These are three main criteria. There are a few lesser ones, but these we shall not discuss. Thus an activity is free in the above sense only if it has roots in harmony, knowledge and love.

Morality can be discussed at several conceptual levels. The true nature of morality can be fathomed only when it is discussed at the level of free activity of the individual. In the present article I wish to mark the outlines of the philosophic road to the concept of free activity.

In the first part of the *Philosophy of Spiritual Activity* Steiner characterizes the thinking activity from various aspects. The following seven statements summarize the results.

1. The thinking process does not take place without the willed activity of the "I." Here lies the starting point of the path leading to an answer to the query, "Who am I?"

2. In thinking we seek concepts that are related to our percepts. This leads to what we call an "understanding" or "explanation" of our percepts.

3. Knowledge is based symmetrically on thinking and observation. (See the little diagram on p. 40).

4. When we relate concepts, the course of our thinking is known to us most intimately and immediately. This relation is self-explanatory.

5. The knowledge of my own thinking is the starting point for all my other knowledge. Here is the beginning of the path leading to certainty of knowledge.

6. To know our thinking we must perform thinking, then observe it. The observation does not alter it. No representation of my own thinking can be truer than my own representation of it.

7. Thus, I have thinkingly observed that I know the thinking process better than any other process.

These statements form a complete spectrum, relating the inner observation of the thinking process to various parts of human nature. How does one build a philosophy on this foundation?

Steiner's book does not discuss the question of building up a philosophy as such. The "philosophy of spiritual activity" is built by Steiner before our mind's eye as we progress through the book. But it may be helpful for understanding this structure if we single out some of the main arteries of thought-flow.

Let us recall our primary elements. Our starting points were observation and thinking. Associated with these through the observation of our own thinking activity, is the "I" through whose will the thinking is carried on. Thus all elements of the sentence, "I will think about observations," are primary experiences and are understood.

Steiner develops a set of secondary elements out of these primary ones. These are (in the order in which Steiner introduces them): concept, consciousness, subject and object, conceptual content, relation, percept, inner and outer world, and representation (*Vorstellung*). The scope of these articles does not permit us to discuss all of these secondary elements and their interrelations at length. The following comments must suffice as indications.

1. Concept.

Hegel remarks that one cannot define with words what a concept is. Indeed, to define means to explain in terms of something else. So concepts would have to be defined in terms of non-concepts. However, no words exist for non-concepts. Thus the notion of what a concept is cannot be reduced to anything else. Hegel concludes therefore that concepts are an absolutely basic ingredient of all philosophy. The reader should admire the airtight logic of Hegel's reasoning in order to appreciate with awe the very refined intelligence of anyone who finds a flaw in Hegel's reasoning. Steiner agrees with Hegel in the first part of his remark, but finds a flaw in the last part, and thus is led to an entirely different conclusion. Steiner's reasoning has a natural scientific flavor and runs in essence thus: Even if one cannot define with words what a concept is, it might be that one could observe and describe how concepts are produced. What can be observed to produce concepts is more basic than the concepts themselves, according to Steiner. Hegel missed the mark here because he failed to realize that one can observe the thinking activity as it produces concepts.

Spencer followed a different approach. Observation is the basic ingredient in his philosophy. According to Spencer, concepts are produced by repeated observation of similar events. The reader should appreciate how in a certain sense, Spencer has an edge over Hegel because of his emphasis on observation. However, as Steiner points out, no matter how often we observe a thing or a situation, without our thinking activity we shall never produce a concept. Spencer missed the mark here because he failed to realize that one must engage the thinking activity in producing concepts.

In a way Hegel and Spencer are opposites, the former looking for a starting point in the inner world of logic, uncontaminated by outer observation, the latter wishing a starting point in the outer world of observation, uncontaminated by inner activity. However, both have this in common—they are not aware of the significance of our own thinking activity, where these two worlds are joined. Steiner starts from this very observation as a basic self-sustaining ingredient. This leads Steiner to the position: One can observe how our thinking activity produces concepts and how these concepts are then linked to our observations. Thus, a concept is a derived or secondary ingredient, our underlying thinking activity is primary, and we know this through the introspective observation of our thinking activity.

2. Consciousness.

Steiner compares consciousness to a theater stage where thinking and observation meet. This was explained in the preceding article.

3. Subject and Object.

By means of the thinking activity the "I" designates itself as the (thinking) subject. What is "given," that is, present without the activity of I, is designated as object. The thinking activity is neither subject nor object but transcends both. However, as we think, we make concepts our own, we individualize them. Thus our logic is subjective.

4. Conceptual Content.

True thinking finds itself directed from concept to concept through their conceptual content.

5. Relation.

The concepts show relations by their conceptual contents. A notoriously difficult question inquires as to the relation between concepts and observable objects. As our thinking grasps concepts one may easily be misled into saying that if three people think the concept of a circle, then there are three concepts. On the other hand, circles are circles for all three persons equally. According to Steiner, in grasping the meaning of what a circle is, all three people lay hold on one and the same concept. There is only one concept of a circle. With this concept many minds can unite without interfering with one another. This uniting is accomplished by our thinking activity, particularly through its faculty of intuition. And what was stated here for a circle holds equally for other concepts.

Thus all objects of observation are related to their concepts. In many instances the relation between the object of observation and the concept is given, that is, no activity other than observation and thinking is required to find this relation. In that case we say that the concept is "in" the object. The concept of a circle is "in" every circle we see. On the other hand, the concept of a house we are about to build is not "in" the building materials. After the building activity is completed and the house is built, the concept will be "in" the house. Thus we find that some concepts are "in" the objects and other concepts require our activity (in the example of the building activity) before they can be "in" their object. These are not the only two classes of concepts, but for our present discussion we wish to single them out.

6. Percepts; Inner and Outer World.

A percept is the object of our observation in the most general sense. Among all the percepts there are the percepts of the "I" and the percepts of the "non-I." The percepts of the "I" make up the inner world, those of the "non-I" the outer world. We observe that we can have both kinds of percepts simultaneously side by side.

7. Representation (*Vorstellung*).

Steiner devotes much care to the working out of an appropriate concept of representation, because just this concept in particular has suffered through what previous philosophers have done to it. He makes clear what the relation is between percepts and representations, thereby redeeming the "cobblestone" left by Schopenhauer.

As a result of each observation the perceiving "I" suffers a change. This change is the "image of the percept," associated with the "I." It is called memory image or representation of the percept.

Thus, during an observation we are engaged with the object of observation, the percept, while during the act of remembering we are engaged with the image, the imprint, the representation, which past observation has left with us. Thus, representations are part of the inner world. Percepts of the outer world are not representations. This conclusion is noteworthy.

How then should we characterize what a representation is? It is a concept that once (during observation) was connected with a percept, and retains the reference to this percept within the "I." It is, in short, the subjective image of reality.

Steiner's ideas on the nature of memory are anchored here. In the *Philosophy of Spiritual Activity* he does not pursue further a specific inquiry into the nature of memory. This is found in certain of his other works. However, the fundamental notion is that memory images are perceived as changes which the "I" retains after an observation. This is so important that in a great majority of cases, whenever the concept of the "I" is introduced in a lecture, this is immediately characterized as the bearer of the faculty of remembrance.

The topic of memory is complicated through the existence of several very different kinds of memory with very different degrees of consciousness. Although such esoteric matters as reincarnation, for example, are not even hinted at in the *Philosophy of Spiritual Activity*, the reader may be interested at this point to learn from other works of Steiner why, for example, people do not normally remember their previous incarnations. The reason, says Steiner, is that one normally remembers only the incarnations in which one was strongly engaged in thinking activity. This is a relatively new activity in the evolution of mankind, in which, so far, only a few have really actively taken part.

After the development of primary and secondary elements of his philosophy, Steiner is in a position to proceed toward a further expansion of the conceptual horizon by dealing with tertiary elements, such as reality, experience, knowledge, feeling, individuality, explanation, and the way in which all of these can be applied to life. The result is an elaborate thought organism, of which we can again merely point to a few main lines here in the briefest of forms.

1. Reality.

You have no foothold in reality by analyzing percepts alone. The understanding of what is real, as opposed to what is merely imagined, is one of the most perplexing philosophical questions. What for example, is the difference between a piece of metal that is "really" red hot and one that is only imagined to be red hot? To the practical man the difference seems obvious, mainly because of his lack of imagination. Nothing is gained here by the use of a thermometer. If our imagination can fool us by telling us that the metal is red hot while it "really" is not, then we may also be a prey to a false imagination about the reading of the thermometer.

As we think our way deeper into this question we can find ourselves at a certain stage with a strange feeling, as if everything around us might perhaps be unreal, as if we were, though fully awake, yet somehow in a state of dreaming from which we hope to awaken to the full and true reality of the world, into some state of super-wakefulness as yet unknown to us. And we long for this super-awaking, because the world of ordinary wakefulness, though admittedly much more real than the world of our ordinary dreams, nevertheless is not experienced as ultimate reality.

According to Steiner this super-awaking exists. We are super awake when we perform the spiritual activity of thinking. This can be expressed in terms of a proportion, almost as if it were mathematics. Steiner writes: "Dreaming is to waking as observation is to thinking."

In thinking we grasp the conceptual part of reality, while in observation we have the perceptual part of reality. Our thinking activity unites these two, and the union so obtained is the whole thing, is full reality.

I want to illustrate this state of affairs by an example. I refer to the gadget without which our civilization would literally fall apart at its seams. I mean the zipper. Suppose you take a piece of black cloth and a piece of white cloth. You label the black cloth "the objective world" and you attach it to one side of the zipper. The white cloth you label "the subjective world," and you attach it to the other side of the zipper. Now consider each little zipper tooth on the black side as a percept, and each little tooth on the white side as a corresponding (individualized) concept. The moving part of the zipper then represents the thinking activity. It is neither objective nor subjective, but embraces both domains. By its motion we transform bit by bit a dualistic world that is torn into an objective and a subjective part, into a world which is one whole, where percepts and concepts interlock to form our knowledge of a full, monistic reality. As we go through life and gain knowledge, we zip the zipper shut. Rudolf Steiner could not have used this example of the zipper because in 1893 zippers had not yet been invented. However, like all examples, this one too must not be used indiscriminately. It can serve to make a person aware of the true nature of man's relation to the world, which cannot be described by black and white alone. Within proper limits it forms an effective illustration for many trains of thought developed in the *Philosophy of Spiritual Activity*.

We always find opposites in the world of the existing, if we take a static point of view. But in life the gap between opposites is bridged by a process, an activity, which unites them into a whole. Thus the polarity of object and subject finds the answer to its antithesis in the thinking activity which transcends and unites both. Likewise, percept and concept are two sides of reality which the thinking activity unites into the single full reality. And in a similar way observation and intuition are united to yield true knowledge.

2. Experience.

Experience is the sum of all of a person's representations. We have mentioned earlier that these are based on a connection between percept and concept in the "I." Thus, conceptless observation leads to no experience, neither does thinking devoid of observation.

3. Knowledge.

Knowledge is a state of the "I" in which it has accomplished the synthesis of a percept and -the corresponding concept.

4. Feeling.

Feeling is the relation between a percept and the "I," as experienced by the I. It is subjective.

5. Individuality.

Through our feelings we are ourselves as separate entities set apart from the world. In a sense we cut ourselves off from the world through our feelings and withdraw in our own individual nature. The duality of "I" versus world thus arises through feeling. It can only be mended by thinking. Through thinking the "I" takes part in a process that lies beyond the division into subjective and objective, a world process. A true individual accompanies and permeates all his thoughts with his feelings.

6. Explanation.

Through our individual nature we are so conditioned that we spontaneously tear the universe apart into percepts and concepts. Thus the observations as such do not inform us about the matrix of relations that exists between them and gives them meaning. In this way a percept appears out of context. Placing a percept into the context from which our nature has separated it, is what we call an "explanation" of that percept.

7. How do we apply this to life?

We strive toward a union of every percept with its concept. This is also true for each individual human being, in particular for ourselves. Each one of us has what we offer to perception, and each one of us is a different living concept, a spiritual being.

We have stated above that some concepts are "in" their percepts, and the connection between the two then merely needs to be recognized. We have also seen that some concepts require our activity before they are "in" the percept. The concept of our own spiritual being is of the latter sort. In almost all of our activities in life we are engaged in bringing concepts into the sphere of percepts. If by our own activity we succeed in bringing the concept of our own "I" into the perceptual world, to some degree then we do accomplish something very special. We perform a free activity.

A free activity cannot just happen by chance. We can only do this knowingly, on the basis of self knowledge. For free activity, the old adage: "Know thyself" is a first prerequisite. We know what we do when we actively unite our own concept with the perceptual world.

The concept of each man's "I" is part of the conceptual (spiritual) world. It is created, as it were, in harmony with this spiritual world, and it waits for the opportunity to be united with the perceptual world. A proper union, an expression of the spiritual content of the "I" in the perceptual world, can only result in harmony, as an image of the harmony that rules within the spiritual world. By its very nature it can never result in conflict. Conflicts in the life of the individual can only arise if concepts that are not a part of the living being of the "I," but can nevertheless be brought into the sphere of its activity, are carried into the sphere of percepts by actions.

Because the deepest essence of the concept or being of the "I" is love toward all the world, we love to accomplish the union between the concept of our "I" and the perceptual world, to express and inscribe our being in its place in the world.

This is why it was stated previously that man's free activity is characterized by the three criteria of knowledge, harmony and love.

VII

The Concept of Morality

In the present age very few people will grant that it is possible to discuss questions of morality, of ethics, in the same spirit as scientific topics. Two attitudes are prevalent. According to the first, morality is something absolute, of divine origin. According to the second, morality is the result of human values that were adopted arbitrarily, and therefore can be changed, or even be dismissed arbitrarily. It is important, when we discuss Rudolf Steiner's concepts in the field of morality, to realize from the start that his views belong to neither of these two classes.

Just as we have explained in previous articles that the division into an objective and a subjective world is not exhaustive but requires a third category, the spiritual, to which our thinking activity belongs, so the division into moral dogmatism and moral relativism—we use these terms in the sense of the two attitudes described above—is not complete and admits of a third approach. The third approach to morality is closely connected with the spiritual category.

The first two approaches are such dominant forces in our culture that they have succeeded remarkably in keeping any really different third approach from becoming widely known. This is perhaps surprising if one considers the completely opposing stands of moral dogmatism and moral relativism toward one another. However, they are both equally opposed to any third view. The reader must therefore be prepared to go beyond these two approaches in order to understand this new approach at least conceptually. The younger generation in particular has a clear need for this understanding.

It is perhaps useful to delineate first the domain of life to which concepts of morality can be applied. The processes, which are generally described by applied mathematics, physics, chemistry, etc. run their course according to natural laws, and these lie outside the domain of morality. One cannot say that the apple that dropped, according to legend, on Newton's head acted in a good or evil manner. Of course there are people who think otherwise, among them, little children. When a small child hits his foot against a stone he may scold the stone or punish it for its evil or unpleasant presence in the place where his foot belongs. To the little child the entire world is colored with moral qualities. However, this attitude is usually lost after a few years, to make room for the concept of necessity and natural law outside of morality. In the second place, a much smaller number of people are attempting to build a concept of morality that includes the world of physics and chemistry. Thus they attempt to make morality more real by placing it into these realms. Their reasoning is approximately as follows: Natural processes have a tendency to transform order into chaos. Anyone with a desk or a kitchen knows what I mean. Stated very inaccurately, the second group identifies good with all that will create or maintain order, and evil with all that leads to disorder, especially when it leads to disorder very quickly. This is a sad example of superficial thinking. By arbitrarily calling certain processes good or evil, one has not established any relation with the quality that we use in a very real and active way as good and evil judgments in life. We conclude that the concept of morality cannot be applied to the mineral world; if this is nevertheless attempted, this attempt is due to a lack of knowledge about the character of the mineral world, as with the child, or due to a lack of knowledge about the moral world, as with the order-disorder theory.

The same that was said for the lifeless world is also true for the plant world. We cannot say that the wild grapevine that grows upon a tree, unfolding its leaves so as to steal all the sunlight, and thus choking the tree to death, is evil. The sting of the nettle or the discomfort of poison ivy may not have our sympathy, but we normally do not feel that the dimension of good or evil is applicable to such things.

The animal world also is not measured with this yardstick. We may be angry at the dog who stole a piece of meat, but we know that this is his nature. We may even be able to train the dog to be a "good" dog and not to do certain things. At this point some people may begin to debate whether perhaps we have here a first trace of morality appearing on the scene. Inasmuch as we are aiming at a concept of morality that is very far removed from training imparted by someone else, we shall not include any behavior of animals in the domain of morality.

It follows that all processes and actions of man, insofar as they belong to the kingdoms of the mineral world, the vegetative world, and the animal world, and are entirely governed by the laws of these kingdoms, lie outside the moral dimension. Only insofar as man possesses something and expresses this in actions that rise in an essential way above these three kingdoms, can concepts of good and evil be applied. Morality is a human force. Those who deny the essential difference between the animal world and man must necessarily deny the reality of morality altogether, if they would only think consistently.

The entire structure of our social life hinges on our approach to the question of morality. There were times when a man was held responsible for his actions in the midst of conditions under which today he would not be considered responsible because his sanity would be in doubt. When man is fully responsible for his actions the question of morality becomes relatively simple. But if man's actions are not fully his own, if he acts under the necessity of natural or psychological laws, under social compulsions, etc., then morality becomes a difficult and, in some cases, an empty phrase.

The difficulty in defining morality is similar to the difficulty in defining health. Health is a very real thing, although it cannot be reduced to a few measurements. Nevertheless, the progress of our medical science leads people to accept the idea that one can discuss health objectively. Health is not a matter of taste or arbitrary decision. Ideas may differ on one or another point of detail in regard to health. Some things are healthy for one person and unhealthy for another. But these things can be studied and can become knowledge. In the matter of morality, contemporary attitudes are very different from those regarding health. Morality is not considered to be a subject for objective discussion, a matter that can be studied and known in the same sense as can health, according to current opinion. According to Steiner it is possible, with all due regard for the difference between the concepts of health and of morality, to arrive at an understanding of morality that is as objective and knowable as that of health.

It is customary to apply the concepts of good and evil to human behavior. The dogmatist accepts certain patterns of behavior as evil, and they are well defined by rules in the form "Thou shalt not . . ." In other cases also, positive action is commended as good. Such rules are usually less specific as to the manner in which they have to be carried out. The dogmatic character, however, is not determined by the fact that there are rules, but by the fact that they are considered valid for all men and all times. Usually such rules are represented as being of divine origin.

The growing child passes through various stages of inner development. Some time during his elementary school year he is attuned to good and evil through the approval or disapproval of his parents, teachers, etc. These evaluations on the part of his adult leaders become at that stage absolute and dogmatic inner norms. Toward the later part of the elementary school or the early high school years these norms detach themselves from specific leading individuals. Parents and teachers are criticized with the same merciless yardstick as are others. The norms that were previously connected with leading adults change and can become deep inner religious moral norms. In essence they are still experienced as dogmatic norms. Usually during the high school age the student begins to realize that there are and were other cultures than our own, where people strongly believed in moral values that are radically different from those alive in our present culture here and now. This is the time when many outgrow moral dogmatism, but soon find themselves behaving as moral relativists of various shades. They appreciate the fact that any and all moral codes of the various cultures one can study in history and in anthropology have been formulated and set up by human beings. They cannot fail to see that in many essentials these moral codes differ among one another. Thus a challenge arises to find one's own position in the matter of morality. Is the latter merely a code of behavior set by ruling monarchs or majorities? Is it a tradition, largely based on superstition? Or is it perhaps the result of economic needs or the struggle for survival? Or is it perhaps some chemical force, locked away secretly in our genetic code? The college student does not have much time to ponder such questions. He may even have given up hope of ever finding a solution. He may find books where it is clearly proved that the question is meaningless and cannot be answered.

Thus moral relativism arises. Morality becomes a code, a set of values, chosen in some arbitrary way, out of motivations and reasons or causes that are rooted in laws of nature, economics, psychology, etc., but not in morality as such. If you know to what set of values, to what moral code, a man subscribes in his actions, you can predict his behavior. That has a certain practical importance. The usual response that one gets if one attempts to describe the approach to morality of Rudolf Steiner's *Philosophy of Spiritual Activity* is: What is the set of values advocated in that book? It takes a long time then, at best, to explain to the inquirer that there is a higher level of discussion of the problem of morality than the level of sets of values; that consequently the *Philosophy of Spiritual Activity* cannot be characterized by any fixed set of values.

The reason for this state of affairs is the uniqueness of every individual and every moment.

The uniqueness of the individual self is expressed by the word "I," that word which each one can only apply to himself, not to another. It is the agent who, according to the first part of the *Philosophy of Spiritual Activity*, performs the thinking activity, and who, according to the second part, performs our willed actions.

The uniqueness of every moment, for each "I," is given by the fact that he accumulates experience, that he lives now in this culture, but perhaps at a certain time learns about other cultures, that it is now winter, then summer, that the stars never occupy the same position twice. Heraclitus, the ancient Greek philosopher expressed this, by saying: "You cannot swim twice in the same wave."

If one appreciates the uniqueness of every moment and of every individual, then one can act creatively; otherwise one acts routinely. Routine action will generally be regulated by a moral code, created by an individual at some time. How was it created? The thinking activity, by means of its intuition, grasped a concept. All laws and rules and codes are first grasped as concept, then formulated. This conceptualizing did not take place arbitrarily, by chance. It was the creative answer of a human being to the challenge of a particular situation, a unique individual in a unique place, time, and conceptual perspective.

The grasping of a concept for moral action is just as intuitive as the grasping of a concept for knowledge. But the "I" performs the spiritual activity in both cases somewhat differently. If we could, as a distant ideal, completely grasp at every instant the uniqueness of the universe at that instant and the uniqueness of our own "I" at that moment within the universe, that is, within our society, within history, etc. then with this wisdom we could grasp a concept for moral action anew at every moment. The result would be actions which are free, in the sense of the "Philosophy of Spiritual Activity." These actions would be carried out with a sense of complete identification of the "I" with them. That is, the "I" brings its power of spiritual love to bear in carrying out actions of this kind. In philosophic language, the concept of moral action which we have here indicated is termed "ethical individualism."

The human being passes through various stages of development with regard to his relation to the concepts of good and evil, of morality. Parents, the school, and society influence these to the stage of moral dogmatism or that of moral relativism. In principle, the final stage of this development can be brought about only by each individual for himself, and that ultimate stage is ethical individualism.

The concepts of ethical individualism form a distant ideal for human development. Most people today do not see beyond moral dogmatism and moral relativism. They have difficulty in understanding what is meant. Misconceptions and objections can arise, some of which will be discussed in a future article. Suffice it here to stress again that, by their very nature, free moral actions cannot clash or interfere with one another. Where there is conflict there is lack of free spiritual activity. And, since all existing moral codes and laws are the result of the free spiritual activity of the individuals who conceived them, it is in the very nature of the free spiritual activity of any individual that it does not run into conflict with these.

For the right conceiving of morally good actions, wisdom is necessary; for the right carrying out, love is required. These two qualities merge into wisdom-filled love. The wisdom raises the love, which can work at many levels, to the level of the spirit. This leads to the conceiving of the actions in harmony with the spiritual world, and this is what keeps them free from conflict. The love raises the wisdom from a state of mere brilliance to a light that is inwardly permeated by warmth. And now let is close this article on this harmonious note, and wish our readers a Merry Christmas and a Happy New Year!

VIII
The Law of the Free Spirit

In the previous article we sketched the concept of morality which Rudolf Steiner develops in the *Philosophy of Spiritual Activity*. It is based on the recognition of the uniqueness of each moment and of each individual "I." If we could, as a distant ideal, completely grasp at every moment the uniqueness of the world at that instant and the uniqueness of our "I" as it is at that same instant within the world, that is, within our society, within history, etc., then with this wisdom we could grasp a concept for moral action anew at every moment. Such actions would at the same time be free in the sense of the *Philosophy of Spiritual Activity*.

This distant ideal can be approached gradually. Some people perform only a few free moral actions in a lifetime. Others may perform actions which are at least partially free. If one wishes to find out in any given case to what degree an action that has been performed was a free moral action in the sense of the *Philosophy of Spiritual Activity*, then it is not sufficient merely to describe the action objectively. A given action can be performed under the influence of very diverse motivations.

For example, a man may support a particular charitable cause because it enhances his social prestige and the gift is deductable from his income tax. Or he may do so simply because in his locality this is considered to be the thing to do (conformity). Or his religion may demand this action from him. Or his social conscience may dictate his decision. In all these instances the action would not be one of ethical individualism.

It may also be, however, that he performs the same action freely. That is, he understands to a degree the nature of the charitable cause; he views this in the context of the world insofar as he knows it, and in the context of his own life as he knows it; it becomes his very own concern to support this cause. He feels that it is part of the dignity of his life that he is able to do this, and therefore he does it at that moment with the fire of his whole inner selfhood, because he feels that this action is a living part of his being. He loves the action, and any other action would make his individual "I" feel stunted.

For an external observer this action would be indistinguishable from a similar unfree one. But for the person himself and for anyone whose understanding goes deeper than the external facts and also encompasses the motivations, there is a whole world of difference between the two.

To the ethical individualist, life is like a musical composition in the process of becoming. It is creative at every moment. Although what follows is consistent with what went before, the later cannot be derived from the earlier. Each composer, even when starting similarly, goes on to make a different work out of it. Even as the musical composer is free in the aesthetic sphere, so the ethical individualist is free in the moral sphere.

The casual observer may raise many objections against the ideas of ethical individualism. It is well to consider some of these here in the spirit of the *Philosophy of Spiritual Activity*. They all arise out of a misunderstanding of what is meant by ethical individualism.

A first objection can be stated thus: It appears that Steiner's view of morality favors non-conformist behavior; however, it is not good always to act "different." Such a remark is based on a misunderstanding. The ethical individualist attaches no absolute value to "being different," to non-conformity as such. Neither does he attach an absolute value to conformity as such. He does not attach absolute values to any abstraction disconnected from the uniqueness of each moment in real life. He has the good sense to see the potential value of both conformity and non-conformity, and he decides for each action what he feels as most appropriate in the world context in which his action is to occur. Indeed his actions will often be indistinguishable externally from those of the conformist. But for the ethical individualist the idea of conformity is not a compelling force. Hence, sometimes he will act in a nonconformist manner; he will inaugurate progress or renewal. For all progress and renewal is due to non-conformist action. An ethics based on conformity alone is an ethics of the status-quo, of stagnation, and can never be fruitful in the ever-changing conditions of actual life. An ethics based on non-conformity alone is not fruitful either. We must use free personal judgment as to when to apply the one or the other.

A second objection fears that the ethical individualist is a dangerous individual, because he does not accept the binding force of social regulations. This misunderstanding arises from a deep-rooted prejudice, namely that no man will behave in accordance with laws and social regulations unless these are enforced so as to become compelling, or binding forces. It was pointed out previously that the free actions of the ethical individualist cannot lead to conflict. The free individual either accepts the law as a manmade, useful part of the universe in which he lives, or he may undertake legal steps to bring about a change in the laws if he feels that such a change is timely, or he may emigrate to another part of the world where the laws are more in accord with what he considers necessary. The *Philosophy of Spiritual Activity* is very explicit in stating that: "... the free spirit never needs to act in direct conflict with the laws of society."

But in the world do we not see what happens when law enforcement is not in strict hands? People from whom one would least expect it, take all sorts of liberties. This certainly is true. But these people have not yet ascended to the level of ethical individualism. The stage of ethical individualism is a stage of human development. Nature and nurture develop the human being up to a point. If that were all, man would not be a free spirit; he could not act freely and morally in the sense of the *Philosophy of Spiritual Activity*. He would have to be bound by rules which regulate his behavior outwardly by means of all sorts of overt and hidden compulsions. However, one of the most wonderful mysteries of creation that one can become aware of, is that man has the possibility, from a certain point in his development onward, of raising himself more and more to the stage of a free human being, living and acting out of the moral intuitions with which he is able to answer the world at each moment. In the physical world one cannot pull oneself up by one's own bootstraps. However, in the spiritual world this is the rule.

The human being is not born fully prepared to act out of moral intuitions as an ethical individualist. He has the potential to reach that level later, provided the spark is not extinguished. As long as man is not yet at this level, the existence and maintenance of laws and regulations in a compelling form are necessary, useful, and beneficial for his further development. However, what is useful at the earlier level loses its compelling character at the level of ethical individualism.

A third objection might run thus: Is not the free ethical individualist really a very inconsistent and whimsical figure, because at every moment he must generate anew intuitive love for whatever he carries out? Today his moral intuition may lead him in one direction, tomorrow in another. This again is a misunderstanding of the nature of moral intuition, which in reality takes into account not only the spatial world around us but also the world of time. Both the world and the "I" change with time in a consistent manner, and thus moral intuitions cannot be inconsistent with the past. They do possess a flexibility and adaptability that allows for greater consistency with the past than any routine behavior. A study of Steiner's biography shows clearly a highly consistent life pattern, and thus affords perhaps one of the best examples to counter this misunderstanding.

A fourth objection could be that the ethical individualist is likely to be a very selfish person, of the type known as a "rugged individualist," because he is so much concerned with self development. Underlying this objection is the notion that one who develops himself can do so only at the expense of his environment, while one who is truly good must sacrifice himself to his surroundings. Ideas like these are derived from an unfree state of development. It is not true that self development necessarily exists at the expense of the environment. For the ethical individualist, the situation is more aptly characterized by the old saying: "When the rose adorns itself, it also adorns the garden." To bring out the best in a man requires conscious efforts by himself, but the resulting development, if rightly understood, does not make him indifferent to his surroundings. Rather he becomes a stimulus to his surroundings that other people also rise to what their innate possibilities contain as silent promise. The deeds of true goodness do not impoverish the "I" but rather awaken it to its full life.

A fifth objection is that the ethical individualist may be expected to neglect his duty because he does not recognize it as the true basis of ethical judgment. Kant set up duty as the great norm to which the individual must subject himself, silencing personal inclinations. According to Kant, a man should act so that the ideas underlying his actions are valid for all people. To accept this as a norm is indeed the end of all individual action. Duty can be conceived at many levels and the level at which Kant conceives it is certainly not the highest. Previously, Schiller remarked ironically that he was afraid he did not stand very high on the scale of virtue because he so often did what duty prescribed, with enthusiasm instead of with a sour taste in his mouth. The personal touch has value, and this is different for different individuals. The ethical individualist will not derive the concept of duty from a world picture in which all people are interchangeable. He will reckon with the world as well as with his "I." Thus, as it is raised to a more complete recognition of existence the concept of duty loses its abstract impersonal quality and dissolves in the more encompassing concept of moral intuition.

A sixth objection is that the ethical individualist must be a fanatic because he is completely given to some idea that took hold of him. Nothing could be farther from the truth. While the fanatic is indeed possessed by an idea, the ethical individualist possesses ideas. The fanatic therefore is intent upon holding fast to a picture of the world that is distorted by the singleness of his idea. The ethical individualist constantly tries to adjust and enrich his picture of the world in order to make it as true as possible. The fanatic will attempt to shun or to eliminate individuals whose ideas do not agree with his. The ethical individualist is intent on understanding other ideas, each in their context, and on rising to concepts which will make possible the coexistence of individual differences through insight.

The nature of free moral activity was formulated by Steiner in clear philosophical language. Thus it became explicit knowledge. But in terms of implicit knowledge many leading personalities in history were to a greater or lesser degree ethical individualists, and this is also true today. Such personalities know how to bring themselves into accord with the forces surrounding them. It is easy to misinterpret all their actions as being the result of compelling motives such as excessive greed, vanity, power hunger, lust for adventure, and other selfish drives. The habit of interpreting their reasons for action only within the framework of compulsion is in some instances insufficient to match the true inner facts. But this habit results in an outlook on history as a patchwork of accidental irregularities. On the other hand, an outlook is possible that sees history as a series of moral intuitions: how certain individuals knew what they were doing and worked in a new direction with wisdom and with complete but free identification of their "I" with their actions. Moses, Leonardo da Vinci, Columbus, William the Silent, Lincoln, and too many others to name them all, are in this class. Enough is known about many of them to make clear that they were no fanatics but had achieved a great deal of ethical individualism in the sense of the *Philosophy of Spiritual Activity*.

A last objection against ethical individualism may be that it is a utopian ideal that does not permit realization in the world because the world is full of conflict, and one cannot live without running into it. Whenever a new idea has arisen, conservative forces have waged war against it in one form or another. Even as a circle is an idea that cannot, strictly speaking, be realized in the world but can be approximated and is therefore a useful concept, so ethical individualism is a distant ideal that can only be approached gradually, yet it is a useful idea without which the ethical side of man would miss an essential ingredient. The force of moral intuition is such that it resolves conflicts, but other forces may make its application difficult. It is a question of optimism or pessimism, whether or not one is inclined to believe that the force of ethical individualism has a future. But we must rise above mere optimism or pessimism and think the problem through most carefully. The *Philosophy of Spiritual Activity* devotes an entire chapter to this antithesis. It is important not to confuse conflict with suffering. The *Philosophy of Spiritual Activity* devotes careful attention to the whole problem of suffering versus pleasure in connection with the motivation of actions. Even in the case of the most elementary desires and needs man accepts a certain amount of suffering in order to achieve his goals. Certainly a man with knowledge of the world as it is, is fully aware of possible sufferings, difficulties, and counter forces, when he grasps a moral intuition. Moral intuition expands the view, and to this view the difficulties are as much part of his motivation as the goal. Because he accepts the difficulties as a necessary part of his actions—for he is a realistic person—they are not a conflict in the ordinary sense. The ethical individualist tries to resolve antagonistic forces in the only possible way, by educating them toward insight and truth. The clearest examples in answer to this last objection are found in the descriptions of the life of Christ. From the viewpoint of the unfree, his opponents were in conflict with him. From his side, he was inaugurating a further step toward insight and human dignity, and was educating those around him in this new direction. He knew the impending suffering, but accepted it as part of what he came to earth for. From his standpoint this therefore was not a conflict. The *Philosophy of Spiritual Activity* does not mention Christ. It does not touch upon issues that tend to arouse passionate stands in many readers, such as matters connected with religion often do. It tries to educate the reader to deeper insight into man's stature. But later works of Steiner seem to warrant the view that the above comment is not inconsistent with his understanding of the problem of conflicts.

The discussion of the last three objections in particular has led us far afield into domains of life well beyond philosophy as such. It is reasonable to ask how the idea of moral intuition worked itself out in Steiner's own life.

In our discussion we have remarked that a new view of history is possible, for which the nucleus is contained in the *Philosophy of Spiritual Activity*. And indeed, Steiner elaborated this in numerous lecture courses.

It was also pointed out that through nature and nurture the human being has to grow up to a certain point of maturity before he is able to act as a really autonomous "I" and thus can become an ethical individualist through further self-development. This growth has to be guided carefully so as not to extinguish the spark of the "I." There is a certain parallelism between historical development and the growth of a child toward adulthood. Before the time of ethical individualism, history shows periods of rigid "moral" laws, in what would properly be called a pre-ethical stage. Likewise, there is a period in child growth where authority serves a positive function, to be outgrown later. One can observe today how very many young people don't know what they want to do in life. In Steiner's educational work, which is another free development for which many thought-seeds can be found in the *Philosophy of Spiritual Activity*, we find very clear conclusions to the effect that lack of authority or the soul-vacuum which all-permissiveness causes, especially during the elementary school age, leads to just these uncertainties in adult life.

It is not the purpose of the present series of articles to enter into a discussion of Rudolf Steiner's educational work. We merely intended to show that an inner and consistent connection exists between the latter and the *Philosophy of Spiritual Activity*.

Rudolf Steiner's ethical individualism was not confined to his own person. He wished to contribute to raising the dignity of man from the level of compulsion to the exclusively human level of moral intuition. His own life is an illustration of how moral intuition works, how it tends to fit itself into the world. In his life this often took the form of someone coming to him with a question, a request for help or advice. The inquirer would then find to his surprise that Steiner had accumulated skills and information for years, which now suddenly found a field of fruitful application.

Thus one can characterize Steiner's life as one of self-development and active service. He adorned the garden of civilization with what he recognized as its most urgent needs. But his many-sided contributions in fields of the arts, of education, agriculture, and many others all have as one of their pivotal points the *Philosophy of Spiritual Activity*. In it we read: "To live in the love toward one's actions and to let the other person's volition live in one's understanding is the basic law of the free human being."

Steiner rarely spoke of purely personal matters. The mission and purpose that he had undertaken shone out into the world through his free deeds, rather than out of words of personal self-concern. But near the end of his life, he once characterized his personal destiny in beautiful words, which at the same time sum up the essence of the idea of moral intuition as the spirit-union of the cosmos and the unfolding "I" as meant in the *Philosophy of Spiritual Activity*, thus:

> I want with Cosmic Spirit
> To enthuse each human being
> That a flame he may become
> And fiery will unfold
> His being innermost.
>
> The other ones, they strive to
> Take from Cosmic Waters what
> Will extinguish flames
> And pour paralysis
> Into all inner being.
>
> O joy, when human being's flame
> Is blazing, even while at rest!
> O bitter pain, when the human thing
> Is put in bonds where it wants to stir!

(translation by E.K.)

IX

Prediction and Retrodiction

Rudolf Steiner's *Philosophy of Spiritual Activity* sparkles with many fundamental new ideas. Some of these are very difficult for the contemporary mind to grasp. The purpose of the present article is to discuss one of these ideas, by focusing attention on it more extensively than is done in Steiner's book. We are concerned with the idea that may be named the "principle of causal asymmetry of time." Let us first explain what this means.

The contemporary mind follows reasoning such as this with ease: If a process is intelligible to our thinking, it is governed by certain causal laws. These laws are what we grasp in thinking about the process. If we understand the laws of a process we can, starting from certain initial conditions, predict what will follow.

For example, if we understand the law of gravity we can *predict* where a stone will strike the ground when it is thrown from a certain place with a certain velocity in a certain direction. In a similar way a large part of the scientific knowledge of today is used to predict what will happen at a later time on the basis of what is known to happen at an earlier time. Thus causality enables us to predict.

However, there is yet another aspect to causality and the laws of nature. In terms of our example, if one knows where the stone landed, with what speed and at what angle it came down, then one can trace its path backward and reconstruct the place from which it must have been launched. This working backward in time is called *retrodiction*. Retrodiction is practiced in many scientific pursuits, especially in archeology, geology, cosmology, etc. The theory of evolution is also a retrodictive theory; it tries to relate the observed present to unobserved past causes with the help of certain causal laws. Criminologists and detectives also often work with retrodiction. And, to a certain extent, everyone in the practice of daily life uses the same ideas.

In summary, our concept of causality leads us to the statement: Knowing the causes we *predict* the effects; knowing the effects we *retrodict* the past causes.

It is usually considered self evident that in any process where retrodiction is possible prediction is also possible to the same degree, and vice versa. This is a tacit assumption with many thinkers. This assumption should be brought to light and examined. It may be called the "principle of causal symmetry of time."

The principle of causal symmetry of time is so thoroughly valid in much of the material world that surrounds us that one tends to accept its truth unquestioned. Even the introduction of the concept of chance has not affected the validity of this principle. Where chance operates one is not able, with full certainty, to predict from the present what the future will hold, but one is equally restricted in certainty for retrodicting from the present back to the past.

Rudolf Steiner does *not* accept unconditionally the principle of causal symmetry of time. He shows that there are cases where retrodiction is possible but prediction is impossible! Such cases establish what should properly be called the principle of "causal *asymmetry* of time."

The knowledge of the causal asymmetry of time is something of tremendous consequence. It may be expected gradually to reshape the entire future ways of thinking of mankind. In calm and simple language the reader finds presented in the *Philosophy of Spiritual Activity* something that is so world-shaking, that if he were to grasp its significance fully he could not possibly remain calm and casual. To anyone who knows how thoughts and ideas have influenced the course of human history it is exciting in the highest degree to experience this thought of the causal asymmetry of time with all its potential development. One can see how the future of human dignity and responsibility, of inner freedom, of morality and creativity, are indissolubly tied to the insight of the causal asymmetry of time. If the latter is not recognized, all of the former will wither and must of necessity eventually be dropped from human civilization. Further, the understanding of all that the life and death of Christ stands for will be impossible in the long run without the insight of this principle, and will gain immeasurably through it. Indeed, a beginning of this gain can be found in some of the other works of Rudolf Steiner.

The idea of the causal asymmetry of time is really a very natural one, and Rudolf Steiner introduces some of its applications without much ado in the twelfth chapter of the *Philosophy of Spiritual Activity*. It is only through our present thought habits that the idea is sometimes found difficult. These thought habits are attuned to the lifeless world. But even in the lifeless world the question of symmetry or asymmetry of time has plagued the experts. This has happened especially in the science of heat (thermodynamics). This science contains a basic law, known as the "second law of thermodynamics." It is the only basic law of physics that shows an asymmetry of time. Great scientists for more than a century have felt challenged to probe into the mystery of this lone asymmetry. But from the standpoint where science stands currently the matter is still wide open and awaits further progress.

The mystery of the nature of *time* lies at the bottom of all of this, and connected with it are the twin mysteries of creation and evolution. Those whose thinking is confined to rearrangements of the existing come here to a parting of the ways with those who recognize creativity.

Whenever an activity is truly creative its outcome is unpredictable. The most complete knowledge of the past does not suffice to predict the outcome of a creative act completely. On the other hand, whatever is being created becomes a part of the existing universe, and is fitted into its ways and laws. Thus one can find things explainable after a creative act, in retrospect. In other words, retrodiction is possible because what has been created fits into the observable universe, but prediction is impossible because it is created out of unobservable relations. This constellation of affairs lies at the bottom of the one-way character of our experience of time.

Undeniably, time "flows" one-way, from the past to the future. We experience it thus through our double connection with the world—on the one hand, with the given world of observation, on the other hand, with the creative world of thinking and its possible expression through action.

The one-way character of time allows retrodiction but does not allow prediction in relation to a creative activity. This is an idea that Rudolf Steiner uses in many areas, though he does not emphasize it in an abstract way. This idea comes forth directly if one has understood Steiner's approach to the inner experience of the thinking activity.

The thinking activity is a creative activity insofar as new concepts are conceived by our intuition. A complete inventory of a person's concepts at a given moment cannot lead to a prediction of what will be the next concept he acquires or creates in addition to what he has. But any newly acquired concept is integrated with those already present; it does not remain as a foreign element separate from the rest. Thus, in retrospect everything in the mind of this person may appear connected and logical, that is, in accord with the laws of thought, but at the same time every new concept is unpredictable. Intuition, in this sense, is a creative activity, or, as we have called it before, an inwardly free activity. An inwardly free activity is of necessity creative.

Thus, the inner experience of the thinking activity leads us to the direct recognition that this thinking activity is an example of a case where retrodiction is possible but prediction is not necessarily possible, in other words, a case of the causal asymmetry of time. The consequences of this finding are very far reaching. We shall discuss here a number of these consequences in the spirit of the *Philosophy of Spiritual Activity*.

A first area of consequences of this one-way concept of time can be found in the field of ethics. We have seen in a previous article that man passes through a number of pre-ethical stages of development, both in regard to the growth of the individual from childhood to adulthood, and in regard to the growth of culture from primitive antiquity to modern times. The development through the pre-ethical stages is governed by what is commonly called nature and nurture, or the inner and outer influences to which the growing and maturing individual is subjected. These influences act according to causal laws. But then there comes a point when these processes have reached a certain degree of completion, and man's further development is now in his own hands. It is at this point that man's free inner activity can begin to emerge. He then has the possibility of creating by his free intuition new concepts for action. Thus he can perform his own moral actions. Only insofar as actions are free (that is, conceived in this way) are they subject to the yardstick of morality, according to the *Philosophy of Spiritual Activity*. This means that truly moral activity is dependent on creative intuitions that bear a direct relation to the will. Steiner calls such intuitions "moral intuitions."

When moral intuitions are carried out in actions, then these intuitions have the same one-way character described earlier. No amount of previous knowledge could have predicted such a moral action with certainty. By means of moral intuition the individual being has created a new impulse or motivation at the conceptual level. Nevertheless, the action belongs to the world and fits into it. Nowhere are the laws of the world violated. Thus, at a later time one can retrodict the course of events that have taken place. In addition, one can retrodict how a particular moral action is related to previous moral actions, performed by the same or by other individuals. But again, knowledge of these past moral actions is incapable of predicting any future moral action. In this sense all moral actions are "first sources." From them new chains of events take their course causally into the future, but the first sources do not have previous causation at the perceptible level. If everything were completely causal in the customary sense, without such first sources, then the world picture, including man, would be that of a complicated machine. This conclusion is not changed by broadening the concept of causality to include chance. Only by the interplay of causally compelled activity and free activity is man introduced into the world picture as a being instead of as a thing.

In regard to human life Rudolf Steiner develops—elsewhere—many applications of the idea of the causal asymmetry of time. For example, when considering a good biography of a person, one can find in retrospect that all actions can be linked to previous influences of nature and nurture in an orderly way. But in the forward stream of time these influences are not sufficient to determine the actions, insofar as free activity is realized. A good biography should show where and how a person introduced new impulses freely into the causal stream of life circumstances. One can apply this reasoning to one's own life. It is possible, and often very useful, to review one's own past and to identify the causes that contributed to the shaping of the present. Retrodiction is possible. But, insofar as one is free, prediction is not possible. One can even go further and consider the human being at birth (or conception). One can link the germinal human being with the past through the laws of heredity and the influences of the environment in retrospect. But all possibly available data, taken beforehand, will not allow one to predict fully all that matters for a human being who is about to be born. The human being comes to earth harboring within himself, in a way that is not accessible to sense observation, a set of first causes that constitute his individual spiritual nature or "I." This "I" cannot be gauged or predicted from any amount of sense data prior to its actual coming. Thus, the gate of birth (or conception) is again an instance where spirit is woven into the causal pattern of the observable world, where retrodiction is possible, but prediction is, in principle, impossible in the areas where the "I" is manifest. The birth of a human being and the birth of a free moral action are thus seen to be quite similar in regard to their relation to the principle of causal asymmetry of time.

In Rudolf Steiner's works on historical subjects one again encounters the same one-way concept of the causal asymmetry of time. History can be described as a causal happening. One can ask of all present events what led up to them. Everywhere in the present one can see the remnants of the past. But one cannot fully predict the future on the basis of even the most complete knowledge of all historical facts, for the future is not made only by the stream of remnants from the past, but, in addition, by an ever-self-renewing stream of free actions of human beings. Thus, to the sense-bound (and document bound) observer it can appear that new first causes are constantly being inserted into the stream of civilization. A particularly crass example is the case of Joan of Arc, because there even retrodiction finds itself baffled to some extent. But also an example such as Abraham Lincoln's decision to work toward the abolition of slavery could not have been predicted. Afterward, of course, it can be made plausible. Not all free actions that enter into the stream of history are of such magnitude in their effects. A multitude of smaller free actions enters into history from day to day, shaping it and altering its course. This influx is not predictable by the laws that can be gleaned from even the most complete record of the past.

Rudolf Steiner applies the same one-way concept to the evolution of life on earth, from the most primitive lower forms of life to one of the latest forms, the human being. One can sensibly ask what led up to the present state of life in the human, the animal, and the plant kingdoms. The fossil record provides the principal answers through retrodiction, but one cannot predict the future on the basis of a full knowledge of the past biological facts. This is true not only at the present time, but would have been true at any time. Consider, for example, the time that there were reptiles on the earth but no birds as yet. Later the birds would develop out of the reptiles. Somewhere, for the first time, feathers were developed. Steiner insists that the new line of development, represented by feathered birds, could not have been foreseen by any (hypothetical) observer who lived before it had come about, on the basis of all possible knowledge about reptiles that perception and thinking could yield. Thus in the birds we have a new creation. In retrospect they can be explained as emerging from the reptiles, but they could not have been predicted before they appeared. Steiner implies that it is not a matter of insufficient knowledge, but rather that it could not have been predicted *no matter how complete* our sense-information and the knowledge derived from it, concerning the reptiles might have been. With the emergence of birds a new creative impulse inserted itself into the stream of evolution. And it was the same with all evolving species of animals in their times.

The concept of reptiles, that is, the innate law of organization of reptiles, does not contain within itself the concept of birds. Thus reptiles will remain reptiles until a *being* introduces a new concept, to become effective in the perceptible world. A world of creative spiritual beings becomes manifest through such new creative impulses. While the reader is brought near to this last conclusion in the *Philosophy of Spiritual Activity*, it is not stated there explicitly in this form. But this same avenue of thought is followed to this conclusion in later writings of Steiner. Its germ, however, is clearly indicated in the twelfth chapter of the *Philosophy of Spiritual Activity*. Thus at every step evolution shows a creative process at work. This process has finally led up to man. And in man the same process appears again, as man's own moral intuition, by means of which he inserts new impulses creatively into the world. Along such lines of thought can perhaps become clear what Steiner means when he speaks (elsewhere) of man on the one hand as constituting a kingdom of nature, and on the other hand as being in the process of becoming a new member of the kingdom of spiritual beings.

Steiner carries the same one-way concept of the causal asymmetry of time still further. Not only the various stages of the evolution of life come under its sway, but also the stages of cosmological evolution of the earth, the solar system, and all the heavenly bodies. It is well known that cosmological evolution has gone through stages.

The history of present day science shows that the ideas concerning the cosmological evolution of our solar system, as well as those concerning our galaxy, have been subject to rather rapid changes. The ideas prevalent today would have been impossible thirty years ago, and these in turn would have been impossible sixty years ago. One cannot ascribe very much weight, therefore, to currently accepted present day cosmological theories. However, Steiner contends that enough is known today about the observed facts to enable us to see that our earth is a complex system of delicate balance. Without this balance of various factors such as the temperature, the conditions in the atmosphere, the chemistry of minerals, etc., life as we know it would not be possible on earth. And this balance and complexity is not something that concerns the earth alone, but includes most obviously the relations between the earth and the sun. Thus one can realize that the present solar system is delicately organized.

It is likely that the present solar system went through more primitive stages. Whether one considers these more primitive stages as similar to the nebula postulated by the Kant-Laplace theory of old, or whether one uses some later scientific model is not significant. The more primitive state of the solar system, whatever form it had, would have yielded a concept to a hypothetical human observer of that time, who would have made the greatest possible effort to gather observations and data. And according to Steiner, the essential thing is that out of this concept of the primitive solar system as it actually was, no thinking, observing, scientific mind (in the sense of today) would have been able to deduce the state of the present solar system.

Thus, again we see that the later form, because it is richer in essentially new ways, cannot be derived conceptually from an earlier form, although they follow factually out of each other. In the *Philosophy of Spiritual Activity* Steiner touches this cosmological case only briefly, but in later works we find much further exploration of this idea. A cosmology results that is only fully described when at each stage account is taken of the new creative intuitions. These intuitions can be discovered only in the world of intuition and thinking, in the spiritual world.

A road of understanding has here been traced that leads toward Steiner's Anthroposophy. We can sense and probe in thinking, in intuition, how in cosmological evolution, in biological evolution, in historical evolution, as well as in the biographical evolution of the single individual human being, the remnants of the past are constantly being interwoven with new impulses, new beginnings, spiritually free moral actions. Human life as well as the physical world thus acquire more and more impulses, are more and more regulated according to this influx out of the self-consistent, self-supporting world of spirit. It is then perhaps no longer surprising that Rudolf Steiner often says of the truths of Anthroposophy: Customary thinking cannot find them, but once they are found, customary thinking can understand them, can fully take hold of them.

Here again we have an application of the same one-way concept of the causal asymmetry of time. Indeed, in order to find anthroposophical truths one has to be at home in the world of intuitions to a degree which ordinary thinking is not normally trained to achieve. But once a new intuition has been brought into the stream of ordinary thinking it is connectible with all other concepts.

In the *Philosophy of Spiritual Activity* Rudolf Steiner has taken great pains to see that its contents make no demands that cannot be managed with ordinary observation and ordinary sense-bound thinking, provided only that the inner observation of the thinking activity itself is admitted. Through this last proviso the character of this philosophy has received its stamp, and only through it can the principle of the causal asymmetry of time be fully understood. In observing one's thinking activity one observes the principle of causal asymmetry of time in operation, when in inner freedom the individual creates his moral intuitions.

One can try to connect all the creative moral impulses (intuitions) that a man experiences during a lifetime. One then has the deepest possible elements of his biography, of that which made his life the life of that inner entity we call the "I."

One can also try to connect conceptually all the original intuitions, which one can discover in a survey of world-evolution as was indicated above. One then has the elements for an understanding of a great cosmic spiritual being or beings.

Finally one can try to confront the concept of the "I" with the concept of cosmic beings, and to connect the two. This leads to the highest possible intuitions.

Goethe attempted something like this when he let his Faust, the man who could not yet quite grasp his "I" encounter the "Spirit of the Earth," who thus describes himself:

In storms of action, in tides of life,
Up and down I wave,
Back and forth I weave!
Birth and grave,
An eternal sea,
Weaving changingly,
Living glowingly,
Thus I create on the buzzing loom of time,
And fashion the living raiment of God.

Wonderfully wrought are these words of Goethe, expressing in a few poetic lines a world of wisdom! In the light of what we have tried to present in this article these words show clearly that in his way Goethe knew about the causal asymmetry of time, and its connection with creativity, human life and evolution.

But Goethe certainly did not live with this idea as a philosopher, and only to a preliminary extent was he able to apply it consciously. Thus Goethe's confrontation of Faust with the Spirit of the Earth results in a premature experience that almost shatters Faust and comes close to destroying his life. From Goethe's works one could not have predicted the wide scope and fundamental function that the idea of the causal asymmetry of time can yield.

In Rudolf Steiner's work one also finds the intuitions of world-evolution confronted with the intuitions of the individual "I." Perhaps the most concise and also the most profound expression of this is formulated in the so-called "Foundation Stone Words," but the idea appears in many places in his work. In retrospect, one might perhaps be able to see how Rudolf Steiner carried on where Goethe left off. But, because this continuation, by the very nature of the problem, was a creative one, it could not have been predicted. How can we characterize this creative continuation?

Rudolf Steiner outlined a path of creative growth that can lead the spirit of man to the spiritual powers of the cosmos. This latter, in a sense, is the "definition" of Anthroposophy. At various stages we find expressions of the confrontation of cosmos and man from the most diverse points of view. We have already referred to the Foundation Stone words as probably one of the most illuminating versions of this. In three stages or parts this confrontation is formulated. There are wonderfully wrought words of Rudolf Steiner, possessing in addition to deepest wisdom, the power to arouse and awaken the human mind to the recognition of its own Spirit nature. These words are much too intricate, much too rich and subtle, to be discussed adequately at the end of an article dealing in the main with something else. But there remains the question of what the intuition is, which arises at the highest level out of this confrontation. This intuition must indicate the source from which the mysteries of creation and of time are constantly renewed. And the words expressing this highest intuitional source are given in a fourth part of the Foundation Stone words, which, unlike those of the first three parts, are surprisingly simple in form. They are not designed to shatter the reader, but rather to show him the greatest example of the working of creative-spirit in the causal world of time, as an inspiring archetypal image for his own striving toward spiritual activity and inner creative moral freedom:

> At the turning point of Time
> Came cosmic Spirit Light
> Into earthly stream of being.
> Night darkness had ceased from holding sway,
> Day-brilliant light rayed forth in human souls,
> Light that gave warmth to simple shepherd's hearts,
> Light that enlightened the wise heads of kings.
> Light Divine!
> Christ–Sun!
> Warm Thou our hearts,
> Enlighten our heads,
> That good may become
> What from our hearts we are founding,
> And from our heads we will guide.[2]

The three fundamental traits that determine the relation between the individual and the world are characteristics for the three ranks of birth. They influence our life in a similar way as our sex determines our character. Whether we are male or female reaches deep down into the formation of our character and into the shape of our personality. To recognize this as clearly as possible is a task for our age. If it is properly understood it will help parents and teachers to understand much better their children and pupils and to comprehend the underlying motives of their reactive behavior.

The ranks of birth imprint their traits on each one of us. From birth onwards we are under the yoke of this great law and it will be the task of the following pages to explain in some detail the various characteristics of first-, second- and third-born people. As I said already, this law determines our relation to our environment in a similarly fundamental way as does our sex. A man has different forms of behavior than a woman. From early infancy we are modeled by being either male or female. We are equally modeled and destined by our rank of birth.

Much too little attention has been paid to this great rune so far. May this thesis help to make it better known so that its realization in turn will help to build a better world!

X
The Ingredients of Moral Action

In previous articles we have described the concept of morality which Rudolf Steiner develops in the *Philosophy of Spiritual Activity*. The origin of morality lies in the same sphere of consciousness as the thinking activity. The free human spirit creates or grasps a moral concept by means of its intuitive faculty. Thus he answers the challenge of the moment, seen against the perspective of the past and the purposes of the future, without being determined by these. In the sense of the *Philosophy of Spiritual Activity*, moral intuition, the intuition that individualizes moral concepts, is certainly a first and indispensable ingredient for free moral action.

However a concept is not yet an action. It does not even completely define an action. The concept acquired by moral intuition lacks the concreteness and definiteness that is required for an action. We shall see that two other essential ingredients must accompany moral intuition in order to achieve effective moral conduct. These two ingredients are called moral imagination and moral technique.

Let us first inquire why the concepts for moral intuition are by themselves not sufficient for effective moral conduct. In this respect the concept for an action does not differ from the concept for cognition or knowledge. Let us therefore clarify the relationships first for concepts in regard to knowledge. Consider the concept of a circle in comparison to an actual "circle." The actual circle has a definite center and a definite radius; the concept of the circle does not have these two data fixed, it allows for any center and any radius. As a result we can conceive a concept, we can think it, but we cannot imagine it in our mind. We can only picture or imagine certain instances or examples. And as we look out into the world we perceive such instances (at least approximately). In the world we can perceive very definite circles. Each one of these perceived circles, these percepts, has the concept of a circle "in" it, as a hidden ingredient, which perception alone cannot reveal, but of which we become aware by having our thinking activity go to work on the percept. Thus our thinking activity bridges the original gap between concept and percept.

When we remember what we perceived earlier, we have on the scene of our consciousness a representation, which can be fully as definite as the original perception to which it refers. Perceptions and representations of memory have in common that they are definite images, containing the concepts "within" them in a hidden way.

If we ask a person to draw or to construct a circle we are really setting up a very difficult task. The difficulty lies in the fact that the task is not wholly prescribed. As the person gets ready to carry out the necessary action he must make a decision where to place the center of the circle and how large to choose its radius. This requires first an act of his imagination. He must imagine first in all concrete definiteness the circle which he is about to draw. Then, as he draws, he constantly compares the percept which he produces with his mental image; he steers his hand so as to make his action conform to his mental design. In this way, by means of our imagination, we can act so as to incorporate a general concept into a specific object.

In what has been said it is not implied that the imagination is always of a visual kind. There are visual, auditory, and motor imaginations; and in addition many other kinds. What kinds of imagination we use in any given case depends on the situation we face and on our experience and preference. However, we do use imaginations of various kinds as guides for all our conscious, meaningful actions. Without the imagination we find ourselves at a loss to act; we cannot carry into reality any action that is conceived merely on the conceptual level.

Even as, for the purpose of our gaining experience, our thinking activity recognizes concepts "in" the percepts or "in" the memory representations, so our imagination must, for the purpose of our carrying out an action, relate the general conceptual basis of the action to the definite circumstances of the perceptual world. Our imagination is the tool which we use to incorporate our conceived actions "into" the perceptible world. All this is true for any intuition that is to be carried from the conceptual level into real action. In particular this is true for moral intuitions.

Moral intuition is powerless if it is not supported by moral imagination. One can illustrate this statement by many examples. One example, which is perhaps as pertinent as any is the following. Suppose a person has understood the *Philosophy of Spiritual Activity*. He understands the nature of free spiritual activity as described. He knows what is meant by moral intuition. Suppose further that this person finds all these ideas beautiful and enthusing. He has a moral intuition that brings him to the realization that this is a force with which he considers it good to link up. He feels that his own activity in life must manifest, bring to expression, this free spiritual activity. Then he faces the problem of moral imagination. How to act here and now in order to accomplish this? Unless he can find answers to these questions by means of moral imagination, his intuition will remain in the sphere of ideas.

Here people can help one another. It can happen that some persons are more gifted with moral intuition, others more with moral imagination. The two types of persons can work together as a team, one conceiving the general and communicating it to the other, and the other giving it a concrete and definite form.

The above relations find a kind of precipitation in modern forms of government. We have a constitution and a body of laws and regulations. The constitution is general and conceptual, the laws are more specific. The constitution is for the government what the moral intuitions are for the individual, and the laws correspond to his moral imaginations.

A classical example of moral intuition and moral imagination is to be found in the Old Testament. Moses conceived the Ten Commandments as a moral intuition. The detailed laws and regulations that follow it are moral imaginations. They connect the intuitive general content of the Ten Commandments with the situations and problems as they arise in the practice of the daily life of that time and culture. In the case of Moses the faculties of moral intuition and moral imagination were both highly developed. These examples have perhaps shown sufficiently what is meant by moral imagination, and why it can be considered as a second essential ingredient of moral action.

There is a third ingredient, no less essential than the other two. It is called "moral technique" by Rudolf Steiner. There is a difference between moral imagination, which gives in image form a concrete goal for action, and the actual carrying out of the action that will lead toward that goal. It is a fact of life that we can imagine a lot more than we can actually carry out. Doing requires a certain experience or skill.

In the example of the constitution and the laws, we find the equivalent of this third ingredient in the judiciary branch of the government, the courts, and judges, etc. There the laws are interpreted and applied, and thus are carried from the books into the practice of the ever changing conditions of life. The practical activity of the judge is based on the law, but in addition also on his knowledge of local custom and precedent. The latter form elements of cumulative experience that enter into the activity in a way that is analogous to moral technique.

In the example of Moses, we find the aspect of moral technique described with some emphasis (Exodus chapter 18, 13-27): Moses tried to settle all the disputes of the people individually as they came up. His father-in-law, Jethro, points out that this method is not practical and will over burden Moses. He advises Moses to appoint judges who are to be instructed how to handle simple issues. Only the difficult issues should be brought before Moses himself to judge.

This example is interesting because it shows two things. First it shows how Moses practiced judging from morning to evening. This is described just before the conception of the Ten Commandments. Moses applied his ideas to the actual situations of life. Thereby he developed a good deal of moral technique. Second, the example shows that this moral technique can be learned and taught. It can be delegated to others.

Moral technique is not always of such weighty proportions as in the above examples, which were chosen for the sake of clarity. The simplest act of goodness or kindness has the three basic ingredients of moral action interwoven:

- Moral intuition conceives what is morally good at this moment for this acting individual.
- Moral imagination forms this general concept into a specific image that can be incorporated into the perceptual world.
- Moral technique performs the moral action in accordance with the other two ingredients.

There are people who are weak in moral intuition, but possess the other two ingredients. They must be given moral intuitions, conceived by others, on which they are completely dependent until they have overcome this weakness. They are not free. If such people are given a fixed set of values they can be "very good people" in the customary sense. But in the sense of the *Philosophy of Spiritual Activity* they can grow further. From the standpoint of free inner activity they are bound. They are in this sense in a pre-ethical stage of evolution.

There are others who are weak in moral imagination, but possess the two other ingredients. They would do well to associate themselves with other men of imagination, in order to avoid a certain incongruence between the loftiness of their moral ideals and the moral smallness of their actual deeds.

There are finally those who are weak in moral technique, but possess the other two ingredients. They may wish to speak a kind word, but somehow the tone makes it unacceptable to the receiver; they may wish to put a person at ease, but somehow manage to create an uncomfortable situation; and so on. From the most insignificant to the most far reaching moral actions, they accomplish something quite different from what they have in mind. They must acquire skill, through instruction and practice. Self education is possible in this respect, if carried on persistently.

In order to be morally most effective one has to have all three ingredients at once at one's command: moral intuition to conceive the direction of a moral impulse; moral imagination to form this impulse in a definite way; and moral technique to act according to the idea that has thus taken shape, and to effectively incorporate it into the existing world.

In the first part of the twelfth chapter, we find information about these three essentials of moral action.

3

About Your Relation to Rudolf Steiner

Preface

How many years will have to pass till the mystery of this man will have been fully fathomed?

This significant question stands out in the fine biography of Rudolf Steiner, written by my esteemed friend, the late Dr. F. W. Zeylmans van Emmichoven, M. D., as a volume in the series *Heroes of the Spirit* (which included biographies of Hegel, Plato, Kant, Goethe, Nietzsche, and other great figures) published in Holland (in Dutch) in 1932.

At present, more than fifty years later, this question still has not been answered fully. If the present booklet takes the reader one step closer to an answer, its purpose will have been achieved.

When people study some of Steiner's writings or behold some of his artistic creations it happens often that they feel addressed in a part of their being that normally lies dormant or fallow, and they wonder then about the nature of the unusual reaction that his work calls forth in them. This booklet attempts to provide some understanding of this situation, by drawing on Steiner's work and on biographies of persons in his environment.

The content of this booklet has grown through more than a decade. Some of its ideas were first expressed in lectures that I gave for anthroposophically oriented audiences in Ann Arbor on February 26, 1974, and in Chicago the following day. The booklet's form, a series of simple short chapters, was chosen in order to meet the needs of modern readers who, in today's hurried life, have only short intervals of time available for reading.

Ernst Katz,
Ann Arbor, Michigan, 1985

I
How a Contemporary Author Found Rudolf Steiner

Around the turn of the century there lived in France a man who had devoted the greater part of his life to research of the great civilizations of antiquity. It was his particular concern to research the secret mystery centers, whose founders and leaders were known as the "great initiates," from whom radiated the spiritual substance of these ancient cultures. For many years this researcher, though not an initiate himself, had gathered information which could bear witness to these great individualities.

In addition, he had diligently trained himself as a writer, in order to be able to present the results of his researches in a worthy form. Finally, after many years of such labors, he had produced a splendid book: *The Great Initiates*,[1] which soon became a classic. In this work he described in sensitive, beautiful prose the lives and missions of the great founders of ancient civilizations: Rama, Hermes, Moses, Pythagoras, and others. The author—Edouard Schuré was his name—knew that one can hardly imagine today the wonderful spiritual power, wisdom, and human goodness which permeated these great initiates and radiated from them through their deeds.

When Schuré had completed this splendid work, only one great question remained in his soul: Might it be, perhaps, that in this life the privilege would be granted him to meet a living "great initiate?" Through his researches his sensitivity was sharpened and he felt sure that he would recognize an initiate immediately when he met one. Destiny led to an encounter with Rudolf Steiner.

About this event Schuré wrote in his diary somewhat as follows: For many years have I spared no efforts to describe to my contemporaries the "great initiates" of the distant past. I have tried to present in a true light the nature of their being and the powerful effects of their initiation. Then it happened that I met Rudolf Steiner—immediately it dawned on me, and I knew with absolute certainty that I stood now in the presence of a living "great initiate."

This encounter led to a remarkable result. The two men became friends. Perhaps you wonder: Is it possible at all to be a friend of an initiate without being an initiate oneself? For only the initiate has free and conscious access to the world of soul and spirit.—To this question Steiner answers:[2] "You may live in intimate friendship with an initiate, and yet a gap severs you from his essential self as long as you have not become an initiate yourself. You may enjoy in the fullest sense the heart, the love of an initiate, yet he will only confide his knowledge to you when you are ready for it." Therefore, only in this limited, modest sense can we speak here of a friendship between Schuré and Steiner.

The above quote refers to initiates in general. Regarding Steiner we may add: His task was to make a major part of the science of initiation accessible to the public. A rich treasure of knowledge and practice, which used to be kept secret in past ages, was to be made openly available in accordance with the needs and requirements of mankind at its present state of evolution. The creation of a public mystery science was his great achievement.

What Steiner imparted to mankind of our time was and is of tremendous, far-reaching value. On this account one can feel great respect for him. And this respect may turn into awe if one ponders how incredibly much more he must have known, of which he kept silent.

II

How People Find Their Way to Rudolf Steiner Today

It is a strange fact of life that events can look well-ordered when you look at them in retrospect, whereas they appear chaotic and chance-driven at the time when they happen. Different people find their way to Rudolf Steiner's work along the most diverse paths of life, which often manifest this fact. An account of these individual paths with all their rich variety would make highly interesting reading. In the English-speaking world most of these paths fall into one of four main "avenues."

The first avenue involves an encounter with a physically manifest application of anthroposophy, such as a Waldorf school, a biodynamic farm or its produce, a building designed in a certain style, Weleda cosmetics, a eurythmy performance, anthroposophic medicine or medical research, etc. Sometimes it may take a long time till the person wakes up to the fact that all of these disciplines originated with a single very special individual: Rudolf Steiner.

The second avenue involves a book in which Steiner is mentioned more or less in the background by another author. Nevertheless, such a book may leave a decisive impression of Steiner with some readers. They may feel drawn to pursue this impression further. Fine examples are *Humboldt's Gift* by Saul Bellow, and *The Spear of Destiny* by Trevor Ravenscroft. There are many other books that perform the same function. In the mind of the reader who travels along the second avenue, a picture of Steiner arises that may be quite vague and unclear at first, but which is nevertheless much more conscious than the picture of those who travel along the first avenue.

The third avenue leads the traveler to an occasion where someone speaks or writes in a stimulating way about Steiner and his work. It may be a teacher, a friend, the author of a book, or the events at a conference. Essential is that attention be purposely focused on Steiner and his work. Often what seems to speak most effectively to the interest and the needs of people who travel along this avenue is the growth or the scope of the person or author encountered in this way. It is felt that Steiner is revealed through his effect on him as a human being.

The fourth avenue leads the individual directly to a book by Steiner, which arouses a more than usual depth of interest and calls for further reading and study. Here the person enters, as it were, into direct conversation with Steiner, without a mediator or interpreter.

Still other avenues may be described, but these four cover the large majority of cases. Each reader may ask himself: Along which of these avenues did my destiny guide me?

All of these avenues have one thing in common. The traveler feels addressed, or touched, in a part of his being that is usually untouched. This results in a slight awakening to the fact that something is at work here, or can be experienced, which has to do with the deepest longings, goals, and impulses of human life. Again, each reader may ask himself: How did I experience this "being touched by anthroposophy?"

Naturally, the freedom of each individual is thereby fully respected. Consequently, very different reactions to this "being touched by anthroposophy" can and do occur. If the response is positive, one may wonder in retrospect how this was possible. It was possible because it was a well-ordered path by which the individual traveler found Steiner at a definite point in time in his or her life. Finding Steiner in such a way is qualitatively different from finding most other individuals. In the following chapters we shall try to discover some of the reasons why, and in what ways it is different.

III

Your Relation to Rudolf Steiner and the Future of Mankind

When you feel touched by anthroposophy you have entered into a relation with Rudolf Steiner. In the course of time this relation may pass through various stages. It may deepen, and even become a real friendship. In what way this is meant will be explained later.

At first the relation with Rudolf Steiner is often rather undefined. You read some of his books, perhaps you admire some of his artistic creations, you get to know some biographical facts. Meanwhile you learn from him about the great worlds of soul and spirit, which are hidden behind the veil of the sense world, the world that can be seen, heard, touched, or perceived by means of our other senses.

Fully human beings need to be alive and conscious both in the sense world and in the higher worlds of soul and spirit. In our time attention is customarily focused on the sense world, while we tend to lose sight of the higher worlds. Usually no independent reality is ascribed to the higher worlds. If they are spoken of at all, they are seen as derivatives or side effects of the sense world. To most of our contemporaries only the sense world is real.

Degeneracy and atrophy befall any organ or function that is not used for a long time. This is a law of the living world. If over a long period of time the human soul and spirit functions are not recognized and consciously actuated and developed, they will eventually waste away. What does this really mean?

The materialistic image of man, though false at present, tends to build a future in which it becomes true. A self-fulfilling prophecy; a self-accelerating process! What at present man fancies himself to be, he will in fact become in the future through the effects, the power, of this fancy: a material creature, whose appearance and behavior will in no way express his independent soul and spirit. For lack of actuation the independent soul and spirit will then have wasted away. The result is a dire state, where human life would have lost all meaning. A subhuman condition!—Is this disastrous long-range future unavoidable?

It can indeed be avoided. Namely if, and only if, human beings of our time learn to *know* (not merely to believe in or talk about) the hidden worlds of soul and spirit. Belief is not enough because our relation to the sense world is based on knowledge, which is more powerful than belief. If our relation to the higher worlds is to stand with the same firmness and independence, it too must be based on knowledge. Only by developing knowledge of the higher worlds can mankind avoid sliding down to subhuman levels. In this knowledge quest Rudolf Steiner stands out as a pioneer and guide of the highest rank.

As you learn to know more of his work, you cannot help but wonder who this unique person was, and what the nature of your own relation to him may be. Surely this relation must have something to do with humanity's need for knowledge of the worlds of soul and spirit.

IV

Why the Ideas of Anthroposophy Remain Linked to Rudolf Steiner

People ask: Why do anthroposophists make so much of Rudolf Steiner? Are not his works more important than the man? Is it not immature hero worship that attracts some people not only to his ideas but to his individuality as well?—Indeed, that may be true for some, but for most this whole matter is to be seen in a very different light. Let me explain. Three domains of human productivity can be distinguished.

In the first domain, the product is soon detached from its original producer. Many creations in science and technology belong here. We feel no need to commemorate the anniversary of Henry Ford if we drive a Ford car. We experience the product, the car, as detached from its original inventor.

In the second domain, the product bears more strongly the stamp of its original producer, who has imparted to it a timeless, universal quality. Many great works of art belong to this domain. A work of Leonardo da Vinci bears his stamp and remains connected with his name and with his individuality. We recognize a work of his hand by means of this individual stamp; thereby, also, we distinguish it from works by other great artists.— Another example: Consider the year 1985, the tricentennial of Johann Sebastian Bach's birth. In this year the music of this great composer is performed everywhere in abundance. Scholars research every detail of his life. Articles and books about him roll off the press. Nowhere have I heard anyone ask: Why do people make so much of Bach? Is not his music more important than his person? No one speaks here of hero worship. From these examples we learn that in the domain of art, especially of great art, it is an accepted fact that the work bears the stamp of its creator, and remains connected with his individuality.—In the case of Rudolf Steiner we assert that *all* of his works are, in a sense, works of art: his paintings, the Goetheanum, his mantric verses, the mystery dramas, his lectures, indeed everything he created, even the organization of his thoughts.

There is, however, yet a third domain. What is produced there retains an even more intimate bond with its creator. Matters of a spiritual nature belong to this domain, for example anthroposophy. Something timeless and universal shines through the products of this domain. If you understand their nature, you know that a lasting bond exists between author and product. For anthroposophy this means that the spirit individuality of Rudolf Steiner was not only essential when he created it, but remains as essentially connected with it today.

Of course, many other individuals have contributed to the development of anthroposophy. But they could do so only because they were, to a greater or lesser degree, friends of Rudolf Steiner, in the sense that they worked out of their own strength toward the same great goals and tried to coordinate their actions with his, as also he coordinated his actions with those of his predecessors.

The laws of spiritual productivity resemble those of artistic productivity more than those that govern the domain of science and technology. Unlike the latter, they require that whatever is created spiritually by a human being may not be separated from its original creator if it is to maintain its living character. This is an important reason why many who develop a real interest in anthroposophy feel not only appreciation or gratitude toward Rudolf Steiner, but even something more, which rightly can be called a kind of friendship.—But what can be the meaning of calling "friendship" a relation to an individual who is no longer living? An inquiry into the nature of friendship seems called for at this point.

V

About the Nature of Friendship

In ancient times friendship was a relation that was valued highly, even more highly than marriage. Betrayal of friendship was considered one of the worst depravities. Friends would help and defend each other in need and in the various undertakings in life. They would share or loan possessions freely, and inspire and counsel each other to steer a right course in life. A high code of ethics governed friendship in those ancient times.

In modern society, many of the functions that were formerly concentrated in one human being, the friend, are now distributed over several impersonal institutions. If one needs a loan, there is the loan department of a bank. If one needs protection, there is the police or the lawyer. If one needs counsel, there is the psychologist or the psychiatrist, etc. As a result, friendship becomes more and more rare.

To define friendship is difficult, perhaps impossible. Plato attempts several definitions in his dialogue "Lysis," but in the end concludes that none are satisfactory. C. S. Lewis[3] characterizes friendship pictorially: Lovers would have to be pictured facing each other, while friends would have to be pictured side by side, facing the world. Certainly a charming characterization. But not quite satisfactory if you dwell on it seriously.

Perhaps the most profound, and at the same time most touching, description of the various aspects of friendship is given in the most ancient great epic of humanity, the story of Gilgamesh,[4] the heroic Babylonian king, and Eabani or Enkidu, the strong and primitive nature-youth. These two men of contrasting origin are poised against each other in fierce combat. But on account of a dream they both had of each other, they suddenly decide to become friends. Henceforth they share in all undertakings and adventures of life. Their friendship is a source of strength, growth, and happiness for both. Then Enkidu falls ill and dies. Gilgamesh is left in grievous loneliness and despair. For the first time in his life he is afraid of death. He starts out on a search for the timeless, the eternal life of the spirit. Though he does make progress, his soul strength fails him in the last decisive stages. Then he searches for his friend in the realm of the dead, but he cannot return him to life. Gilgamesh cannot solve the problem of friendship after death.

The story of Gilgamesh deals with many fundamental problems of life with which modern man also struggles. But to modern man possibilities of solutions are open that were not available to ancient man, not even to ancient kings. For modern man friendship can become a meaningful spiritual experience even beyond death, though naturally this experience differs somewhat from the experience of friendship with a living person.

We do not allude here to alleged mediumistic relations with a departed human soul, nor to other parapsychological phenomena of a "psychic" nature. These are all excluded from our considerations. What we mean here as a meaningful spiritual experience of friendship beyond death may be illustrated by the following example. It is concerned with an individual who might have fallen into oblivion if Steiner had not described him intimately in his autobiography.

Karl Julius Schröer (1825-1900) was a Viennese professor of German literature and a noted Goethe-scholar[5] of that time. Schröer may be seen as a friend of Goethe (1748-1832) in the above sense. In everything Schröer thought and did he would ask himself, "How would Goethe have thought and acted in these circumstances?" In this way, Schröer became gradually more and more open to what lived in Goethe. Questions in Schröer's mind could find answers through his inner closeness to Goethe's spirit. Or, one might say that Goethe's spirit was a source of inspiration for Schröer. On the other hand, one can also maintain that Schröer helped Goethe, for example, by inspiring his students with enthusiasm for Goethe's work.

We see in this example a spiritual two-way relationship which is based on normal, fully waking consciousness, without any admixture of mediumistic or spiritualistic paranormal phenomena. In a similar way a conscious and direct two-way relationship of the nature of friendship with a departed soul, on a spiritual level, is possible today.

To many contemporaries this may seem fantasy. Like Gilgamesh, they cannot free themselves of the bonds of materialism. But today, more and more persons know, or can learn to know, the reality of such a relationship. For such persons it is possible to conceive of a friendship with the spirit individuality of Rudolf Steiner, even though his earthly life ceased long ago. When friendship with Rudolf Steiner is mentioned in this booklet, it is to be understood in this sense.

VI

A Deeper Aspect of One's Relation to Rudolf Steiner

So far the question of one's relation to Rudolf Steiner has been discussed at an elementary level. There is a deeper sense in which one may find oneself related to him. Quite a number of people are aware—sometimes dimly, sometimes quite clearly—of a soul-spiritual bond, stemming from past incarnations, which connects them with Rudolf Steiner. Upon becoming acquainted with his work—or, during his life, with him personally—such a person may suddenly realize that he knew Rudolf Steiner already, and now recognizes him anew. With this recognition, the person experiences a direct confirmation of the reality of reincarnation.

One of Steiner's students, the late Dr. F. W. Zeylmans van Emmichoven (1894-1961) describes how such a recognition became clear to him.[6] At the mature age of sixty-three this experienced Dutch doctor and psychiatrist writes about this event in retrospect:

In December of 1920 I journeyed to Dornach. My relation to anthroposophy had aroused in me the intense wish to meet Rudolf Steiner. This became the most decisive event in my life. It happened as follows.

On the evening of December 17th I sat in the "Schreinerei"—the carpentry workshop building near the Goetheanum—together with my fiancée, who studied eurythmy in Dornach. We were very happy to be together and were waiting for Rudolf Steiner's lecture. Outside it was bitterly cold. Dornach was covered with deep snow.

Suddenly the blue curtain beside the stage parted and Rudolf Steiner, whom I knew from photographs, went to the lecturer's rostrum. At that instant I experienced in an immediate way a renewed recognition (*Das unmittelbare Erlebnis des Wiedererkennens*). This went so far that within me there arose all at once a whole series of images, which pointed somehow to past situations, in which I saw him as my teacher through thousands of years. It was the most powerful experience I have ever had in my whole life. I sat there, but my mind was elsewhere, and only after a while did I realize that the lecture had already started.... When I came to myself again from the state just described and saw Rudolf Steiner there on the rostrum I had a most peculiar sensation. I felt: Here I see for the first time a truly human being. It is not easy to describe this impression. I had met with many great persons of fame and renown: professors, artists, etc. I had frequented in circles where one could experience a lot; I had not led a philistine existence. But only now did it dawn on me: This is the way man was meant to be.

Zeylmans analyzes this impression as a thoughtful psychiatrist would do, and then continues:

When the lecture was over, my fiancée said, "Come with me, I will introduce you to Rudolf Steiner. He likes to meet young people." I had not expected this, but if this was the custom I was willing to comply. So I went with her to the front and was introduced. Dr. Steiner said, "I have been expecting you here for a long time." (*Ich habe Sie schon lange hier erwartet.*) I thought he meant that I had been in Dornach for some time, so I replied, "But Herr

Doktor, I just arrived in Dornach this very afternoon." He smiled merrily and said, "That is not at all what I mean."

In this account Zeylmans describes how he became conscious of a deep bond with Steiner, rooted in past incarnations, extending over thousands of years, and how Steiner also was aware of this bond, and confirmed Zeylmans experience by saying that he had long expected his coming, which implies having known Zeylmans before.

It is implausible that this knowledge was only based on communications from his fiancée, for in that case it would have been more appropriate to say something like, "Your fiancée has told me that you would come and I am pleased to meet you now." The phrasing of Steiner carries the distinct overtone, "I have long known you and I have known that our paths would cross; I have waited for this event to happen."

Experiences of a similar nature as described by Zeylmans, though often less fully conscious, are alive in the souls of many anthroposophists. What is it that underlies experiences of such a recognition of Steiner?

In the course of past incarnations Steiner has connected himself with a great many souls who, in their subsequent lives, have been scattered in time and in space, over the whole earth, over the past, the present, and the future, in accordance with their individual karma. All of these souls have one feature in common, a hidden mark of a bond with Rudolf Steiner as a friend. This bond may come to expression in a very conscious way, as in the case of Dr. Zeylmans. It may also work more indirectly, as will now be described.

You can learn to recognize this hidden soul mark by paying attention to certain subtle, intimate experiences when you meet people for the first time. To this end, you must learn to distinguish between two kinds of encounters. The first kind is related primarily to your own karma. The second kind usually has hardly any such relation to yourself. Externally the two kinds of encounters are indistinguishable. Internally you can learn to notice the difference. How is this difference observed?

With encounters of the second kind you can notice a subtle inner stirring, like an admonition of conscience, whose message speaks somewhat like this, "Be very quiet now; this soul does not come to meet you. It comes to find its way to Rudolf Steiner. Be very quiet now, and listen deeply, lest you block its path." In this way you become aware of a subtle force that works subconsciously in the other soul, but which can easily be frightened away by the crude ways of modern life. By paying attention to this kind of inner experience you can learn to recognize this soul force. It is the expression of a dormant relation, a dormant friendship, with Rudolf Steiner. This relation is present in a germinal form and wants to unfold, but can do so only through encounters with others in whom the relation with Steiner is more conscious.

The encounters of the first kind are devoid of this kind of subtle message.

VII

About the Thread of Tragedy in Rudolf Steiner's Life

If you learn to test encounters in the way described in the last chapter, three powerful feelings arise. First you can experience a feeling of grave responsibility to the powers of karma that lead people to their encounters. Then there can be a feeling of great joy about the large number of latent friendships with Rudolf Steiner, of which you become aware in this way. Finally, you can feel a great sorrow, as you notice how many of these latent friendship-relations fail to germinate and to develop to maturity. Thus, this domain of experiences usually contains a tragic element. A corresponding thread of tragedy runs through Steiner's life.

Central in Steiner's life-task or mission were his researches of karma. They culminate in the recognition of the Christ spirit as the "Lord of Karma," that same spirit who passed through the Mystery of Golgotha, the mystery of Death and Resurrection. Karma research and research concerning the light and warmth that radiate from the Christ spirit into all parts of the spiritual world formed principal elements of his mission in life.

It lies in the very nature of this mission that it cannot be carried out alone. It requires the cooperation and the help of others. But alas, all too often, too little of this cooperation and of this help was forthcoming too late. That seems to be the major cause of the thread of tragedy that runs through Steiner's life. We shall return to this theme more fully later. Here we describe only one single event of characteristic significance.

On September 28, 1924, Steiner addressed for the last time a gathering of members of the Anthroposophical Society. The illness that would eventually consume his life forces forced him to cancel all engagements thereafter. This last address[7] he gave in the *Schreinerei* to an audience of

600 to 800 members of the Anthroposophical Society who had gathered for the Michaelmas festival conference. In this lecture he felt impelled to say: "When in at least four times twelve people in the near future the Michael thought can come to full life—in four times twelve people, who are recognized as such not by themselves but by those who direct the Goetheanum in Dornach—when among such four times twelve people there arise leaders for the Michael festival mood, then we may look forward to the light which is to spread throughout humanity in the future through the Michael stream, the Michael activity."

Forty-eight bearers of Michaelic thought were not there, and one had to hope for them in the future. That was the deep tragedy. Yet it was presented in such a selfless, objective, and artistic way, that those present hardly realized its tragic aspect. In retrospect it appears tragic to an almost unbearable degree that the forty-eight needed to form the human vessel for this most sublime sun-archangel, Michael, the herald of Christ, could not be realized at this most decisive point in time, when Steiner had given all of his wisdom, love, and strength.

VIII
Rudolf Steiner as a Teacher

Rudolf Steiner was engaged in teaching activities for the greater part of his life. Already in high school, and later at the University in Vienna, he tutored fellow students extensively in order to earn his upkeep. Then he became the tutor at the home of the Specht family in Vienna, where he was charged with special care for a severely retarded hydrocephalic child, whom he brought back to normalcy in the course of about two years. Later he taught courses at a workmen's evening school in Berlin. Reports indicate that Steiner's courses were so lively and interesting that their enrollment swelled, while attendance in other courses of that school declined. Understandably this caused considerable jealousy among his colleagues.

Later his lecturing activity covered most of Europe, from Norway to Sicily, from Finland to England and Hungary, with a total of more than six thousand lectures. During the height of his lecturing activity, the largest halls in major cities were crowded to capacity. Often many people had to be turned away. His innovative ideas in primary and secondary education have given rise to the Waldorf School Movement, the second largest nondenominational private school movement in the world. The teachers of the first Waldorf school were trained and guided by him as a teacher of teachers.

From 1909 to 1914 he also developed an esoteric school for the training and inner spiritual development of members of the Theosophical Society, later the Anthroposophical Society, in Germany. He discontinued this activity at the outbreak of the First World War in 1914, but resumed it in a transformed way in 1924 as the School of Spiritual Science at the Goetheanum in Dornach. This school still functions today.

It is fair to say that teaching, in a variety of forms, and at various levels, runs as a major thread through Steiner's life. Quite early he developed exceptional didactic skills. Having noted this, we must not forget the multitude of other creative activities in which he was also engaged productively.

What kind of teacher was he, and what were his ideals as a teacher? This question can be answered at several levels. We need to inquire first what types of students can be distinguished, for effective teaching must meet the predispositions of the students.

I should like to posit that one can divide adult students or learners into four main types. No real student fits one of these types exactly; most students will be mixtures of all four types with one type clearly dominant.

The first type of student cannot learn through presentations in verbal form, only by doing. Textbooks are useless to him except for the illustrations. Learning proceeds for him by experimentation and by imitating what others are doing. This type of student requires a teacher who does not teach in traditional ways, but who brings to the environment of the student such circumstances as will encourage—and are worthy of—imitation, and which will challenge him to expand his "do it yourself" knowledge. Often the preschool child has many traits in common with this first type.

The second type of student has a need to believe with absolute trust in his teacher as an authority and as an expert. Whatever comes from his teacher is accepted unconditionally and uncritically. If this type of student finds a good teacher he may learn a great deal. However, he is subject to two great dangers.

The first danger is that he may become a parrot, repeating the words or actions of his teacher without having made their meaning sufficiently his own. The second danger is that he may close himself to learning from other sources. Thus he may become intellectually dependent on his teacher. This type of student requires a teacher who, on the one hand, will respond with understanding to the student's need to attach himself to an authority, without which he would be unable to learn, and who, on the other hand, possesses the wisdom and moral strength to guide the student gradually toward overcoming his dependence on his teacher and to stand on his own feet. This can best be accomplished by stimulating the student's creative artistic activities. This student attitude is quite normal in primary school children. It is also found in certain adult esoteric schools of inner development that are rooted in Eastern traditions.

The third type of student is the most successful one, given the state of consciousness of our time. He is able to learn from a teacher and he can make what he learns his own by using sound judgment. In addition, he is free to go beyond his teacher, both by learning from other sources and by his own independent research. One might say that the whole world is his teacher, but he knows that the whole world has also been the teacher to others, and therefore others may teach him. This type of student requires a teacher who acts as a guide, as a friend, or as an older brother. His teaching is not based on authority, but rather aims at awakening and strengthening the student's self, his faculty of sound judgment, his "test all things and hold fast what is good," his ability to find his way in new situations. This student attitude is normally expected, or encouraged as an ideal, at the high school and college level. Also a few esoteric schools of self-development acknowledge this ideal.

There is a fourth type of "student," hardly worthy of the name, whose intent is not to learn, but to achieve a semblance of learning, for social purposes such as for conversation, entertainment, etc. This eclectic type of "student" may be stimulating company. He may also be an impostor. He will never take knowledge very seriously in his own life. He may seek out all sorts of teachers, but will end up with none.

We return now to the question of what sort of teacher Steiner was, and what his ideals were as a teacher. From what has been stated, it should be clear that he was able to benefit students of all four types. However, when dealing with adults, his main emphasis was directed towards the third type. He often directed attention away from his own person by referring to many other great figures in history. Regarding matters of esoteric self-development he wrote:

"No teacher of spiritual life wishes to establish a mastery over other persons… He would not tamper with anyone's independence. Indeed, none respect and cherish human independence more than the spiritually experienced."[8]

"The teacher (of esoteric training) can never offer anything unless the recipient comes forward to meet him of his own free will."[9]

"It must be emphasized that higher knowledge is not concerned with the veneration of persons, but with the veneration of truth and knowledge."[10]

"... for one seeking spiritual schooling... a direct relation to the spiritual world is of far greater importance than a relation to the personality of the teacher. The latter will gradually become merely the helper; he will assume the same position in spiritual schooling as a teacher occupies, in conformity with modern views, in any other field of knowledge."[11]

"All who apply to those possessing knowledge and experience... must realize that what they seek is the advice of a friend, not the domination of a would-be ruler."[12]

These quotes could be amplified by many more to show that Steiner saw his role as a teacher, be it for exoteric or esoteric instruction, as a stimulator of interest and insight in the student, with avoidance of any kind of pressure or coercion; as an adviser and helper, as a guide and wise friend where guidance and wisdom were sought.

Steiner often would answer a question or a request put to him in such an amazingly profound way that he clearly must have worked at this subject for quite a long time. Yet he would never show his profound grasp of a field unless a question was put to him. This is merely one aspect of his biography that illustrates that he adhered to the above statements in his own life.

Among the students of his works all four of the types described can be found. Steiner has something positive to offer to all of them. His main emphasis is always toward awakening a keen sense for truth, a wide-ranging and delicate sense for beauty and harmony, and a deep sense of responsibility; all of these in a fluid and meaningful process of evolution, in which the unique and divine spirit of Christ is central.

Though I have never met Steiner, I have had the privilege of meeting many of his students. They all were fired with enthusiasm for life and full of creative originality. Their lives, achievements, and personalities were a living testimony of Steiner's ability to bring out the best in his students, more so than any words of conventional praise could convey. It is therefore understandable that even today, more than sixty years after his death, many people feel that they can learn from Steiner, either first-hand through his books (his complete works, including the published lecture cycles, comprise about 350 volumes), or second-hand through students of his works. They feel they can learn from him in several respects. First, they can learn about many facts in a new, integrated, meaningful perspective. Second, they can learn to improve their own skills and faculties, especially the faculty to steer their own lives in a meaningful way in the context of humanity.

Though many people today are in great need for much of what Steiner has to offer, and are aware of their needs, they hesitate to devote a great deal of time and effort to exploring the works of a man who is not widely known in the English-speaking world. When this subject comes up in conversation one often meets with the response, "I should like to know first who Rudolf Steiner was." This attitude is not only quite understandable, it is fully justified. For it is well known—as Steiner also often states—that *what* is said or written may have a very different meaning, depending on *who* says it or writes it. There is a fair number of biographies of Steiner available, but it is not easy to gain from them a picture of the inner man, Rudolf Steiner. How can we approach this inner man? In the following chapters we shall try to point out ways to approach Steiner in this sense.

IX

A First Step in Approaching Rudolf Steiner

A good first step in approaching Rudolf Steiner today consists of seeking out one single concept that was particularly important in guiding him to the highest summits and to the deepest abysses of the spiritual world, not only to other human souls and spirits, but also to the spiritual beings of the cosmos, the angelic hierarchies, and the various kinds of elemental beings.

There may be several answers to this quest, but certainly one major concept of this kind is selfless selfhood (*selbstloses Selbstsein*)

Steiner refers to this concept in numerous places. Many allusions to it may be found in the verses of his *Calendar of the Soul*,[13] for example in the last lines of the thirty-fifth verse. Selfless selfhood implies being fully true to oneself, yet in a selfless way, that is, in harmony with the cosmos. Precisely through Steiner's exceedingly highly developed selfless selfhood was it possible for many cosmic beings to speak through him, with his fully conscious control and cooperation. The noted German poet Christian Morgenstern (1871-1914) has formulated this beautifully in the following poem, written in 1912 upon hearing a number of Rudolf Steiner's lecture cycles, which he had attended from 1909 on whenever it was possible for him to do so.[14]

Er sprach. Und wie er sprach, erschien in ihm
Der Tierkreis, Cherubim and Seraphim,
Der Sonnenstern, der Wandel der Planeten,
Von Ort zu Ort.

Das alles sprang hervor bei seinem Laut,
Ward blitzschnell, wie ein Weltentraum, erschaut,
Der ganze Himmel schien herabgebeten
Bei seinem Wort.

Admittedly an intricately wrought poem of this sort defies translation. Here follows my attempt at translation:

He spoke. And as he spoke, there shone in him
The zodiac, the Cherubim and Seraphim,
The sun-star, planets wand'ring, orbs entwined,
From place to place.

This all sprang forth now as he told,
Like a cosmic dream, in lightning to behold,
And all the heavens seemed to earth inclined
At his word's grace.

True it is that all that Steiner spoke was an expression of his personal experience and was permeated by his personal will. Yet, equally true it is that at the same time he was a vessel through whom the wisdom of the Akashic record—that living spiritual record of the complete past of man and world—could find utterance; through whom also the spirit of the present time, the lofty archangel Michael, found voice to make his guidance known; through whom at times even higher spirits chose to find expression. All of this was only possible through his selfless selfhood.

Once this quality of selfless selfhood is understood as the leading trait of Steiner's nature, it can readily be seen that a positive relation to him can only be established insofar as one is able to partake, oneself, in this quality of selfless selfhood. To this conclusion we are inevitably led by our contemplation of this first step in approaching Steiner. This conclusion may be put in another way:

Those persons whose selfhood lacks selflessness, in other words, those who are entirely selfish and self-centered, may be expected to be unable to establish a positive relation to Steiner.

Those persons who lack selfhood, either as a result of training in this sense, or as a result of circumstances of life, also may be expected to be unable to establish a positive relation to Steiner.

Only those in whom a living balance between selfhood and selflessness is maintained are likely to establish a positive relation to Steiner.

X
A Second Step in Approaching Rudolf Steiner

A good second step in approaching Rudolf Steiner is the study of reports of contemporaries who experienced him personally. We pointed already to Schuré, Zeylmans, and Morgenstern. Many others could be added, resulting in a mosaic of impressions in a wide variety of settings, described from a wide variety of viewpoints. An interesting collection may be found in the periodical *The Golden Blade* of 1958.[15]

A particularly telling addition to all of these is the moving description which Dr. Guenther Wachsmuth gives of Steiner's visit to the ruins of King Arthur's castle in Tintagel, England. Wachsmuth writes:[16]

> He spoke there, standing on the cliff, about the experiences of the Knights of King Arthur, who experienced in this external struggle of the forces of light with the elements of the earth a reflection of their own inner battles ... As he then surveyed from the highest point of the cliff the remains of the walls of the ancient castle, which indicated the structure of the mystery place of King Arthur in its external lines, the past became present for him in his spiritual vision, and he described to us in living pictures—pointing with his hand to the various parts of the castle—where the hall of the round table had once been, the rooms of the king and of his knights. The immediacy of the spiritual vision in this place was so intense that, during his description, the entire reality, the external life and action, as well as the inner willing and achievement of the circle of King Arthur's Knights stood before us as actual experience.

Why is this story so particularly telling? Wachsmuth describes here one of Steiner's most outstanding and remarkable soul-features: his faculty of *spiritual envisioning*. This faculty he was able to actuate in broad daylight and in the presence of many people. At this occasion it seemed to work almost contagiously on those present. One could also say that those present were awakened a little toward the spirit.

Similar experiences with Steiner have been reported independently by many contemporaries. There can be no doubt that he was a "seer," who had access to the worlds of soul and spirit while simultaneously in full control of his waking consciousness. His seership was permeated by a most human quality. Always it tended to link the unseen world with the world of the senses, so that the latter would become more transparent and meaningful. It was never in opposition to the world of the senses, therefore never in trance or other states of dimmed consciousness, but always with heightened wakefulness.

Steiner possessed this faculty already as a child. Later he was able to transform this natural spiritual vision into a consciously directed faculty. His work gives ample evidence that not only was he in full possession and control of this rare faculty for himself, but also, that he saw this as a dormant power in every human being, and he taught methodical ways of self-development and self-education toward awakening such a faculty. In a distant future he expected such faculties to become the common possession of all of mankind.

Here it seems reasonable to ask: How can we ever hope to approach Steiner if we do not possess the faculty of spiritual envisioning, which is so central to his whole being? Are we not in a position that many express bluntly by saying, "*He* saw it, but *we* see nothing?"

This manner of stating the question stems from a thorough misapprehension of the problem, and therefore is not fruitful. For the results of Steiner's supersensible perceptions were always cast into a logically understandable form in order to make them intelligible. We should be alert here to the difference between belief and understanding. Belief in what a person says means to give one's own assent to his statements. Understanding means that one understands the meaning of what the other person says and, as yet, gives it neither assent nor dissent. To the degree that a person can meet Steiner's statements with the understanding of his sound, unprejudiced mind, he is able to approach Steiner. In fact, the response of this kind of understanding is all that Steiner asked for and hoped for from the public. What Steiner had to say about any matter, he intended to be a stimulant. As a helper and as a guide he tried to lead his readers or listeners to finding their own relation to any content presented. Therefore, he casts his presentations in a noncompelling, logically consistent narrative form.

If we wish to approach Steiner's being, we must meet his work, including his statements about the supersensible, with the kind of understanding here described, namely an understanding that holds a clear and perfect balance between blind belief and negating disbelief.

We conclude, therefore, that in approaching Steiner we must reckon with his highly developed faculty of spiritual envisioning. We must recognize it and acknowledge it, rather than evade it or place ourselves completely outside of it. What is needed is an attempt at entering with empathy and understanding into his power of envisioning, as far as we are able to do so, while all the while maintaining our full wakefulness and our unprejudiced and logical mind. Through selflessness we can enter into an understanding of this aspect of his being; through selfhood we guard against illusion and error. In the next chapter an example of such an approach will be given.

XI

Rudolf Steiner's Faculty of Spiritual Envisioning as Manifest in His Fairy Tale of the Wonderous Spring in the Rocks

Between 1910 and 1913 Rudolf Steiner wrote—and directed performances of—a series of four mystery plays. In the second play, "The Soul's Probation,"[17] the fifth scene is set in a remote mountain landscape, where Felix Balde, a recluse, lives with his wife Felicia. When the central figure of this play, professor Capesius, a renowned historian, feels utterly burnt out, he visits the Balde's lonely mountain cottage, where he feels his vital energies recharged by listening to fairy tales, which Felicia's creative imagination is able to generate spontaneously. In this scene she tells to Capesius the famous fairy tale of the wondrous spring in the rocks.

In summary, the fairy tale tells of a sensitive boy whose soul is wide open to the influences and moods of nature around him. He often spends many hours on moonlit nights at a lonely mountain spring, where water gushes forth and forms a spray-mist as it tumbles down from one rock to another. One night, as the boy gazes into the sparkling mist, he discerns three fairies, who fashion from the mist-droplets a gleaming silver chalice, filled with moonlight, which the boy then receives from them as a gift. But in the night that follows, he dreams that a fierce dragon robs him of the precious gift. Four times these wondrous events happen, then no more.

Twenty-one years later this boy has become a young man who lives in a big city. One evening he is exhausted from work and wonders what life may still have to offer him. Suddenly he feels transported to the spring he knew so well in his youth, and the same three fairies appear again. This time they speak to him. They tell him that he may turn to them for help whenever he is in difficulties. Specifically, the first fairy advises him to turn to her when he feels lonely. She will then strengthen him with the "draught of hope in life." Likewise he is told to turn to the second fairy when he feels discouraged. She will help him overcome this condition by providing the "power of faith in life." And when he is confused about life's problems, the third fairy will enlighten him with "living rays of love." The three fairies have been his invisible companions all the time. And now, at a more mature station of life, he dreams again of the dragon who formerly robbed him, but who cannot approach now, owing to the protection by the fairies.

Like most good fairy tales, this one can be interpreted at many levels. At a superficial level one might say: Felicia tries to tell Capesius: "Don't let loneliness, discouragement, or confusion depress you. Draw strength and confidence from revitalizing the dreams and ideals of your younger years, which motivated you to steer the course in life as you did." In order to reach through to Capesius she had to bypass his abstract intellect; therefore she chose the picture form of a fairy tale.

An interpretation at a deeper level might run as follows: We assume that Steiner in his younger years had himself the spiritual experiences with the fairies described in this tale. In support of this assumption we note:

a) This fairy tale is completely original. The fairy tale literature offers no analogue from which he might have borrowed.

b) The events are described with many details.

c) We know that Steiner spent his youth in a mountainous part of Austria, also that a jar of sparkling spring water from a spring a couple of miles away from home was considered a special treat at the meals of the family. Young Rudolf often went to fetch this water.

d) Steiner describes in his autobiography and related literature several instances in his youth of inner envisioning experiences whose content differs, but whose character is similar to the one described in this fairy tale.

Our assumption is not contradicted by what Steiner stated in a lecture on June 8, 1923, twelve years after the fairy tale was written, "This is ancient mystery wisdom: In the daytime one sees light with one's physical body, but at night one does not see merely the sunlight, but the sunlight is caught in the silver chalice of the moon. The moon was the silver chalice which caught the sunlight at night. And this sunlight which was caught at night in the silver moon chalice the soul would drink; it was its soma-drink."

The fairy tale tells of a special gift of elemental clairvoyance—the chalice filled with moonlight—which young Steiner derived from his intimate relation to nature, of which he would be deprived temporarily through the influence of the materialistic culture that surrounded him. (He uses the "dragon" as a symbol for materialistic culture at other occasions.) But he was to regain this faculty in a more articulate form as a young man. In this new form it was not only proof against the "dragon," but provided a source of strength for coping with the difficulties which the young Steiner encountered in life.

In summary, we see that this beautiful fairy tale can be interpreted as a stylized and adapted form of personal spiritual envisionings that Steiner experienced as a child, and in a transformed and matured way, as a young man twenty-one years later.

Finally, we interpret the fairy tale at a third level, by making use of Steiner's anthroposophical ideas. This interpretation aims at a meaning that transcends the personal and deals with issues of human nature in general. To do so seems justified because the thrust of these mystery plays is not merely personal. Rather, they reveal through their characters broad problems and developments of human nature in general, so that anyone can identify to some degree with each of the characters of the plays.

We note several specific traits in this fairy tale: In the first part, experiences are described at the level of imaginative consciousness, in silent pictures. The imagination derives here from the silvery moonlight. It is connected with the "spiritual moon sphere."[18] In order to arrive at a higher level of consciousness, the pictures of imaginative consciousness must first be extinguished. One can then achieve inspirative consciousness, where intent and meaning are expressed in a kind of inner speech. This domain refers no longer to the "moon sphere."

Accordingly, in the second part, no mention is made any more of the moon. But the fairies now speak. Moreover, in this domain everything is permeated by a moral dimension, which provides the strength to overcome the dragon. The fairies speak of ways to solve major moral problems that beset mankind today. They speak at a level to which the dragon no longer has access. Traditionally, the dragon is slain, or at least subdued, by Saint Michael, the archangelic representative of the sun. In other words, the second part of the fairy tale is connected with the "spiritual sun sphere."[19]

In this fairy tale, personal experience is transformed in a selfless way, so as to become an expression of ways to deal with the great life problems of contemporary man: loneliness, discouragement or fear or insecurity, and confusion or lack of meaning. The fairies indeed offer what is needed in order to cope with these life problems. The roots of these problems lie deeply embedded in human evolution.

The first problem, the problem of loneliness, arises from the realization that man is born out of the divine. Divine as man's origin may be, this birth leads to a painful feeling of estrangement or loneliness. This loneliness can only be overcome by generating interest in the world that is spread out around us in space. To achieve this one must feel part of life, that is, a connectedness with one's environment. Pictorially speaking, one needs the "draught of hope in life." In Rudolf Steiner's fairy tale this is precisely the gift that the first fairy offers to the young man.

The second problem comes from the realization that all life ends inexorably in death. This can drain all courage and enthusiasm. It can lead to discouragement, apathy, fear, and insecurity. Here it is necessary to realize that Death has been transformed through the Mystery of Golgotha, Crucifixion, and Resurrection of Christ. One who realizes this in depth will be able to maintain courage even in the face of death. Pictorially speaking, he obtains the "power of faith in life." This is the gift that the second fairy promises.

Finally, the third problem takes hold of us if the world seems so confusing and poses so many unsolved and seemingly unsolvable riddles that our own life seems devoid of sense and meaning. Then we must turn to that spiritual power which leads man to inner freedom. This freedom can be achieved only by first illuminating our motivations and then by awakening love, permeated by insight, for our actions. This is explained in detail in Rudolf Steiner's main work, *The Philosophy of Freedom*.[20] What better picture is possible for this love, permeated and borne by the light of wisdom, than "living rays of love?" Just this is the promise of the third fairy.

The three gifts or promises of the fairies, hope, faith, and love, are here pictured in a selfless, artistic way as the forces that modern man needs in order to deal effectively with these three major problem areas of life. In this way we can learn to see this fairy tale as a beautiful manifestation of Steiner's faculty of envisioning, here directed at the basic life problems of modern man.

One question remains to be considered: Whence do these three forces, these three fairy gifts, originate? They originate in the spiritual sun sphere![21] Therefore, in order to get to know Rudolf Steiner more intimately, we must learn to understand his relation to the sun sphere. That can take us one step closer to him.

XII

Rudolf Steiner and the Sun Sphere

Since Old Testament times it has been known that among the seven principal archangels one was most exalted, namely Michael, the ruler of the spiritual sun sphere. The seven archangels rotate as regents of human evolution, each one leading in turn for a period of about 300 years, so that a complete cycle of all seven is accomplished in 2,160 years,[22] the duration of a cultural period. In other words, each cultural period has the benefit of the guidance of each of the seven archangels. What is the situation of our own time in this context? Michael, the sun archangel, became the regent of human evolution in the latter part of November of 1879. Did anything special happen on earth at that time?

If you study Steiner's power of envisioning, you come soon upon a mysterious point in his life. He is guided to his initiation. We know that his friend, the herb gatherer Felix Koguzki, took him one day to a person in Vienna, whose name is not known.[23] This person "stimulated in Rudolf Steiner those things with which one must be familiar in the spiritual world." That happened in November of 1879! Thus, Rudolf Steiner became the first initiate of the present period of Michael's regency! This event awakened in Steiner the power that would enable him to wage the fierce battle "against the dragon of the materialistic world conception and against the bull of public opinion." The unknown master released his pupil into the world with the words, "You know now who you are—act accordingly—always true to yourself."[24]

Thus the present Michael period was ushered in by this outwardly completely unnoticed event of the initiation of Rudolf Steiner, who became thereby the representative of Michael on earth, charged to do battle for the spiritual well-being, nay, the spiritual survival, of mankind.

All friends of Rudolf Steiner, all of his students, and all those who bear in their soul that hidden mark of a connection with him, as described earlier, are of necessity deeply involved in this battle. Indeed, already before their life on earth began were they deeply involved in it. When they went on their way toward their present incarnation, starting from spiritual heights, contracting gradually from cosmic distances, they had to pass through the spiritual sun sphere. There they—who now on earth feel a bond with anthroposophy—were imbued with this bond. From angelic spirits who serve Michael they received in the sun sphere an extra measure of spirit strength and light—more than was to be expected according to their individual karma—in order to help thereby on earth toward a spiritual awakening of humanity. Acceptance of this sacrificial angelic gift in the sun sphere implies, of course, a great responsibility to bring this gift to the fullest possible fruition on earth. This is a deeper aspect of the positive relationships that people feel toward Rudolf Steiner.

From 1879, Steiner had conscious access to the sun sphere. From his position as an initiate of the sun sphere, he was able—by surveying the Akashic record—to provide mankind with new concepts and forces, which present human evolution sorely needs. He was able to illumine the unique cosmic and earthly significance of the Mystery of Golgotha with new light that had never shone before, but which can answer deep soul longings in our time. The Christ mystery encompasses an earthly and a cosmic mystery. The latter is a sun-mystery. The "Foundation Stone Verse"[25] hints at this sun-mystery with the call "Christ-Sun!"

The sun initiate created in Dornach (Switzerland) a new mystery center, which has—in the sense of Michael—branches throughout the whole world. Its central building, the first Goetheanum, was built in a most original style of wondrous beauty. It conformed to form laws which, as was the case with all true mystery centers of the past, imbued it with an attractive force or vortex for the etheric formative forces of the cosmos.

Creative work on earth always runs the danger of provoking evil counter forces. Though the forces of the spiritual sun sphere are in themselves proof against all abuse, they may encounter among men on earth conditions that may render them ineffective here. This is the root cause why even in the most wonderful sun impulses there weaves usually a tragic motif.

It was tragic that Steiner had to speak so often for ears which did not hear; tragic also that he had to build in a world where destruction has a free hand; most tragic that he had to work in a world where all around the "wars of all against all" are being prepared. Externally this motif of tragedy is most poignantly manifest in the arson that caused the first Goetheanum to burn down in 1922/23.

It is true that soon a second, more effectively fortified, Goetheanum arose on the ashes of the first one. It is also true that Steiner's productivity rose to incredible heights in answer to this event. Nevertheless, the impulses of this mystery center, as well as Steiner's own life forces, suffered a sensitive blow through this tragedy.

The high moral quality that permeates Steiner's work in all domains of life can be comprehended only from the sun sphere. When he returned to this sphere after his death, to the council of great initiates and masters, one may well assume that his stature had grown so much during his earth life that his spirit-word carried a particularly incisive significance. (By "spirit-word" we mean a spiritual activity in the sun sphere that expresses intent and meaning.) Through this spirit-word, which has to be reborn ever and ever again out of the spirit fire of the sun sphere, and only through this, does anthroposophy still exist on earth today. For it is highly remarkable how anthroposophy grows, slowly, quietly, steadily, sixty years after Steiner's death.

The meaning of a positive relation to Rudolf Steiner, a friendship, must include ever anew the kindling and the bringing to radiance of this sun-spirit-word, the power that was his source of inspiration. Some further aspects of this will be described in the next chapter.

XIII

Benedictus, Representative of the Sun Sphere, and Rudolf Steiner

In Rudolf Steiner's mystery plays,[26] we meet with a figure named Benedictus, who reveals in stylized form many personal experiences of Steiner. Benedictus appears always at the right time and the right place when one of his pupils needs guidance for the next step in inner development. He is also the golden hierophant in the sun temple.

Whether or not Steiner intended Benedictus as a kind of self-portrait is a controversial question of little merit. It is clear on the one hand that Steiner was an initiate of the sun sphere, and on the other hand that Benedictus represents the typical initiate of the sun sphere. Therefore the two must conform to one another in all essential aspects.

For an uninitiated friend today, there is no better way to approach Steiner than to add to the study of the usual biographical sources, and to the approaches mentioned earlier in this booklet, a thorough study of the words and deeds of Benedictus. From these plays, one can begin to understand the tremendous discipline, love, and strength, which he developed and placed in the service of those cosmic powers that work in the sense of the spiritual revitalization of mankind. Also, one can gain a better understanding of the adversary powers, "Lucifer and Ahriman," who tend to thwart or to abuse all efforts towards man's spiritual reascent.

A study of Benedictus in these plays is an extensive task, too extensive to be carried out within the scope of this booklet. We shall therefore limit ourselves to one carefully selected example. In the fourth mystery play,[27] "The Soul's Awakening," the fifth scene is entitled "The Spirit Realm." There Benedictus identifies himself as a representative of the sun sphere. He also states the conditions under which one may approach him and establish a positive relation to him:

Ihr druckt gewaltig meinen Weltenkreis
mit euren dichten erdbeladnen Sphären.
Wenn ihr den Selbstsinn weiter kraften lässt,
So findet ihr in diesem Geistessein
Mein Sonnenwesen nicht in euch erstrahlen.[28]

This may be translated as:

You weigh down heavily my cosmic sphere
With the condensed earth-laden spheres of yours.
Should you let self-indulgence grow too strong,
Then you will find that in this spirit life
My own sun nature cannot shine within you
   (ray forth within you).

These lines are worth pondering deeply. A great deal of information is compacted into them. Benedictus speaks here unambiguously of his sun nature; his nature belongs to the spiritual sun sphere. And what is required, if one wants to approach him? This is expressed in the form of an admonition. In speaking this admonition he avoids forms such as, Thou shalt not do this or that. Rather: <u>If</u> you do *this*, <u>then</u> you yourself will find that the consequences are *that*. This form is also typical for the way Steiner taught.

And what is the content of his admonition? In earthly life we tend to overemphasize our own selfhood. It becomes a kind of indulgence in the self ("Selbstsinn"). If one is to enter the sun sphere this must be tempered. It must be transformed into selfless selfhood, as described earlier. Only if this transformation is achieved are the conditions right for entering the sun sphere, and for establishing a positive relation with Benedictus—Rudolf Steiner. For a positive relation with a being in the sun sphere can only be established if it is established in conformity with the conditions of that sphere.

What is the character of such a sun-relation? The essential being of the one is to light up and shine in the other one and radiate from him, and *vice versa*. This type of relation has long been known. The Gospel of Saint John alludes to relations of this sort. Of the numerous instances given there, a few are quoted here:

14:11 I am in the Father and the Father in me.
14:20 Ye in me and I in you.
15:4   Abide in me, and I in you.
15:5   He that abideth in me, and I in him, the same bringeth forth much fruit.

Of course, Christ is a being incomparably more exalted than Steiner. The point, however, is that Saint John sets forth here examples of the rules that obtain in the sun sphere. These rules must be adhered to for establishing a positive relation to any being in the sun sphere.

If your relation to Rudolf Steiner is to be in the nature of a friendship, then his essential being must gradually shine within and ray forth from you, in the way which is characteristic of the sun sphere. This may be possible only to a very limited degree; this then is the limited degree to which such a friendship is possible.

In the moon sphere it would be sufficient to keep the *image* of a friend alive in one's soul. In the sun sphere his "essential being" must become radiant within us. Within the friends of Rudolf Steiner his sun-spirit-word must ever anew be born, kindled, brought to radiance, to the degree that this is possible.

In this connection it is good to remember another aspect of Benedictus—Rudolf Steiner. His words were not intended merely as instruments to convey information. His words were intended as forces that awaken dormant faculties in the soul.[29] Benedictus expresses this as follows:

Es wollen meine Worte nicht das allein nur sagen,
was als Begriffeshüllen sie verraten,
sie lenken Seelenwesenskräfte
zu Geisteswirklichkeiten

Zu führen an Erkenntnisquellen
ist dieser Worte Eigenheit.

This may be translated as:

I do not wish my words to say merely
what they convey as a vehicle for concepts.
They turn the natural forces of the soul
to the realities of spirit.

It is in the nature of these words
to guide to founts of knowledge.

Especially this aspect of his words—to carry a force that tends to guide or lead to sources of knowledge—reveals a quality of the sun sphere. It is this aspect that enables one to become gradually more and more a "friend of Rudolf Steiner" in the sense described.

Summary and Outlook

In summary, a way has been described that can lead gradually to a better and better understanding of Rudolf Steiner, even to the development of a friendship relation with him. Such a development may show a great deal of variation from one person to another. Usually it will pass through the following stages:

1. Getting acquainted with Steiner's work.
2. Recognizing the significance of his work for one's own life.
3. Becoming aware of the personal-superpersonal stamp of his work.
4. Studying biographical sources, such as reports of his contemporary students as well as his autobiography.
5. Realizing that the connection with him points beyond the present life.
6. Recognizing the importance of his work for our time.
7. Recognizing him as the leading initiate of our present Michaelic age.

Rarely did Steiner speak about his own person, and when he did, it was always filtered through selfless selfhood, reluctant and with great objectivity. Indeed, the writing of his autobiography, unfinished through his untimely death, was only undertaken because of the persistent urgings of friends. Even so, it tells more about other people who influenced him than about himself.

Once, however, in 1925, only a few weeks before his death, he wrote a mantric verse in which he expressed concisely what was the driving force of his will, the task to which he had dedicated his life. Exceptionally, this verse begins with the word "I." If you wish to develop a friendship with Rudolf Steiner, you would do well to ponder from time to time what was the goal of his striving, and what opposing forces this striving will encounter:[30]

Ich möchte jeden Menschen aus des Kosmos' Geist entzünden
Dass er Flamme werde
Und feurig seines Wesens Wesen entfalte. —

Die Andern, sie möchten aus des Kosmos' Wasser nehmen
Was die Flammen verlöscht
Und wässrig alles Wesen im Innern lähmt. —

O Freude, wenn die Menschenflamme lodert, Auch da, wo sie ruht! —

O Bittern is, wenn das Menschending gebunden wird, Da wo es regsam sein möchte.

This may be translated as:

I want with cosmic spirit to enthuse each human being
That a flame he may become
And fiery will unfold his being innermost.

The other ones, they strive to take from cosmic waters
What will extinguish flames
And pour paralysis into all inner being.
Oh joy, when human being's flame
Is blazing, even when at rest.
Oh bitter pain, when the human thing
Is put in bonds when it wants to stir.

In this verse the first part expresses Rudolf Steiner's ideal as perceived from the sun sphere. It describes his very "I."

The second part describes the hindrances—they are of an Ahrimanic nature—which emanate from the moon sphere. These are "The other ones."[31] The third part reflects the earth situation, which is a give-and-take dynamic balance, midway between these poles, swinging now more to the joyful sun side and then again more to the tearful moon side. During his life on earth Steiner always strove to find in this way a right balance.

What will be the pragmatic meaning of friendship with Rudolf Steiner in the future?

As the number of people who recognize Steiner's sun nature grows—for the time being this growth process is bound to be a very slow one—it is likely that destiny will cause two things to happen. On the one hand such "Friends of Rudolf Steiner" will find themselves scattered to rather isolated places on earth, where it will become their wish and their self-imposed task to inject into the culture of our age something of the impulses of the spiritual sun sphere of which mention has been made. On the other, hand they will learn spontaneously to recognize each other as brothers, whenever their paths cross. This will eventually give rise to a "Brotherhood of Friends of Rudolf Steiner," not in any formal organization, on the contrary, a brotherhood whose bond is effective only by way of the spirit, without any outer organization. Nevertheless, effective.

Well do I know that in our time such a perspective sounds to many fantastic, utopian, or irrelevant. Let me therefore end by reminding the reader of a phrase from the early pages of this booklet, "This booklet is written out of a concern for the spiritual well-being of man in the future, a sense of responsibility toward future generations. It is intended as a conversation reaching out across future times. Contemporaries are welcome to participate."

4

Meditation — An Introduction

When you undertake a single step forward in the knowledge of spirit realities, take at the same time three steps forward in the development of your character toward the good.

— Rudolf Steiner

MERELY A DECADE or two ago the word "meditation" was hardly current in this country. Today a host of occult movements, often based on Eastern influences, have come to be known by many people, and most of these movements practice what they call meditation, though the word refers to somewhat different practices in each movement.

Representatives of one movement will teach you their technique of meditation in four easy lessons for just $75, other movements make their information available essentially free of charge. Some teach daily meditation, others meditate primarily on Sundays. Some meditate in solitude, others in groups. Some meditate in special positions or postures; others just assume any relaxed position. Some insist on the essential role of breath control (among them many students of Yoga), others feel that breath control does not matter, or is even harmful. Some feel that common sense should not be abandoned ever, others emphasize that the irrational in man is to be aroused in meditation. And many other relatively superficial externalities of meditation can be discussed in a more or less journalistic style, without coming to grips with the question of what meditation is really about. In this article I wish to address the more basic questions of meditation.

A first question is: *Where to find a teacher?*

It is often thought that one can learn meditation only from a teacher, a "guru." In olden times this was generally true. A teacher or guru first had to accept a student or "chela," and the latter would then become inwardly quite dependent on the former. For a modern person such a state of dependence would be far from beneficial. A basic modern question is: Is it possible to teach meditation so that your inner freedom and independence is not curtailed but, on the contrary, enhanced?

Rudolf Steiner[1] worked out of what this question implies. Therefore he is no longer a "guru," a teacher in the old sense. He is something higher, for which no word has yet been coined.

It is true, of course, that Rudolf Steiner had students during his lifetime. This author has had the privilege of meeting a considerable number of students of this "first generation." It is a striking fact, which I have experienced over and over again, that all of these students have become so very different, each one himself, each one creative in his own way, each one attuned to the world at the place where he stands in life. This experience bears out that Rudolf Steiner showed to these students a practical path, based on real freedom.

But the influence of Rudolf Steiner far transcends the range of his first generation of students. Anyone can find out for himself the actual meaning of this statement, by reading carefully the book *How to Know Higher Worlds* and related literature on meditations.[2] Then it can become clear what Rudolf Steiner means when he writes that his personal presence as a teacher is no longer necessary. The book just referred to, if read carefully and applied carefully, can teach a great deal. Through it Rudolf Steiner guides the student gently onward, into a world of meditation, in such a way that he becomes more and more free and autonomous.

The more one gets acquainted with this work of Rudolf Steiner through actual practice, the more one stands in awe of its encompassing wisdom, the completeness with which everything has been taken into account, the expertise and humanness. One can then recognize that this book has been written by one who is a master of the highest order in this subject. Once this recognition dawns on a person, it can become clear why one will not find anyone in the Anthroposophical Society today who sets himself up as a teacher of meditation, as a guru. At best you can find a friend who can give a little help here and there. The ways have been charted by Rudolf Steiner for the totality of modern humanity! I shall therefore consider meditation here in the sense in which Rudolf Steiner writes about it.

Let us now turn to the question: *What can motivate a person to practice meditation?*

The forces that govern the evolution of the sense-perceptible world—the world we see, hear, feel, etc.—are rooted in another world, an invisible world, a spiritual world. A person can strive toward developing his own spiritual potential by such means as meditation for three kinds of reasons:

1. For self-satisfaction, self-aggrandizement, to be able to earn more money, or for the purpose of acquiring more power over more people. If meditation is carried out with this kind of motivation it will ultimately damage or destroy the person.
2. For the withdrawal into the purity and bliss of one's own "Nirvana," away from the world of the senses, which is felt as a dissatisfying world. If meditation is carried out with this kind of motivation it will retard rather than enhance the person's actual development.
3. The only right motivation for meditation is that one is willing to accept a burden—an almost crushing burden—because one has recognized that one can become in this way a more effective servant of world progress, a more effective helper of mankind and of the spiritual world.

Compassion and love toward humanity must be the basic motivation for meditation. Otherwise, the cross one has to bear on the path of self-development, of which meditation is a fundamental part, becomes too heavy.

Many people want to be of service to mankind. Often they concentrate on short term goals and don't wish to work at deep changes within themselves. Many, for example, go and help underdeveloped countries, or they become social workers. But also those whose jobs do not have an aura of benevolence earn their living by means of activities that society values and needs. They are all of service. But all of their services could be much more significant if they would start to upgrade themselves, slowly and gradually, along the path of training that Rudolf Steiner describes. What matters here is not merely service to the outer, immediate needs of society—important as these may be—but especially service to the deeper needs, to the world as a whole, even to the spiritual world, in which our true home lies.

There is no reward, in the ordinary sense, for undertaking such a demanding self-training. The reward is only that one is allowed to shoulder heavier responsibilities. If you expect to *get* something in return for your efforts, you had better forget about the whole undertaking. It is not going to work. If, on the other hand, your source of love to mankind and the world is flowing freely, then this is a great reward, for it enables you to *give* more to the world.

Meditation is the way that leads slowly and gradually to a consciousness of the spiritual world. This supersensible world is always actively present within us and around us. *Why then are we not normally conscious of it?*

It is through the working of Divine Grace that this world is not open to our normal consciousness. Were we to become aware of this world suddenly and without sufficient preparation, we would be so severely shocked that we would be unable to pursue life normally any more. Therefore it is Grace that keeps this world sealed. Only those who develop gradually the requisite qualities of inner strength and perfection can experience the supersensible world. Meditation is the road that leads to experiencing of the spiritual world. What is to be encountered on this road is not coarse, like the world of the senses. The experiences are, especially at first, delicate and tender. They are very different from the impressions conveyed by the senses. Do not expect the spiritual world to be a world of visions. Visions are, after all, woven out of the same kind of impressions that the sense world offers: forms, colors, sounds, etc. The expectation of such impressions is a preconceived notion concerning the spiritual world that actually hinders your progress. Rudolf Steiner devotes much attention to this question. It should be studied carefully, so that one knows quite clearly what spiritual experience is NOT like. It is *not* the content of a vision, nor a voice, nor a dream, nor a fantasy. Such illusory experiences usually arise out of the subconscious. To take such illusory experiences at face value reveals a lack of judgment, an almost pathological condition, which should first be overcome. Misconceptions in this regard arise sometimes because the vocabulary used for expressing spiritual experiences must of necessity be taken from our ordinary language, which is adapted to our impressions from the sense world. Consequently, modes of expression are used for spiritual experiences, which careless readers might misinterpret as descriptions of illusory experiences. But then, Rudolf Steiner's works are never intended for careless readers.

Meditation is a road to real insight into the spiritual world. There exist a few examples of spiritual experiences, which every modern person can have without special training. The most typical one can be brought into focus as follows: Think of a statement that you have examined from various aspects. Suppose you have come to the conclusion: this statement is clearly true. Actually the statement may or may not be true; that is not what matters. What matters is your inner experience when you conclude that the statement is true; when you say to yourself: "Yes! I see its truth; it is quite clear." Ask yourself what you experience when you reach this conclusion with clarity. This is a very subtle experience: the experience of insight, of truth. This is one of the few spiritual experiences that we can have in our ordinary consciousness.

If you grasp this, the road is open to the understanding of Rudolf Steiner's statement: "The spiritual world is made of the same substance that thoughts are made of." Thoughts are not a product of the brain, neither are they made of any material substance. They consist of something much more alive and active than is usually recognized. And this something is of the same quality as the spiritual world. That is why meditation, an activity closely related to thinking, can lead to consciousness of the spiritual world.

Anyone who considers starting on the path of meditation should ask himself: *Am I properly prepared for such a momentous undertaking?* For most people the answer is: NO! And so we shall now turn to the question: *What preparation is required?*

Rudolf Steiner emphasizes that people will not achieve anything worthwhile in meditation if they do not first prepare themselves properly.[3] And this is accomplished by practicing the famous six *introductory exercises*.

If there is a tendency to disregard these six introductory exercises, meditation will at best be *ineffectual*, and it can even be *harmful*. People who are at first quite "normal," and who undertake work along the path of meditation without diligently practicing these six exercises, may develop psychological weaknesses such as living in illusions; being unable to distinguish truth from error; becoming confused; losing the power to direct their own lives or to conduct their own affairs effectively; becoming drifters; becoming obsessed with all sorts of fears, superstitions, inhibitions, etc.; becoming jealous, vain, conceited, quarrelsome, willful, angry, intolerant, prejudiced, negative, nosy, harsh, frivolous, overly talkative; and neglecting one's duties in daily life.

There is absolutely no danger that any such harmful qualities might develop when progress along the path of meditation, as outlined by Rudolf Steiner, is attempted, provided his instructions are followed carefully. These instructions are designed to strengthen sufficiently the positive aspects of a person's character. But, if a student picks and chooses only what he likes, and disregards what he does not like, then distortions and imbalance are likely to result.

You cannot just play around with these matters or take them lightly, just as you cannot walk into a chemistry lab, pour liquids from various bottles randomly together and hope to remain unharmed. For you are releasing real forces. You had better be cognizant of these forces and handle things according to exact rules. Likewise, very real dangers exist if you approach the path of meditation in a careless or flippant mood. It would be better not to touch this field at all, until the attitude of dabbling is replaced by one of systematic careful work. The six introductory exercises are simple, but not easy. Their regular practice is indispensable as a preparation for the path of meditation. They are called:

1. Control of Thought.
2. Control of Action.
3. Control of Feeling (Equanimity).
4. Positivity (Tolerance).
5. Openness (Receptivity).
6. Harmony (Perseverance).

They should be practiced in this order. First one takes up the first exercise and practices it daily until one feels that one has gained a reasonable degree of mastery. Then, keeping up the practice of the first exercise, the second one is added to one's daily tasks. When this is mastered the third one is added, and so forth until the sixth. If these exercises are done correctly they will become a daily source of inner strength. Rudolf Steiner suggests that a month of practice for one exercise leads to a readiness for adding the next one, and so forth. Thus, after six months one is ready to begin with the practice of actual meditation. For students of the early part of this century a period of one month per exercise may have been a practical average time. However, for many people today one month is not enough time to gain mastery of each of these exercises to a sufficient degree. It is then advisable to choose longer intervals, as needed. Nothing is gained by haste.

The order in which the exercises are given is not arbitrary. What is gained through one exercise is required as a basis for the ones that follow. Therefore, the order should in general be maintained as here described. A practical description of these six introductory exercises will follow.

How does one go about practicing these six introductory exercises?

1. Control of Thought.

This exercise should be done daily, preferably at the same time. It should take only a few minutes. The student shall pick a simple thought (sentence) or a simple concept (word). The simpler the better. For example: "Paperclip." The purpose of this exercise is to control one's thoughts so that one *admits* for a period of say five minutes only such thoughts as connect with the concept of "paperclip." One *forbids* the drifting of associations and the involuntary jumping from one idea to another.

The following train of thought is an example of how this might be carried out:

> A paperclip is used for holding papers together. But not merely to hold them together. Its function is to hold them together in such a way that they can easily be separated again. In that respect paperclips differ from other means of connecting papers together. Stapling, for instance, also holds papers together, but unstapling is not so easy as taking off a paperclip. Moreover, stapling does a slight damage to the papers, whereas a paperclip holds papers together without damage. This is the great virtue of a paperclip that it performs its function without doing any damage. This feature of a paperclip, that it does no damage, is based on the circumstance that the force which a paperclip exerts on the papers remains external to the paper. The staple, on the other hand, exerts a force that does not remain external to the paper. Thus, the usefulness of a paperclip is connected with the fact that its force remains external to the papers that it holds together..
>
> A paperclip exerts this force by virtue of its elasticity. The material of which a paperclip is made provides this elastic force.
>
> Paperclips are usually made of metal because metals are good materials for providing elastic forces. Nowadays, however, plastic materials have been developed with elastic properties approach-

ing those of metals. Why, then, do we not use plastic paperclips? Indeed, these are used, but they tend to show undesirable side effects; they break, rather easily. Consequently, plastic paperclips are not yet used as widely as metal ones. The price of a metal paperclip is exceedingly low, and this is in part due to the fact that such very large numbers of paperclips are being produced. It is, for example, not difficult to estimate the rate at which paperclips are used in the greater New York area. It could easily be a million paperclips a week, which would be about a ton of paperclips a week. Just imagine the flow of paperclips that our civilization must keep up in order to satisfy this demand of the greater New York area alone, not to say anything of the whole nation....

We shall stop here, but it is not difficult to see that one could go on for a much longer period of time, thinking about ever different aspects of the paperclip. Not that a paperclip is such an important thing. It is only used here as an object for the training of our thinking. The above sequence of thoughts does not stray. It relates all the time to the concept that was placed in focus. The purpose of this type of exercise is to learn to hold our thoughts at will for a few minutes in continuous relation with one concept or with one thought.

In order to make this exercise entirely clear a counter-example will now be given: a train of thought that starts out very much like the other one, but which does go astray.

A paperclip is used for holding papers together. I remember seeing a paperclip used to hold together two pages of a letter which the president had written. It was a private letter of the president. Ah! The private letters of the president! They would undoubtedly make most interesting reading. How much insight into the real behind-the-scenes forces of politics might not be gained through access to the private letters of the president!

Now you see, by this time the relation with the paperclip is completely lost. The thoughts followed their own current instead of my directing them. As a result I found myself soon fluently passing from one association to another and the relation with the initial concept, the paperclip, was no longer part of my thought process. Instead, all sorts of matters having no relation with the paperclip emerged and took over. If one catches oneself doing this kind of insufficiently controlled thinking, then one must try again the next day, either with the same concept or with a different one.

If this first exercise is carried out regularly for many days a definite result can be noticed. It consists of a feeling of certainty or firmness within one's mind, even within one's head. This feeling one should learn to know and to cultivate by one's own experience through these exercises.

2. Control of Action

After reasonable progress has been achieved with the first exercise, the second exercise can be added, meanwhile keeping up the practice of the first one.

The second exercise concerns one's actions. Most of our actions are performed rather unconsciously. They are usually determined by inner and outer causes, of which we have at best only vague notions. The second exercise demands that we conceive of a simple action that we *can* carry out daily at the same time, and that we set ourselves the task of performing this action daily at the set time. One may, for example, decide to turn one's ring around at noon every day. Or, one may decide to look at the sky and observe the clouds at 3 p.m. daily. Or, one may tear a page out of a daily calendar before going to bed.

If you set yourself any such task you will find that it works beautifully for the first two days. On the third or fourth day there usually arise quite reasonable circumstances that seriously interfere with your plans for carrying out this particular action. It takes great effort and perseverance to try it every day again, regardless of the number of past failures and skippings, caused either by circumstances or by mere forgetfulness. After some time, sometimes after several weeks, you find that at the right time you do *not* forget. Even if you are in the middle of doing something quite absorbing, when the appointed time comes, an awareness arises spontaneously that it is now time to perform the exercise. It feels as if something within you were suddenly saying to you: "Now it is time to do your thing."

In this way one learns to know what it takes to establish a habit, a pattern of action. And one learns to know more intimately than ever before the inner force of will with which one carries out initiatives.

3. Control of Feelings.

Again, after reasonable progress has been achieved with the second exercise, the third exercise may be added, while keeping up the practice of the first and second one.

The third exercise refers to the control of feelings. Some people have this control of feelings already to a large degree, through life. It is by no means intended that a person shall *avoid* deep feelings; what matters is that the feelings do not run out of control. They must not overwhelm a person. There should always be a little inner distance between oneself and one's feelings. Thus one should always be able to ask: What message does this feeling bring me?

In some stories you might read: "She burst into tears and sobbed passionately until sleep overtook her." Or: "When she learned about the good news, she was beside herself with joy and did not know whether to laugh or to cry." These are instances of uncontrolled feelings: feelings that overwhelm and almost drown a person.

If a person tends towards such feelings, he or she must practice controlling them. In particular, feelings of futility sadness, despair, rage, and similar negative emotions, must be controlled.

The third exercise consists in trying to become aware of one's own feelings and in introducing equanimity into the realm of these feelings. This cannot be practiced at set times, but should be done whenever feelings arise that tend to possess us instead of being our possession. Once you become aware of this balance—this subtle difference between your having feelings versus the feelings having you—then hardly a day will pass without several opportunities for practicing this control.

The practice of equanimity will not tend to make your feelings shallow. On the contrary, a great enrichment in the quality and range of one's feelings is the result.

Equanimity in feeling must enable a person to face a dangerous situation, and though he may be afraid, he is not panic-stricken; he must be able to face an insult without becoming angry, to face pain without losing his reason, to face success without becoming conceited, etc. Too many people who think that they have gained success in some enterprise lack this equanimity. They do not have success: The success has them!

The result of practicing this equanimity, this control of feelings, is a feeling of relaxation, of quiet strength, which gradually permeates one's whole body.

4. Positivity (Tolerance).

When the first three exercises are well under control, the fourth exercise may be added. It consists in the practice of refraining from unnecessary critical or downgrading thoughts. Its purpose is to develop a sense for the positive aspects of all things and situations, even of very bad or objectionable ones. Of course this does not mean that one should call positive what is clearly negative, or beautiful what is ugly. It does mean, however, that one should learn, in all situations, to seek out—not to overlook—the positive, the beautiful, etc., even if it has to be found amid much that is negative or ugly.

As one works at this exercise, it can happen that one becomes aware—suddenly or gradually—of the enormous number of negative prejudices, attitudes, feelings, words and actions that one hurls into the world daily. Little by little these have to be transformed, as more attention is focused on the positive aspects of the world. This exercise should be practiced as opportunities arise. They arise usually at least several times daily. If one is so engaged during the day that one is unable to practice consciously the search for what is true, beautiful, noble or good, one can do so instead during a few quiet minutes set aside for this purpose in the evening. One should then make it a practice to remember an occurrence or a scene in which one was involved during the day, and one should now put special emphasis on finding its positive aspects.

Such ponderings of a few minutes daily result in a gradual transformation of one's relation to the world. One becomes aware of a richness in the world that was previously not within one's ken. The world shows you more of its qualities. As a result, a blissful feeling of being in touch, in communion with the world, can arise; gradually the so-widespread feelings of loneliness and isolation vanish. And as one learns to see more and more the positive aspects of one's surroundings one becomes gradually more truly tolerant.

5. Openness (Receptivity).

The fifth exercise again builds on the previous ones. It consists of a striving to meet every experience with a fresh, unprejudiced, open mind. This is difficult. Through our culture and our education we perceive the world, as it were, filtered through many prejudices and preconceived ideas. Of many of these we are not conscious. We must be able to push these filters aside, at least for a short moment, in order to allow the world to communicate to us a wider range of its content, in order to be receptive to this wider content.

If we learn to perceive really in an unprejudiced way, we can become aware of a very subtle quality around us, which is difficult to describe. It is as if the space around us were imbued with a subtle life of its own; a life that communicates with us, into which we are embedded—lightwise, soundwise, and warmthwise. As a result of the fifth exercise, the awareness, at which the above expressions hint, should grow in clarity and strength.

6. Harmony (Perseverance).

During the buildup of the five previous exercises the accent was generally on the newest one, while the previous ones, though kept up, required less attention or effort. Now that all five exercises have become part of one's daily activities, a certain balancing between them must be accomplished. It takes a great deal of perseverance to arrive at a systematic harmonization of these five exercises, so that their results become part of our own nature.

As this harmonization takes place, we become filled with inner peace. Not a peace of inactivity, yet, peace. Peace with ourselves and peace with the world around us.

When these six introductory exercises have been practiced singly and together, and when the results described for each exercise have been achieved at least to a degree, then one is ready to start with exercises in meditation. For gifted persons, this stage can be reached in six months, but many people require longer. It is a sign of maturity and self-knowledge if one can find one's own proper speed.

Work at these exercises should proceed actively and steadfastly, but without anxiety, stress, haste, or pressure. Joy and peace should be the dominant mood. And it is good to refresh one's awareness of the proper motivation for this work from time to time.

The reader who has familiarized himself with the six introductory exercises will understand why a certain degree of mastery of these disciplines is an indispensable prerequisite for successful meditation. Indeed, these exercises are designed as safeguards against all negative, and possibly harmful, influences on the soul, as well as reinforcements for all of its positive qualities. These exercises and the qualities they foster are valuable as an introduction to meditation.

For effective meditation a basic mood is essential. It is a mood of devotion and reverence toward truth and insight. Our culture scarcely supports this mood, and seldom is the connection acknowledged between this mood of devotion and reverence, and growth of insight. Information is treated in wide circles without such feelings. And yet, even in regard to the tiniest bit of information, if one really wants to make it one's own, if one wants to become aware of its meaning, one has to meet it at least briefly with a certain measure of devotion. The great and lofty truths of existence are meaningful only to a mind that is prepared to receive them with great devotion, reverence and awe. Indeed, the great scientists, philosophers, artists, and religious geniuses of all times have always agreed that it is this devotion and reverence toward truth and insight that led them toward their spiritual heights.

Many people practice meditation punctually, dutifully, with an almost grim perseverance, and with very little success. The reason why they actually accomplish so little often lies in their uncontrolled or wrongly directed basic mood. A certain subtle pride in one's own righteousness, a hidden fear to meet with living truths that are much greater and loftier than those of one's own little self, can seriously thwart all meditative progress. Therefore it is a matter of conscious self-direction that the right basic mood be established: the mood of devotion and reverence toward truth and insight; not toward people, but toward truth and insight. This devotion can be considered as a manifestation of love, one's love for the world. The world will only communicate its deeper secrets to us if we approach it with this love. And this love presupposes an inner quiet, a receptivity, and the silencing of all the everyday helter skelter that traverses the uncontrolled, undisciplined mind.

Rudolf Steiner describes many meditation exercises.[4] I should like to describe only two very elementary ones, to illustrate the character of meditation in general. The purpose of these exercises is to become aware of two kinds of forces: on the one hand the forces associated with growth, living, sprouting; on the other hand the forces associated with decay, dying, withering.

Observe a seed, a real seed. Look at it carefully. Then think that it has life, the potential to grow into a full plant when placed in suitable surroundings. An artificial imitation may appear deceptively similar, but it cannot grow into a full plant. It is not alive. The life force in the real seed is invisible. But if the seed grows into a plant, then what was at first invisible will in *time* become visible.

If this thought is strengthened sufficiently it can result in a feeling, a perception of the invisible life force. This feeling, which can be cultivated to the point where one is quite familiar with it, is something new; a feeling with which one was hardly familiar before. It is akin to the feeling that a sunrise stimulates in us. (In stating this, it is assumed that the reader has actually looked at a real sunrise, and has experienced it with an open, receptive mind, unclouded by modern cosmological concepts and abstractions.) It is a feeling for which poets and composers through the ages have been receptive, a feeling of great power and harmony.

Now, likewise, observe a full-grown flowering plant. Then reflect how it is at the height of its unfolding, ready to start withering and decaying. It, too, has life. But its life is of a different quality than that of the seed. We can think that in time its life will cause the plant to shrivel back into almost lifeless seeds; seeds in which the life is present as a potentiality to unfold anew. Thus there is invisible in the full grown plant a protective force that carries its life beyond complete decay.

If thoughts such as these are strengthened sufficiently, another feeling can result: a perception of another, second kind of force. This feeling, for which awareness can be cultivated, is again of a new kind. It is akin to the feeling that is aroused in us by the rising moon.

In this way one enters into a new dimension of the world in which we live, the dimension of the life forces, the forces of growth and decay, in all their detailed variations. This is the world of the formative forces; and the feelings, to which reference was made, are articulated according to the various processes of that world.

A great deal more could be said about these meditations and their results. You find this described in the works of Rudolf Steiner, referred to earlier. Here only the following remarks seem pertinent: *First*, some people will perhaps prefer the meditation on growth above the one on decay. The meditation on growth has an outgoing, rejuvenating quality that tends to be enjoyable, whereas the one on decay has a reflective quality of serenity that does not call forth joy so spontaneously. It is important, however, that both be done with the same surrender, the same attention and love.

You will find, in general, that Rudolf Steiner describes meditations in sets of two (or more), in order to achieve the required balance. Indeed, one's sense of balance must become like a compass in this inner work.

It enables us to steer a course of harmonious development into the spiritual world.

Only a few meditations form an exception, in that a complete and perfect balance is achieved within a single meditation, so that one does not need to pair them with other meditations. One example is the meditation of the Rose-cross, described in chapter 5 of *An Outline of Esoteric Science* (provided one builds the exercise up carefully in the way described there). It is beyond the scope of this article to enter into details concerning this meditation. It is mentioned here only for its self-contained, completely balanced inner "Gestalt."

Second, In order to describe the feelings of growth and decay Rudolf Steiner refers to cosmic archetypal phenomena: the rising sun and the rising moon. These can be observed by anyone. But have you really quietly taken the time to observe these? In olden times people would sometimes get up early for the purpose of observing the rising sun, and they experienced it as a tremendously uplifting impression, through which the divine power, wisdom, harmony and goodness in nature spoke to them. Or, they would quietly observe the rising moon with its strange forces of fertility and of fantasy. Maybe one would have to prescribe for the modern dweller in polluted cities an additional introductory exercise: go out to some place in the country, in nature, at a suitable time, and observe the rising sun, or the rising moon, in various seasons. It is essential that these impressions be received in all purity, uncontaminated by modern ideas of cosmology and space exploration concerning the constitution of these bodies. Then one should experience the feelings as described.

Meditation can thus gradually open up a consciousness of worlds that are normally unobserved, to which one pays little attention, worlds of life forces in which we find ourselves embedded.

Meditation should not be a task, a burden, or a strain. It should become natural, something one loves to perform, loves because in so doing one knows that one is growing in strength, strength for service to the world, service that fits into the world harmoniously; for it is ultimately what the ancients called the "harmony of the spheres" that weaves and works in his domain of formative life forces into which one enters.

One can continue to progress a long way along this path, and the statement that the earth is a living organism can thereby rise from the status of a metaphor or symbol to that of a meaningful reality. But it is not our purpose here to describe his path in any further detail, nor to characterize further the exercises that open up even deeper realms of the soul and spirit world. I wish, however, to point to the fact that through his process of meditative development one does not only become aware of more layers of the world around us and within oneself, one also changes as a person. The goal of these inner changes is what is usually described as the birth of the higher self.

Some will progress fast along the path of meditation and self-development, others more slowly. To some it will be given to put their gifts to uses that are visible for the public eye, while others work more in invisible, hidden ways. Whether one or the other is the case is determined by factors of a spiritual nature, which are often to a large extent beyond the control of the student. One should recognize that both ways are equally valuable and necessary in the world. Much more important than the question of externally visible achievements versus internal invisible work is the quality of the work itself, and this quality one can learn to gauge by means of a gradually developing and growing inner feeling of strength. This feeling tells that one is working in accord with the spiritual world. Meditation also has this important aspect, that it is an offering to the spiritual world, and the feeling referred to above can indicate that this offering is being accepted by that world. A sensitive openness to what is thus communicated can be of great help in shaping one's further progress.

I should like to conclude this introductory article by stressing once more the emphasis that Rudolf Steiner places on the right motivation for all work along the path of meditation. He formulates this in terms of an inviolate fundamental rule, thus:[5]

> This is a fundamental rule of all spiritual science, which cannot be violated without sacrificing success, and which should be impressed on each student who practices any form of esoteric training: All knowledge pursued merely for the enrichment of personal learning and the accumulation of personal treasure leads you astray from the true path. *All knowledge pursued for growth toward maturity on the road of human ennoblement and cosmic development brings you a step forward.* This law must be observed strictly. And only those are genuine students of the path to the spirit who have adopted this law as a guiding principle for their entire life.

5
Meditation According to Rudolf Steiner

Preface

MORE AND MORE people in all walks of life are becoming aware of serious deficiencies in the way human life is organized and runs its course, individually and societally, without a clear sense of purpose or of the dignity of human life, heading towards physical bankruptcy of humanity and of the earth. Few realize, however, that the present predicament is the result of a way of thinking, a world conception, a paradigm, which has guided human actions through some four or five centuries, with undoubtedly great triumphs of "progress," into the present soulless and spiritless isms, such as materialism, reductionism, positivism, etc. The roots of the resulting uneasiness lie much deeper than the merely traditional tension between a younger generation and an older one.

Calls for change abound, without a clear insight into the nature of the causes of the present difficulties, nor into the effects that may be expected of changes towards any particular new direction or paradigm. A major difficulty appears to be how to get beyond the present paradigm at all, without falling prey to illusion or to dogmatism. As a result the calls for change usually result in change within the bounds of the present paradigm, leading to "more of the same misery."

The search must be for something beyond the prevailing paradigm. Against such a change human conservatism, complacency, and inertia, rebel fiercely. Nevertheless a new paradigm is needed, one which should be compatible with the control that modern Western humanity has gained over outer circumstances by means of science and technology, but which should in addition permit a grasp of human nature, not only in its bodily aspects, but equally in its soul and spirit aspects and their interrelations. In the old paradigm one has the polarities of objective and subjective, body and mind, science and human values. In the new paradigm these seemingly opposite tendencies should be harmonized in a balanced way.

The leading, comprehensive, breakthrough in this direction has been achieved by Rudolf Steiner's Spiritual Science (Anthroposophy). His epistemology leads to a broader understanding of what "knowing" means, and how the broadened process of knowing can systematically transcend the boundaries which are set by the inputs of the bodily senses and by what the intellect can add thereto by working these inputs over. The result is a new paradigm, a comprehensive world view, which encompasses besides a physical world an equally real world of soul and spirit and their interpenetration. The balancing force, which integrates and harmonizes the seemingly opposite tendencies of the world of the senses and the world of soul and spirit emanates from a universal, real, spiritual being, which Rudolf Steiner identifies as the Christ spirit, a concept which far transcends conventional concepts of Christ.

The way into this new paradigm is not easy. It requires developing new, valid, habits of perception and thinking. Meditation is the means towards this end, if practiced in a way, compatible with this new Spiritual Science.

On the other hand, ancient Eastern paradigms are invading the Western world. However, in their essence they are usually not compatible with the deeply felt Western will for responsibility for the spiritual evolution of the earth and of humanity as a whole.

The content of this booklet comes from an extensively reworked lecture, which I was invited to present on February 20, 1993 in Chicago at a conference of the Anthroposophical Society in America, titled "Spiritual Development in East and West." One could assume that the audience was somewhat familiar with Steiner's basic ideas. I have tried to recast the material of this booklet in a form of short chapters, which have the tone of a conversation of the author and the reader.

Ernst Katz, Ann Arbor, Michigan, 1993

I
Introduction of Rudolf Steiner's Mandate of Freedom

Dear reader,

In the short space of this booklet it is only possible to present the vast subject of meditation in a very eclectic way. I hope to dwell on a few points that seem essential to me and hopefully are of some interest to you also, especially if you are engaged in a practice of meditation.

Meditation is practiced in a variety of ways in different spiritual movements. In most of these movements one can point to a teacher or guru, whose guidance is such that the student becomes to a greater or lesser degree inwardly dependent on the person of the teacher.

In this sense Rudolf Steiner is not a guru.

Rudolf Steiner tries to make the student independent of his person while developing a direct relation to the spiritual worlds.[1] The freedom of the student is continually called upon. Rudolf Steiner considers meditation to be one of those few activities where a human being in our time is really free.

Not all people who strive for inner development like this freedom, for it requires a certain maturity; a sense of responsibility; a willingness to experiment to some degree with certain details; and a good dose of sincerity, self-motivation, common sense, courage, and other soul qualities that are not in everybody's book. To make this point of freedom clear by way of an example, think of a road map, which tells anyone who likes to travel from a place A to a place B which roads are good roads and where there are repairs, hazards, or dangers. A good road map does not reduce the freedom of the traveler. On the contrary, it enhances this freedom, and at the same time it can save a lot of time and grief by enabling the traveler to avoid byways which are perhaps dead-end streets and the like. What Rudolf Steiner has done can be compared to the making of a map, a very detailed, up-to-date map of roads that lead the spirit of the human being toward communion with the spiritual world, the spiritual beings of the cosmos, with clear indications of how to avoid certain hazards along the way. Meditation is the principal means to travel along such a road, such a path of spiritual development.

Notwithstanding all of this freedom, there are of course certain laws which pertain to such development, and one better take account of these. If one wants to meditate successfully there is one law in particular that one should know. *You cannot serve, or follow, two or more masters for your spiritual development at the same time.* It is well known that Pythagoras[2] went through numerous initiations in different mystery centers, one *after* the other; but you cannot do it at the same time. It is of course fine to gather information about different paths, while following one particular path. But to follow actually the recommended practices of meditation of different paths at the same time and mix them up together in some fashion is not beneficial. It is therefore a definite choice one makes, if one chooses Rudolf Steiner as the guide for one's meditative development.

How did Rudolf Steiner become such a special guide for meditative development? Up to his fortieth year he was essentially silent regarding his spiritual experiences and about esoteric teaching. That is in accord with an esoteric law. To be a genuine spiritual teacher requires a certain degree of maturity that—apart from very few special exceptions—can only be acquired after the fortieth year. I should like to characterize Rudolf Steiner's position in this respect, by referring to a letter thst he wrote to his assistant, later to be his wife, Marie von Sivers. In this letter[3] he writes what moved him to start teaching esoteric matters after his fortieth year. He writes there that he was visited in the spirit every night for a long period of time by what he calls, and what are called in other movements too, the "Masters of Wisdom and of the Harmony of Feelings." These venerable individualities have in the past given decisive impulses, directing human evolution on earth in a spiritually positive direction. In these nightly spiritual visits these Masters came to Rudolf Steiner and urged him, beseeched him, implored him, "would you please take on this mission, which needs to be performed at this time for human evolution, for which you have the basic qualifications, *and which we cannot carry out.*" After long consideration Rudolf Steiner was persuaded to take on this mission, which became then evident in his teaching and to which he devoted all the forces of his life.

By doing this, soon and very rapidly, Rudolf Steiner became a Master himself. This he did not write; I am stating this as a logical consequence. He became a Master, and you might even say, because he took on a task that the Masters themselves could not engender, he became a "Master of Masters," THE outstanding Master for our time. Of course, this is not something which people in general are willing to recognize. But it is important to know that these nightly spiritual visits took place according to this letter, and that this was the stimulus that persuaded Rudolf Steiner to break his silence about his spiritual experiences and insights.

Meditation according to Rudolf Steiner is the greatest thing a person can undertake today. The map he offers is the most detailed, most up-to-date, and most accurate map. When I say up-to-date please realize that the spiritual world as well as the road to the spiritual world is not given as the same once and for all. All these things go through an evolutionary process. Therefore it is important to have a map that is in accordance with the conditions on the way *at the time that one wishes to travel*. The freedom that a map offers is something from which people often shy away. No question it is difficult to bear and to actualize. Many people prefer to be led by the hand, every step, unfree. This is probably one of the main reasons, I believe, that though the works of Rudolf Steiner are widely read today, the Anthroposophical Society is still very small.

I have heard it said that it really does not matter whether you follow one or another guru, or one or another path of inner development, because in the end all will meet at the same summit. I must oppose this view. In the first place, I maintain that different paths lead to very different summits, if one wants to use the image of summits at all. But in addition, I maintain *there is no summit!* There is no summit; it is more like travelling and seeing the horizon: as you travel a mile the horizon moves forward a mile too, and thank goodness, there is always more wisdom to learn and more work to do.

II
Basic Information

What does Rudolf Steiner consider to be the basic reason why there is a human interest at all in meditation? He phrased the answer poetically thus:

Why does the seeking human soul
Strive towards knowledge of higher worlds?
Because when our soul looks
Into the world through our senses,
This question arises with deepest longing:
Where do we find the true spiritual essence, the divine.[4]

That is the reason. But there are many people who don't feel this longing, this deep longing to transcend the world of the senses. For them meditation has no meaning, and we should recognize that. The essence of human nature transcends all sense perception, not because our senses are too crude and their technological extensions, such as microscopes, telescopes, and other instruments, have not been perfected sufficiently, no, our human essence transcends in principle the entire world which our physical senses can perceive directly or indirectly. Never will there be, nor can there be, any instrument enabling a researcher to probe the essence of human nature by sense perceptions.

Anthroposophy, as Rudolf Steiner described it, rests on two premises.[5] First, beyond the world that is perceptible by the physical senses—including their extensions through research instruments—there exists a world of spirit, in which the sense world has its origin and its roots. Second, it is possible to learn to know—not to believe, but to know experientially—this spiritual world, and to act in it. Meditation is the means to learn to know this spiritual world. Meditation is always connected with a development, an inner growth. It also metamorphoses as one develops along the path; therefore you cannot define meditation in any rigid way.

Rudolf Steiner has given many indications for meditation. Of the copious literature I should like to mention only a few major references, among which I distinguish two classes.

There is in the first place the general literature. Here the principal works are:

Knowledge of the Higher Worlds and its Attainment[6]

An Outline of Esoteric Science,[7] chapter 5

Theosophy,[8] chapter 4

And, again, different approaches are given in Rudolf Steiner's *Mystery Plays*[9] and in the lessons of the School of Spiritual Science.[10]

These are all general paths.

There is in the second place literature on specifics, containing a wealth of the esoteric work and meditative teachings of Rudolf Steiner, especially in the pre-World War I years. Here you often find very specific indications, given to a particular person or to a particular group; some are suited to a particular time or to a particular occasion or emergency. They cannot always be generalized without further ado. In this class I should like to mention especially:

Verses and Meditations[11]

Guidance in Esoteric Training[12]

A Way of Self Knowledge[13]

and two volumes of the complete works of Rudolf Steiner, numbers CW 264 and CW 265.[14] In addition to these principal sources there is a very large number of further literature references, too many to mention here.

III

The First Steps

I should like to say here something about several specific questions concerning meditation. The first question I want to address is: What is the first step toward meditation? It is the cultivation of a feeling! A feeling that you are seeking the truth about a higher world, a world that is the soul's true home. This is a divine world, a world so lofty, so exalted, that you can only enter with the deepest reverence and devotion toward what may come to you from that world as your experience, as truth. This higher world is holy ground. That is a major hurdle for many people in our time.

How can we cultivate this basic mood of reverence without which all efforts of meditation yield either no results or sometimes even quite negative results. The first step of meditation is to realize that we are seeking to enter a holy world. That is essential. Personally, I find it helpful to dwell on the Lord's Prayer as a preamble to meditation. Other people surely have many other ways to establish the right mood of reverence.

This brings us to the question of the relation between meditation and prayer. It is not possible to draw a sharp boundary between these two fields. There is a difference but also an area of overlap. To make this clear let us look first at one example Rudolf Steiner gave in lectures about color.[15] He suggested there a meditation in which one imagines, and immerses oneself in, a disk of fiery red, which has some rays or protuberances of red, and then again likewise with regard to a blue disk. One can learn thereby to experience the expanding quality that lives in red and the contracting quality of blue. This kind of meditation is very powerful in its effects. But it has no prayer-like quality at all.

Second, let us look at another example, a verse that Rudolf Steiner gave for meditation. He has given it to several people, every time slightly modified, but basically the same. When used for meditation, this verse has a healing power for all those illness-causing influences to which every one of us is exposed in the present conditions of our civilization. It sounds thus:[16]

> O Godly Spirit, abide in me,
> Abide in me within my soul,
> To my soul grant strengthening force,
> Strengthening force too for my heart,
> For my heart that seeketh Thee,
> Seeketh Thee with deepest longing,
> Deepest longing for good health,
> For good health and trust in life,
> Trust in life which through my body streams,
> Streams as a precious gift divine,
> Gift divine from Thee, O Godly Spirit.
> O Godly Spirit, abide in me.

This is a very beautiful verse, also a very powerful meditation. It is a prayerful meditation or a meditative prayer, whichever you like to call it, a prayer or a meditation at the same time. It seems to me to be particularly effective in the morning. This example shows that no sharp boundary can be drawn between the two fields of prayer and of meditation.

IV

Meditation and Intellect

A question which is asked frequently is: How important is it that we understand the meaning of the words or sentences which are used for meditation? Not all meditations have words. There are for example pictorial meditations. I mentioned already the example of the meditation on the red and blue disks. But let us focus on those meditations that are given in the form of words, as a "mantram." There are students of Steiner who believe that a meditative verse or mantram is so carefully constructed by Rudolf Steiner that *any* change is detrimental to its beneficial effect. Therefore they recommend, even for English-speaking people who don't know any German, to meditate these verses in German. Personally, I think this goes too far. I maintain that it is definitely beneficial to understand *something* of what the words mean.

However, to try deepening one's understanding in an intellectual or speculative way is definitely not beneficial for meditation. For example, Rudolf Steiner often suggested as content for meditation the German phrase *"Weisheit lebt im Licht."* I should like to suggest that an English-speaking person meditate this as *"Wisdom lives in light."* I believe that Rudolf Steiner would never give this phrase to a blind person for meditation, simply because a blind person has no conception of what the experience of light is. What I am trying to say is: Where Rudolf Steiner gives verses or phrases for meditation, a certain amount of understanding of the meaning of the words seems to me essential and beneficial. I know, on the other hand, of some Eastern disciplines who give, and do emphasize, meditations on sounds, which in themselves have no meaning. I think this is a difference between Rudolf Steiner and certain other movements.

The importance of silencing the speculative intellect is perhaps best explained in the quotation that follows. In the last year of his activity Rudolf Steiner gave a course of lectures to medical doctors, followed by a question and answer period.[17]

One doctor asked the following question: "What must I do out of my ego when I meditate?" Rudolf Steiner gave this answer:[18]

> Meditation consists of the following: as a modern person you feel, regarding every sentence, that you must understand it. That is a definite activity of the ego in the present incarnation. Everything you do is a definite activity of the ego. The intellect is in the present incarnation, and everything else is covered over by the ego, it works at most in a dreamlike way and is unconscious. In contrast to this, to meditate means to exclude this intellectual striving and to take the content of the meditation to begin with as it is given, I would say purely according to the wording. If you approach the content of your meditation intellectually, you set your ego in motion before you absorb the content of the meditation, for you think *about* the content of the meditation, and so you have it *outside* of yourself. But if you simply let the content of the meditation be present in your consciousness as it is given, not at all thinking *about* it, but let it be present in your consciousness, then there works *within* you, not your ego of the present incarnation but the ego of the past incarnation. You keep the intellect still, you immerse yourself simply into the content of the words, which you hear

inwardly, not outwardly. You hear it as content of words, into this you immerse yourself, and as you immerse yourself into this, there works in the content of the meditation your inner human being which is not the one of the present incarnation. In this way the content of the meditation does not become something you should understand, but rather something that works in you as a reality, and works in you in such a real way that eventually you become aware: "now I have experienced something which formerly I could not experience." Take for example a simple content for meditation which I have often given: "Wisdom lives in light." Now, if you begin to think about this the result may be tremendously clever, or equally foolish. But the content of the meditation is there in order to be inwardly heard: "Wisdom lives in light." When you hear this inwardly in this way, something within you takes notice, something that is not of the present incarnation, but that you have carried over with you from previous earth lives. And this something thinks and feels, and after some time something lights up within you, something that you did not know before, and that you cannot think out of your own intellect. Inwardly you are much further than your intellect, which contains only a small segment of what is there.

This answer of Rudolf Steiner to the doctor who asked the question: "What must I do out of my ego when I meditate?" is very enlightening and characteristic.

V

Supporting Exercises

Inasmuch as meditation is a path of development, you will readily understand that it can only be effective if it is practiced *regularly*. Many people encounter certain difficulties when they try to practice meditation regularly. I should like to indicate some of these difficulties and the ways Rudolf Steiner recommends to overcome them by means of supporting exercises.

Meditative practice should not be felt as a stern duty, but rather as a longing for inner refreshment, like hunger or thirst. In order to develop this free-flowing practice of meditation the soul must be able to dwell on a given content for several minutes without straying, without an outer stimulus. Most people today are not able to do this. They have not developed this ability. So Rudolf Steiner gave an exercise. It is called "The Control of Thought." By means of this exercise one learns to practice keeping one's thoughts on one particular item. But if you have to practice this exercise every day you soon discover that it is difficult to start a new habit and pursue it every day. After a few days you find that you forget, or something seemingly very important interferes, and so forth. So a second exercise is called for, which strengthens the will, so we can actually form such a habit. Figure 1 represents symbolically these exercises as indicated. One line represents the first exercise, "Control of Thought," a second line represents the second exercise, called "Control of Willing." These exercises are very simple, not very time consuming at all, and they are described in the literature mentioned earlier, and in addition in a little booklet from my hand.[19] If you exercise the will in this way you will discover that progress is not forthcoming as quickly as you would want it. It is a long and arduous process, and so you may feel frustrated after a time. Therefore one needs an exercise in "Perseverance" and "Equanimity," "Control of Feeling." This is represented by a third line in the diagram. As one has learned this, a fourth quality is needed for meditation: "Positivity." You see, meditation leads first of all to an awareness of one's own weaknesses. That can be very disagreeable and frustrating. We need to muster all sorts of positive forces, such as courage, to overcome this frustration and to progress further. Positivity helps to overcome this frustration. It is sometimes also called "Tolerance," for tolerance seeks the positive in a situation which otherwise may look very negative. A fifth exercise has to do with what happens when the meditation is successful. As Rudolf Steiner expressed it in the quote given earlier, when the meditation is successful then you will become aware of something that you have never felt or known before. To become aware of this requires a kind of openness for new ideas, new impressions, new truths. The spiritual world is so radically different from the sense-perceptible world that a sensitive openness is required to notice the impressions it leaves on our mind. If we meet the world with a fixed mind-set of preconceived notions, if we are bound to a certain paradigm, then many impressions will be veiled for our mind, they escape us, even though they are clearly there.[20] So we need to cultivate this openness in order actually to become aware of what the spiritual world bestows on us as a result of our meditation.

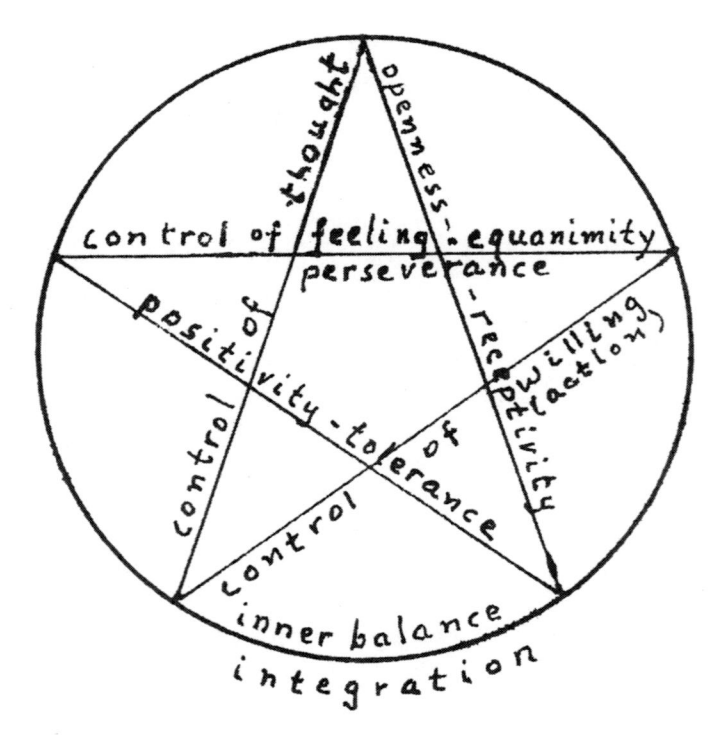

FIGURE 1

Symbolic representation of the five exercises and their integration

To summarize, the five characteristics or attributes are: control of thought, control of willing, control of feeling or equanimity or perseverance, positivity or tolerance, and openness. If we practice the exercises that strengthen these characteristics our meditations will certainly improve. We have represented these five characteristics by the five lines in the diagram of figure 1.

But then we have not had it all, because as long as it takes effort to practice these virtues they are not really integrated into our own nature, they have not yet firmly become part of our own character, as they should. So there is a sixth care, you may call it a sixth exercise, "Integration for Inner Balance," represented symbolically by the circle in figure 1. By these exercises you have as it were prepared the garden, the right inner environment, for meditation, in your own soul. In the soul's garden, thus prepared, meditation will grow properly. The diagram of figure 1 is only intended as a reminder of these five or six exercises and their connections.

VI
The Form of Meditation

Right meditation has an organic structure of four parts. First there should be a beginning and from this beginning you build up a certain content, which you hold, hovering in the soul. But then there comes a second part in which you erase that content, and create an empty, yet alert and awake, consciousness. This is not altogether easy. The danger is that you fall asleep. But it is possible. If you can hold this wakeful empty consciousness in a relaxed way then there follows a third phase, that is, something absolutely new streams in, which could not be known nor felt before. This new thing is the fruit of meditation. Thereby you are touched by the spiritual world. It is the beginning of an awareness of something spiritual. Then there has to be a fourth phase, the end of the meditation. The meditation should not just fade out. At a certain point this new impression is perceived, is recognized, and then you say "thank you," and that is the end. This, or a similar ending, is an act of will to return to ordinary consciousness. This is the organic structure of what meditation ideally should be like.

Rudolf Steiner recommends that during your ordinary daily life you should not allow the experience of meditation to come back into memory or into your mind. It should be there only for the secluded holy moments of meditation. The rest of the day goes its own profane way, and you should give yourself fully to the tasks at hand. But, on the other hand, you should at no time during the day forget that *you are a meditant*. That is very important. Rudolf Steiner goes so far as to say: "Shame at you, if you ever forget during the day, whatever else you are doing, that you *are* a meditant." These two rules of conduct are interesting complements. You don't think or try to recall the meditation as such, but you keep alive a feeling, that can give you a certain strength, or maybe dignity, also humility, that you *are* a meditant.

How long should a good meditation last? Rudolf Steiner writes, if you have no more time to spare, five minutes will do, provided they are applied in the right way.[21] On the other hand, the more tranquil and deliberate the meditation is carried out, the stronger will be its effect. Rather than giving a particular time, Rudolf Steiner recommends that one should develop a sense of tact, you might call it, as to what the right duration of one's meditation should be in any given situation. At a certain moment during your meditation you should sense a feeling:

"now it is enough." That is an important observation. You see, this throws the responsibility for certain details again back to the student. Personally, I find it much harder to meditate five minutes than to meditate, say, twenty minutes, because if you meditate five minutes it has to be very energetic and very precisely focused and yet relaxed. Another justification for a period of twenty minutes for meditation can be derived from Rudolf Steiner's Mystery Plays.[22] In these plays meditations are presented on the stage. It is the first time ever in history that meditations are presented on stage. In these Mystery Plays the duration of meditations varies between about fifteen to thirty minutes. So twenty minutes cannot be too far off. Moreover, studying the meditation scenes in these plays can teach a great deal about the form or structure of meditation at various stages of development.

VII

Toward the Golden Rule

Regarding one's meditative life, Rudolf Steiner has some further recommendations. The meditant should develop four characteristics. They are sometimes called the four basic attitudes, but I think the word characteristics expresses better what is meant here.

A first characteristic is the search for truth. Try everywhere to distinguish between what is true or false, what is reality or semblance, what is essential or non-essential, what is timeless and what is perishable. A second characteristic should be: develop a sense for the moral value of any truth or true information. The second characteristic is different from the first one in an essential way. With the first characteristic you recognize the essential truth aspect, that is a thought criterion, while with the second characteristic you use a moral criterion. The third characteristic is that one has made the five or six exercises mentioned one's own to the point of having their results integrated into one's character. And the fourth characteristic is a love of freedom. Freedom not only for oneself, but also freedom, respected in regard to one's fellow creatures. In the long run this fourfold character development is essential for good progress in meditation. Many of the things stated here seem, and probably are in some respects, similar in Rudolf Steiner's work and in the disciplines of other movements. But when you look into the situation more carefully you will notice everywhere fine distinctions, having to do especially with this aspect of the freedom of the student.

One of the consequences of these four characteristics is expressed in a phrase that sounds somewhat puzzling: "Every idea that you make your own should become an ideal." That means, every idea that is in thought form should become a potential motivation for action. This is not practiced by many people in the world today. Most of us carry with us an enormous amount of information, of ideas, which are there, sitting idly, abstractly, unable to be transformed, or at least we are unable to transform them, into ideals that are potential sources of action. Not necessarily outer action; it could be inner action too, but action of a strenuous kind. That kind of excess baggage is a deadening hindrance for soul development, and as we proceed on the path of meditation we should pay attention to this requirement that our ideas should become ideals. If they cannot become ideals they should not be taken in. Only in this way, by being selective about ideas that can become ideals, can we regain the spontaneous creativity that all of us once had as little children, but which we have lost, most of us, in the process of growing up.

Another implication, related to the four characteristics, is that meditative practice is not only a search for knowledge, not even knowledge of higher worlds. It is a path of moral development. If you look at these four attributes or characteristics you will see that the first one refers to thought activity, recognizing truth, the essence of truth, thought. That is a matter of knowledge. But the other three all have a strong moral component. You can understand therefore the requirement that is often called the "Golden Rule": "For every step forward in knowledge you should take three steps forward in the perfection of your moral character." That is a great hurdle for many meditants, because the work of perfecting three steps in one's moral character is a tremendous amount of work.

VIII

Situation Meditation

Another question will now be addressed, namely what Rudolf Steiner means by what he calls "Situation Meditation."[23] An approach to an answer can be found in Rudolf Steiner's reply to the question of the doctor, related in chapter four. When meditating about the words "Wisdom lives in light" the meditant should hear these words inwardly, not outwardly. Thereby an inner space is entered, you find yourself in a soul situation..

Another example is given in the meditation scenes of the Mystery Plays. There the meditant, his name is Johannes, imagines himself to be amid a mountain landscape where springs spring from the rocks; in his meditation the rocks and springs call to Johannes "O man, know yourself!"—Again, a situation in a soul space that is alive and speaks to the meditant, so that he hears it inwardly, not outwardly.

I should like to consider the idea of situation meditation in connection with the Foundation Stone Verse,[24] which is known to most readers. It starts out with the call "Soul of man!" Then follows an elaboration, and then again "Soul of man!" Another elaboration follows, and then a third time the call "Soul of man!"—This call "Soul of man" can of course be meditated in a more or less conventional way, but implied in Rudolf Steiner's work on meditation is the suggestion that if you wish to meditate on the Foundation Stone Verse you arrange your inner picture so that you hear this call "Soul of man" coming from all directions of the cosmos toward you. When you do that you have created an inner *situation*. This is an example, in fact, a particularly important example, of a situation meditation. We should imagine ourselves in a cosmic situation, where out of the universe this call comes to us, it is heard by us, it is not spoken by us. The situation should be permeated by a moral quality, an atmosphere of reverence and holiness. It is only by developing situation meditation that we can become aware of, and acquainted with, the hierarchies of spiritual beings, the nine ranks of angelic beings, and thereby our own spiritual being grows into its cosmic nature.

IX

Chakra Development in the West and in the East

In the course of meditative practice the inner nature of the meditant acquires gradually new soul faculties, which lead by degrees to a direct perception in the spiritual world. One way to characterize these changes is to say that new soul organs of perception are developed that can be seen in the human aura. They are seen as the so called "lotus flowers" or "chakras." These have of course been known since ancient times. Naturally, a harmonious development must work at all the chakras or lotus flowers. They are said to have two "petals," sixteen petals, twelve petals,

Meditation According to Rudolf Steiner 147

eight or ten petals (it is interesting that this number is not quite defined), six petals and four petals. They are situated in the aura near certain organs of the body, as perceived by clairvoyant perception. Figure 2 represents their locations symbolically.

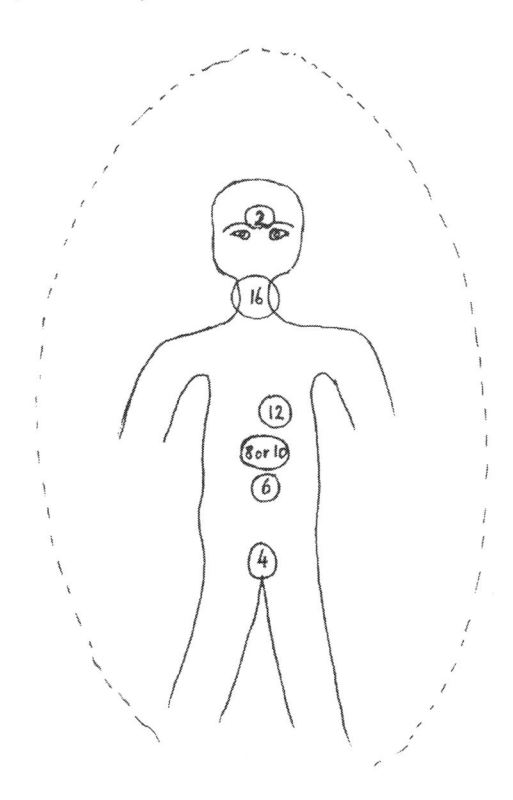

FIGURE 2.
Schematic representation of the location of the chakras or lotus flowers within the human aura, in the vicinity of certain parts of the physical body. The number of petals of each lotus flower is indicated.

An important distinction between many Eastern paths and the Western path, which Rudolf Steiner suggests, has to do with the way these organs are developed. Eastern paths often develop these organs from below up, starting the development of the four petal lotus flower first or at least early. The word "kundalini" always refers to this lotus flower. Then the development is guided toward the higher lotus flowers. Rudolf Steiner, on the contrary, begins at the top, at the lotus flowers with two, sixteen, and twelve petals, and then the development is guided to the lower lotus flowers. One may be tempted to think, what difference does it make? In the end we all meet at the same summit; in the end all the lotus flowers are developed and one perceives the same world with them. However, this is not true to fact. The fact is that one lands in a different world depending on whether one develops the chakras in the order from below upward or in the order from above downward. This is a very significant difference.

For those who develop the chakras from the four petal lotus upward, this development precludes, or at least makes it very difficult, to enter the spiritual world in such a way that they can approach the mysteries that are connected with the Christ spirit. For that it is necessary to guide the development from the top down. This is so, in particular, in our modern times where things have taken on a different structure than in ancient times. This seems to me a very significant difference, although from a merely intellectual viewpoint one would of course expect that it should make no difference as long as all of the petals of all of the lotus flowers are developed.

X

About the Greater Guardian of the Threshold

I should like to dwell now on an experience that Rudolf Steiner describes in *Knowledge of the Higher Worlds and its Attainment.*[25] It is the experience of an encounter with a particular spiritual being, when one has reached a particular stage of maturity along the meditative path of development. It is the encounter with the so called "Greater Guardian of the Threshold," a most far-reaching encounter with deepest meaning. It is a sublime experience, not unlike a near-death experience. It makes clear in an experiential way that the human being must not merely seek individual salvation or liberation. Rather what is needed is a union with the spiritual essence of the cosmos, of the whole world. And this is possible because the human being is in essence a cosmic being. Once this union has taken place, based on freedom and creativity, one can and will return in order to recognize the needs of the evolving world, the evolving earth, and evolving humanity, and also of the evolving spiritual beings that stand behind this evolution. And one can then respond to these needs with works of love. That is what the Greater Guardian tells, teaches as it were. Who is this Greater Guardian? At first his identity is a mystery. The encounter with the Greater Guardian places, on the one hand, a very impressive and glorious personality or being before one's ken, but on the other hand, who this is, is a mystery.

At this point I should like to insert a little digression. Rudolf Steiner has sometimes been criticized because he never mentioned Christ in his book *Knowledge of the Higher Worlds and its Attainment.* If you check carefully you will find no mention of Christ in this book. The reason is that the book stops at the point where the meeting with the Greater Guardian is described, and his personality is a mystery. Only by further development, as described in the fifth chapter of *An Outline of Occult Science* does Rudolf Steiner tell how the student becomes gradually aware at a certain stage of his development who the Greater Guardian really is.

Here I should like to refer to the biblical story of certain disciples who after the crucifixion went on their way to the village of Emmaus. On the way, they were joined by a stranger whom they did not recognize, and who explained to them many things about why the life of Christ had to be as it was. When they finally came to the village of Emmaus they took habitat in an inn and started to eat. When the stranger broke the bread they suddenly recognized that it was the Christ, but then, at the very moment of recognition He vanished from their sight.[26] This story tells of an encounter with a spiritual being whose identity was at first a mystery, and only after a certain development was His identity revealed as being the Christ.

Likewise, the identity of the Greater Guardian is at first a mystery, and only after a certain growth and development has been achieved is his identity revealed, rather suddenly, maybe not quite as suddenly as in the case of Emmaus, but fairly suddenly. The realization then opens up to the student that the Greater Guardian is none other than the Christ.

It makes no sense to say: "You could have told me that much sooner," because it was not a reality to the perceiving soul any sooner than when the soul is ripe to make the recognition, just as it was not a reality to the disciples before they took their meal at the inn. That is the reason why the identity of the Greater Guardian is not revealed in the book *Knowledge of the Higher Worlds and its Attainment,* for that book ends with the first encounter with this Guardian. And that explains why Christ is not mentioned in that book, even though He appears there in this unrecognized form that only further development will reveal.

XI

Influences of Ahrimanic and Luceferic Beings

For encounters with spiritual beings the development of the two petal lotus flower is especially important; also the six petal lotus plays an important role.

The Greater Guardian of the Threshold is not the only spiritual being that the meditant may encounter. Other spiritual beings that may come within the ken of the meditant are the nine ranks of angelic beings (the so-called hierarchies), elementary spirits, souls of departed or as yet unborn human beings, and many other kinds of beings. There are also evil spiritual beings, whose intentionality is to thwart the god-given potential for the development of humanity toward a lofty spiritual future. Among them one can distinguish two classes, Ahrimanic beings and Luciferic beings. There are actually more classes, but these two are the most important ones to be concerned about. In our times, one needs to be especially concerned about the Ahrimanic beings. They inspire the human being in a peculiar way, which Rudolf Steiner describes in essence as follows:

> The ordinary human being, while unconscious during sleep, dwells in a certain way in the spiritual world and undergoes certain experiences. In our time one of the persistent experiences, to which all of us are exposed during sleep, is that we are approached by Ahrimanic beings who whisper as it were into our ears:[27] "Good is evil, and Evil is good." Complete moral confusion is the result when we awake. We cannot find our moral bearings as firmly as people could in former times when this whispering during sleep was not so systematic and so prevalent. If the world drifts farther into an Ahrimanic future,[28] there is reason to be concerned and to pay particular attention to the strengthening of our moral fiber during waking, because during sleep there are constantly efforts at work of these spiritual beings, trying to cause moral confusion by calling good what is evil and evil what is good.

You need only pick up contemporary newspapers or magazines, and you will find the effects of this whispering very clearly in evidence. On the other hand, if we would respond to this situation by saying that we want to leave this world alone, we want to retire into seclusion, we want to flee from this earth when it gets that bad, we want to renounce all earthly responsibilities, then of course we come into the domain of the other, the Luciferic beings. And Rudolf Steiner points to the fact that this is possible. But then one would become a very badly stunted angel, that is, an angelic being that is unable to develop further. It is nice to become an angel, but it is not nice to be a stunted angel.

The recognition of the twofold aspect of evil is not always easy. It can be quite confusing. But what do these evil powers do further? That is again something new for our times. In olden times there was *karma*, and people had to eat up their karma. In our times, however, more and more people come into circumstances where, as Rudolf Steiner points out, karma is in disarray, there is a disorder introduced into human karma. We must learn to notice where such a disorder creeps in, and try to correct it. For this an insight into karma is necessary, which can be achieved by some rather difficult meditations which Rudolf Steiner describes.[29] It is important to know that this information exists, that one can do certain exercises in order to come to grips with regard to questions of karma, that one can gain insight about karma with regard to certain people, and then try to do something about it to rearrange the disorder in a favorable way.

How come there is this tendency of disorder in karma in our time? I believe one major reason has to do with the following. In past centuries it happened that certain groups of people were subjected to tremendous sufferings. All over the world it has happened and it is still happening today. One example, which everyone knows of course, is the suffering imposed on the American Indians by the Spanish invasion in the sixteenth century. Now these people reincarnate, and one can have the impression that a great deal of the unrest in the world today is a direct result of disorder in the karma that has been caused by imposing this tremendous suffering on large groups of people in past times, in past centuries of history. It is then reasonable to ask: Is there perhaps much greater suffering in store for humankind if the dehumanizing Ahrimanic forces are allowed to proliferate without a corresponding growth of the forces of morality, the forces of the human heart, the forces of enthusiasm and warmth, the forces of love and of Christ?

Here I find another very serious sign of our times. It manifests as a paralyzing force in human soul development.[30] It is a characteristic of the present Ahrimanic influence not only to cause moral confusion, good is bad and evil is good, but also to influence souls in a paralyzing way in regard to self-development. Rudolf Steiner expressed this beautifully in a verse, which he wrote only a few weeks before his death. It expresses all the devotion and love that he put to work in his tireless efforts to give gifts to humanity for the task that he accepted from the Masters. It is a very special verse because it begins, like almost no other verse of Rudolf Steiner, with the words "I want" ("Ich möchte").[31]

I want with cosmic spirit
To enthuse all human beings
That a flame they may become
And fiery will unfold
The essence of their being.

The other ones, they strive
To take from cosmic waters
What will extinguish flames
And pours paralysis
Into all inner being.

O joy when human being's flame
Is blazing, even when at rest.
O bitter pain when the human thing
Is put in bonds when it wants to stir.

The other ones, the paralyzers of human and cosmic-divine evolution, they are the Ahrimanic spirits who rune every night into our ears, "good is evil, and evil is really good." For them a human being is merely a thing.

XII

Closing Remarks

In closing, I should like to share with you one of the main reasons why I have presented here these eclectic remarks. It is to emphasize the importance of the new kind of free guidance that can be derived from Rudolf Steiner's work. Because of this new quality of freedom in spiritual development, it is perhaps not surprising that in all sorts of places tendencies crop up, more and more, to distort Rudolf Steiner's work and its significance, even tending to erase Rudolf Steiner from human consciousness, so that his map for meditative development can no longer set human beings aflame with enthusiasm in the right way. Let us take a stand against these pernicious tendencies, so that Rudolf Steiner's work can stand in our time as a fiery beacon within the sea of "cosmic waters," ever anew enthusing human beings, that a flame they may become, and fiery will unfold the essence of their being.

Appendix

The lecture from which the foregoing chapters were derived was followed by a question and answer period. A selection of the questions and answers is reproduced here in condensed form.

Q. What does Rudolf Steiner have to say about meditating in groups?
A. Rudolf Steiner never advised any of his students to meditate in groups. Consequently within the Anthroposophical movement, meditation in groups is not encouraged by the governing council (*Vorstand*) in Dornach. There are people who feel that meditation in groups provides a force that bears them up more forcefully than when they meditate alone. I think that Rudolf Steiner would answer that one can indeed feel this force, but in the long run it is not beneficial, on the contrary. The reason is that this force of group meditation is to a large extent rooted in the astral body, while Rudolf Steiner sees meditation for a modern human being as beneficial only if it is impulsed by the forces of the (higher) ego. If group meditation is successful, one lands in a different "province" of the spiritual world than with an individual meditation, and that province is very limiting for further progress. Therefore, I think it is fair to say that group meditation has no place in a setting that calls itself a setting according to Rudolf Steiner.

Q. What is the relation between the path of meditation as indicated in this lecture and the path given in the lessons of the First Class of the School of Spiritual Science?
A. The School of Spiritual Science offers, for those who seek it, a path of meditative development that is, as it were, a highway on the map to become aware as directly as possible, first, of the Guardian of the Threshold; then, of one's own weaknesses and shortcomings (which is a painful but healthy awareness); and then, becoming aware of several

spiritual levels and of the beings that belong to these levels, including the beings of the angelic hierarchies. Rudolf Steiner calls the School of Spiritual Science also the School of the Archangel Michael who, as you know, is the "ambassador" of Christ. Thus, this is a very clearly drawn path of development. On the other hand there are many students of Rudolf Steiner's work who feel that there is so much material about inner development given in the literature that they have no need for any particular additional instruction. Not everyone has to follow the same path. A wide range is possible.

Q. Are there others who can corroborate out of their own experience results that Rudolf Steiner indicates as occurring as a result of travelling along the path described.
A. I have indicated that Rudolf Steiner is a Master of a high order. As a result he has stated what he had to say in a very precise and appropriate way. It is not easy to clothe spiritual experiences in words of our common language. If you ask other people, you will find that they usually say, "It is much harder than I thought, to progress along this path." However, there are some of his students who definitely describe in books, experiences that corroborate Rudolf Steiner's indications, albeit to a very limited degree. One example is Dr. G. Wachsmuth,[32] another is an English painter, Gladys Mayer, etc. But in general you will find that people are very reticent about such experiences because they feel it is difficult to find appropriate words, and Rudolf Steiner says it so much better.

Once I heard a lecturer from India describe the path of developments traced by his teacher. At the question period that followed his lecture, someone asked: "Before investing that much time and effort I like to know if what you tell us is confirmed by your own experience." The lecturer replied that he had not reached the height of his teacher, but he had had what he called *"glimpses," which convinced him of the reality* of what his teacher was talking about. I think that in the anthroposophical movement there are quite a number of people who would agree that they have had such convincing glimpses. That is as far as I can answer the question of corroboration.

6

Cosmic Secrets in Rudolf Steiner's Health Verses: A Meditative Tale

Introductory Summary

RUDOLF STEINER has given us a beautiful, carefully crafted mantric poem, to which others have added the too restrictive title, "Prayer during Illness." The poem can permeate our daily life and strengthen our whole being. To understand the deeper significance of such a mantric poem, one must be sensitive to elements of meaning that lie hidden behind and beyond the literal meaning of the words and verses. Rudolf Steiner created this mantric poem for the whole human being, its earthly as well as its cosmic aspects. In the poem the words represent the earthly aspects. They speak to the earthly human being. The cosmic aspects of the poem are hidden behind the words as underlying secrets. They relate to the cosmic human being. In this mantric poem the hidden elements of meaning are of particular importance. These hidden elements can be raised to consciousness. Once the deep significance of this poem is discovered, and then developed into a meditative mood, one's daily life can thereby be permeated by a strengthening force.

In a most concise and esoteric way the poem intends to make us aware of the process whereby the human being receives from the spiritual world refreshing health-giving forces, forces that enable us to maintain our health in body, soul and spirit. Every time that we go to sleep, these forces are called upon to undo the damage signaled by fatigue. The regeneration that sleep can bring should not be taken for granted. It is brought about by a cosmic health-giving force, a divine gift that originates in the starry world. Through a process of cosmic contraction, effected by the beings of the spiritual hierarchies, this gift is brought down into the earthly human body.

This health-giving force is mysteriously present in the mantric poem. Once its secrets have been discovered, meditation can enhance the effectiveness of this health-giving force. The present article attempts to raise to consciousness the cosmic process whereby the force descends into the earthly realm. The moods corresponding to each stage of its descent can help one who would work meditatively with this poem discover how to maintain that wondrous condition we call good health.

I. The Verses

Rudolf Steiner created a beautiful mantric poem, which may prove helpful in strengthening one's health if it is taken as content for meditation. For those who work at their inner development, it is especially important to work meditatively with these verses. The first condition that must be met in such work is to strive for bodily and spiritual health.[1] However, the virtue of these verses is by no means limited to such people. Nowadays everyone's health needs strengthening in order to counteract the harmful influences of our civilization, to which all of us are exposed. Consider merely one example. While sleep used to be a source of revitalization and refreshment, an inordinate number of people in our civilization suffer from insomnia and other disturbances of sleep. These verses are intended to be especially helpful in bringing order into just this basic component of human health. The verses read:

1. O Spirit of God — fill my I,
2. Fill my I within my soul,
3. On my soul bestow a strength'ning force,
4. Strength'ning force too for my heart,
5. For my heart that seeketh Thee,
6. Seeketh Thee with deepest longing,
7. Deepest longing for good health,
8. For good health and trust in life,
9. Trust in life that through my body streams,
10. Streams as precious gift divine,
11. Gift divine from Thee, O Spirit of God,
12. O Spirit of God — fill my I.[2]

The form of these verses shows several striking features. Each line begins with essentially the same words that end the previous line. Such repetition reveals a carefully linked series of thoughts, in accord with a strict order of thinking. This ordering of thought is consistent with Rudolf Steiner's advice that one should observe how one connects one thought to the following one in one's thinking process.[3] Such a well-organized process of thinking has a beneficial influence on the health of one's mind or soul.[4] Further, most lines have a trochaic meter (long, short: — –). According to Rudolf Steiner this rhythm facilitates entering into cosmic thought.[5] Lastly, the final line of these verses is identical with the first one. Thus, at the end of this mantric poem one returns to its starting point. In other words, the meditation has a cyclic form. One can proceed through its cycle again and again without feeling a discontinuity. Going through its cycle several times one could go on and on. However, when one goes through the cycle of this mantric poem more than once, one will reach a point where one feels "Now it is enough; it is time to end." When one experiences this feeling one should continue to the twelfth line:

O Spirit of God — fill my I,

and then stop. At times it may be found more satisfying to end with the words:

O Spirit of God, I offer thanks to Thee — Amen.

Of course, those who work meditatively with this poem have to find their own way into such details.

II. The Hierarchical Spiritual Beings and Their Cosmic Domains of Activity

Profound secrets lie hidden in this mantric poem. As a meditation it is formulated in such a way that the soul can experience a kind of cosmic breathing process. This process can be more healthful if certain feelings accompany each verse. A consideration of the open secrets that are woven into this mantric poem can allow such feelings to arise naturally in the course of meditation. To unseal these secrets one must become familiar with certain basic concepts of anthroposophy concerning cosmology and the spiritual hierarchies.[6]

According to a doctrine that may be attributed to Dionysius the Areopagite,[7] the Athenian friend of the apostle Saint Paul, there exist between the Spirit of God and human beings, nine ranks of spiritual beings, which form three hierarchies, each with three ranks. One may refer to these spiritual beings collectively as angelic beings or angels, but within this doctrine the term "angels" has a more restricted meaning. Table 1[8,9,10] lists the names of the nine ranks of spiritual beings.

TABLE 1
The Nine Ranks of the Hierarchical Spiritual Beings

Hierarchy	Classical Name	Name according to Spiritual Science[9]	Alternative Names
First Hierarchy Spirits of Strength[8]	Seraphim	Spirits of Love	
	Cherubim	Spirits of Harmony	
	Thrones	Spirits of Will	
Second Hierarchy Spirits of Light[8]	Kyriotetes	Spirits of Wisdom	Dominions, Lordships
	Dynameis	Spirits of Movement	Virtues, Authorities
	Exusiai	Spirits of Form	Potentiates, Powers, Elohim
Third Hierarchy Spirits of Soul[8]	Archai	Spirits of Personality	Principalities, Spirits of Time
	Archangeloi	Spirits of Fire	Archangels, Spirits of Soul-warmth[10]
	Angeloi	Spirits of Twilight	Angels, Sons of Life, Spirits of the World of Colors[10]

In the first centuries A.D. people still had a living awareness of these spiritual beings and their relationships, but today direct awareness of these beings has practically vanished in the Christian world. Rudolf Steiner describes in great detail the nature of these beings, their evolution, their states of consciousness, their tasks and activities, and their significance for

Cosmic Secrets in Rudolf Steiner's Health Verses

the human being and for the Earth. The different hierarchic ranks have different cosmic domains of activity, which can be described as more or less spherical spaces or spheres, with the Earth at their center. These domains or spheres are listed in Table 2.[11]

Table 2
The Geocentric Spheres of the Hierarchical Spiritual Beings

Spiritual Beings	Spheres
Seraphim, Cherubim	Their spheres extend out to the region of the fixed stars.
Thrones	The including sphere of the orbit of Saturn.
Kyriotetes	The including sphere of the orbit of Jupiter.
Dynameis	The including sphere of the orbit of Mars.
Exusiai	The including sphere of the orbit of the Sun, but sometimes: The excluding sphere of the orbit of the Sun.
Archai	The excluding sphere of the orbit of Venus.[11]
Archangeloi	The excluding sphere of the orbit of Mercury.[11]
Angeloi	The excluding sphere of the orbit of the Moon.

The following astronomical concepts may be helpful in understanding the spheres. Consider a typical geocentric planetary orbit. A geocentric sphere that touches the planetary orbit as to include this orbit is called an "including sphere." A geocentric sphere that touches the planetary orbit and excludes this orbit will be called an "excluding sphere." Figure 1 (below) illustrates both types of spheres for a typical planetary orbit. Figure 2 (below) shows the including and excluding spheres for the orbit of the Sun.

Table 2 requires the following comments. For a description of the activities of the spiritual beings connected with the outer planets one uses the including spheres; for those spiritual beings connected with the inner planets and the Moon, the excluding spheres. The Sun is special. From the geocentric viewpoint (which is the view one experiences from the Earth) the Sun completes one revolution annually along an elliptic path, practically a circle with the Earth a bit off center, as is shown in Figure 2. Its including and excluding spheres differ but slightly. The sphere to be chosen depends on the context. Both will be used in order to grasp the deeper meaning of certain verses of this meditation.

The spheres in Table 2 form a regularly diminishing series if one takes into account a remarkable fact in the history of astronomy. In the fifteenth century the names of Mercury and Venus were switched.[11] The planet which today we call Venus was called Mercury in earlier times, and vice versa. The fact of this reversal of planetary names is not generally known, though it is well documented in authoritative historical records. In Spiritual Science the ancient nomenclature is often used, especially when one is concerned with the forces and beings of the soul-spiritual world that are connected with these planetary bodies. Thus, according to ancient nomenclature, the planet that orbits closest to the Sun is called Venus, the "planet of longing,"[12] while what is called Venus today was in former times called Mercury, the "planet of healing." The present discourse adheres to the ancient nomenclature.

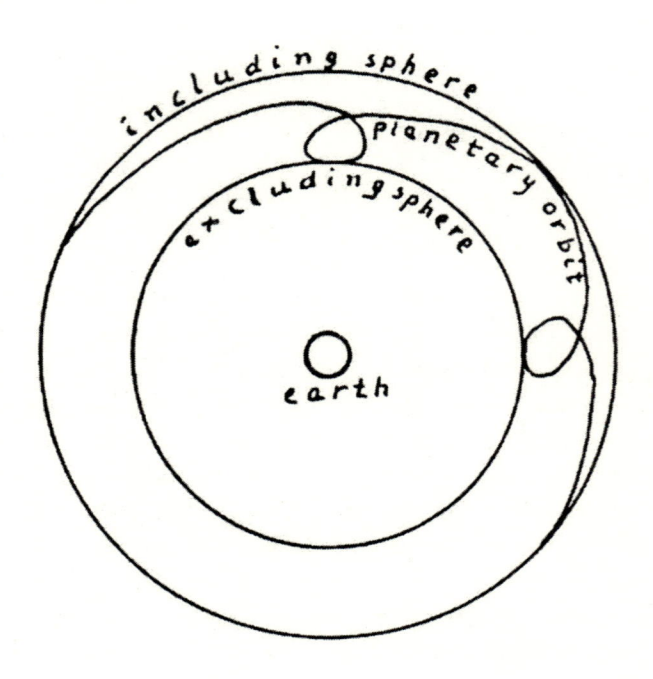

FIGURE 1

A typical geocentric planetary orbit and its including and excluding sphere

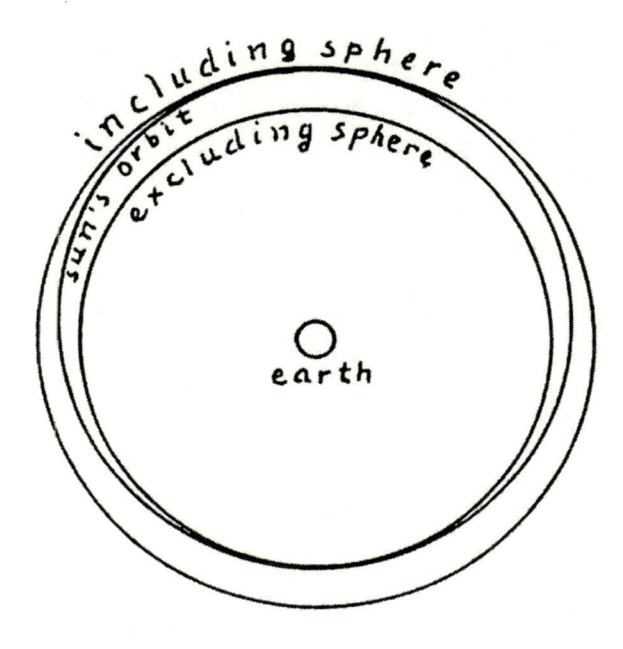

[Figure: concentric circles labeled "including sphere", "sun's orbit", "excluding sphere", with "earth" at center]

FIGURE 2

The geocentric Sun orbit and its including and excluding sphere

Since time immemorial people have felt that the starry sky is a manifestation of the divine Spirit. Gazing with awe and reverence at the majestic starry sky with its innumerable luminous stars, one may even today become vaguely aware of the creative activity of the divine Spirit in a primeval past. Of course, present-day cosmological ideas, based as they are on materialistic concepts only, are incompatible with such an awareness. That one is allowed as a human being to behold this magnificent work of art, the starry sky, can be felt as a great gift. When I open my soul to the spontaneous impression of this great cosmic revelation of the divine Spirit, where am I then really? In a certain sense I am then in the domain of the Seraphim and the Cherubim, spiritual beings who are privileged to behold the Godhead of the Holy Trinity directly, and whose domain of activity is anchored in the fixed stars and reaches down into our solar system, even into the Earth.

According to Spiritual Science, our "I" and our soul expand every night when we go to sleep out into cosmic space. There they receive and absorb subconsciously a kind of spiritual essence that sustains us the following day. Every night we partake subconsciously of the divine-spiritual essence that the beings of the first hierarchy bring to us from the world of the fixed stars, the world of the divine Spirit. The Seraphim and the Cherubim bring it to the sphere of Saturn, to the domain of the Thrones, who in turn pass it on to our "I."

After the human "I" has received the divine-spiritual essence in the Saturn sphere this essence must be brought down through the planetary spheres to our earthly body in order that we may be refreshed upon awakening. In each planetary sphere the spiritual beings of that sphere work upon this essence. They enrich it in a qualitative way before it can take the next step on its earthward journey. In this way, the spiritual essence gradually permeates our astral body, our etheric body, and finally our physical body. Thus every period of sleep is a cosmic journey. First there is an expansion, an out-breathing as it were, toward the Saturn sphere. Then the divine spiritual essence is received. Lastly there is an in-breathing, a return to our body through the spheres of the hierarchies, where the divine-spiritual essence is enriched.

What are the qualitative enrichments that the hierarchies bestow upon the original divine-spiritual essence as it passes through their spheres? In the Saturn sphere the Thrones give the divine essence to our "I." In the Jupiter sphere one enters the domain of the Spirits of Wisdom, the Kyriotetes, who endow the essence with a quality of inner life. In the Mars sphere is added what can be called an inner strength. The Sun is the heart of the solar system. Here the essence is enriched with heart-forces. In ancient times the planet Venus was designated as the "Planet of Longing" (*Sehnsucht*). This designation implied a longing to overcome the effects of the Fall from Paradise, by striving toward that evolutionary goal which resulted from the Fall, namely spiritual freedom. Thus in the Venus sphere the divine spiritual essence is enriched with a longing for spiritual freedom. In the sphere of Mercury, the "Planet of Healing," a health-giving force is added, one that helps the mind and body come into a proper balance. The Moon sphere is the gate to incarnation. Here is added a quality that may be called the "will to live." With all of these qualitative enhancements the divine essence finally enters into the will-pole of our earthly body. Viewed from this aspect, the human microcosm becomes permeated with what is breathed in from the divine macrocosm, enriched by the contributions of the hierarchical spiritual beings. This is health.

However, one can also describe this process of cosmic in-breathing from another, polar opposite viewpoint. Looking at this in-breathing process from an earthly viewpoint, one sees first the human physical body. This physical body is subject to wear and deterioration. It suffers damage through its involvement with waking consciousness. As a result one becomes tired and one ages. During sleep this wear and damage is to a large extent repaired through the activity of the etheric or life body. The etheric body is able to perform such repairs because it contains, and acts according to, the etheric ideal images underlying the formation of the physical body. These etheric ideal images are stimulated by the influences from the Sun sphere.

However, the etheric ideal images need periodic re-enlivening. This re-enlivening comes from the astral body, which contains, and acts according to, forces which Rudolf Steiner calls "prototypes" (*Vorbilder*) of the etheric ideal images. These prototypes are stimulated by the influences from the planetary spheres. The astral prototypes in turn need periodic revitalization. This revitalization comes from the "I," which has received divine-spiritual essence from the fixed stars at the Saturn sphere. The enrichments that are bestowed upon the divine essence during its descent through the planetary spheres are reflected, as it were, as a revitalization of the prototype images in the astral body, and then as a re-enlivening of the ideal images in the etheric body. Thus, when the physical body receives the divine essence with all its planetary enrichments, a harmoniously attuned cooperation of the four members of the human being—the "I," astral body, etheric or life body, and physical body—is brought about. This harmonious cooperation is health.

III. The Verses as a Tale of the Cosmic Journey

Each verse of Rudolf Steiner's mantric poem for health expresses in a most concise way one step of the cosmic journey that was described in the previous section. To appreciate this fact fully one needs to imagine in as lively a way as possible the qualitative nature of the contributions which the various hierarchies are able, at their respective spheres, to bestow upon the descending divine-spiritual essence on its journey down to the human body. Such vivid imagining, combined with the relevant insights of anthroposophy, can help the reader or the meditant to transcend a merely intellectual approach to these verses. Certain feelings can arise naturally at each stage of this journey. These feelings will support one's understanding of the whole process.

The first verse of this mantric poem tells us that the Spirit of God is to enter into and fill our ego or "I." To achieve a living understanding of what this means, let us try to imagine enlarging our being, expanding in all directions of space, expanding our soul all the way to the Saturn sphere, the domain of the lofty Thrones. There, we imagine, we direct our gaze outward toward the starry sky all around us, and we become aware of the venerable Cherubim and Seraphim who are carrying holy divine-spiritual essence from the world of the fixed stars inward to the Saturn sphere, to the Thrones, and we pray that our own being may be filled in its very center, in its "I," with that precious essence. Then the lofty Thrones, following the directives of the Cherubim and the Seraphim, pass this divine-spiritual essence on to the human "I." All of this mighty cosmic happening is implied in the first verse:

(1) O Spirit of God — fill my I.

Why should the expansion of our soul reach out just to the Saturn sphere? The Saturn sphere is the home of new beginnings. In the first incarnation of the Earth, called in Spiritual Science "Ancient Saturn," the beginnings of the human physical body were laid down in the Saturn sphere. In the second incarnation of the Earth, called "Ancient Sun," the beginnings of the human etheric body were developed in what was then the Saturn sphere. In the third incarnation of the Earth, called "Ancient Moon," the beginnings of the human astral body came about in the Saturn sphere. Finally in the present or fourth incarnation of the Earth the human "I" originated in the Saturn sphere, and there its true home is to be found.[13] It is highly significant that the first verse refers to the human "I" as the receptacle for the fiery instreaming of the divine spiritual essence, and thereby implies the Saturn sphere as the locale. How does the "I" prepare itself to be worthy of receiving and holding what comes to it from the starry divine world? The "I" needs to permeate itself for this holy event with a mood of deepest reverence and devotion. Only in such a mood can this heavenly gift be properly received. Figure 3 (below) attempts to picture symbolically these relationships.

The first verse initiates a process. What flows into the "I" from a divine source must be further breathed in. It must be carried through the planetary spheres down to our earthly abode, for it needs to become effective in our physical body. To accomplish this the spiritual beings of the first hierarchy must pass this spiritual essence on to the beings of the second

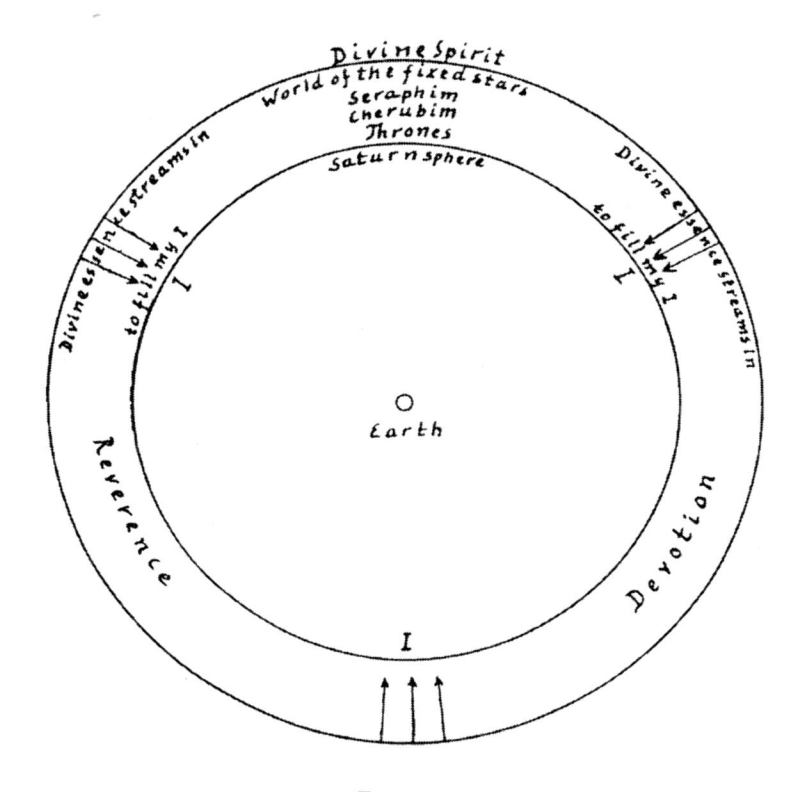

[Figure 3: A circular diagram. At the top outside the circle: "Divine Spirit", "World of the fixed stars". Inside the upper portion: "Seraphim / Cherubim / Thrones / Saturn sphere". In the center: a small circle labeled "Earth". Around the outside of the circle: "Divine essence streams in" (upper left and upper right), "to fill my I" (with arrows pointing inward on both sides), "Reverence" (left side), "Devotion" (right side). At the bottom: "I" with three upward arrows.]

FIGURE 3

Symbolic representation of the cosmic and hierarchical aspects of the first verse

hierarchy, and these again to the beings of the third hierarchy, so that in the end it can descend as a precious gift to the earthly human being.

We will consider the second, third, and fourth verse of this mantric poem in a similar qualitative way as the first verse. The second verse takes us from the Saturn sphere, the domain of the Thrones, to the Kyriotetes, the Spirits of Wisdom, whose domain of activity is the Jupiter Sphere.[6] The third verse leads us further to the Dynameis, the Spirits of Movement, in the Mars sphere, and the fourth verse takes us into the domain of the Exusiai, the Spirits of Form, in the Sun sphere. In other words, each verse corresponds to a transition from one sphere into the next one.

The second verse refers to the descent of the divine-spiritual essence from the Saturn sphere to the Jupiter sphere, the domain of the Spirits of Wisdom. Which imagination can express appropriately the enrichment that the divine-spiritual essence receives through the activity of the Spirits of Wisdom? The Spirits of Wisdom are Light-Spirits.[8] Their wisdom weaves in their light. It weaves also in the light of our own consciousness, in our consciousness soul. Through their light the Spirits of Wisdom enable the human soul to merge with the divine-spiritual essence, provided the human soul is not dull and closed, opaque to their light. This merger can be experienced as an illumination. To become receptive for this experience the human soul must cultivate a rich inner life. Implicitly the second verse of the poem calls for a readiness and willingness to enrich the soul's inner life, to make it as versatile and sensitive as possible.[14] Then the spiritual-divine essence that has filled the "I" can light up in the soul's consciousness:

(2) Fill my I unto my soul.

However, the activity of the Spirits of Wisdom is not restricted to their weaving in soul-light. Their major characteristic is their will to give gifts. Rudolf Steiner calls this quality the "Virtue of Giving" (*Schenkende Tugend*).[15] This quality comes to expression in the third verse of this poem, which describes how the Spirits of Wisdom send us on our way to the Spirits of Movement. Thus, in the third verse the soul prays that it may receive that gift which will enable it to carry the divine-spiritual essence from the Jupiter sphere to the Mars sphere. Granting this gift is, as it were, authorized by the Spirits of Wisdom, while the gift itself is actually given by the Spirits of Movement as the soul arrives in the Mars sphere. In the poem this gift is called "strengthening force" (*Stärkekraft*).

What is meant here by "strengthening force"? Its meaning can be discerned in the characteristic virtue of the Spirits of Movement, the Dynameis, whose domain is the Mars sphere. Spiritual Science tells how in the course of cosmic evolution, specifically during the ancient Moon-incarnation of the Earth, certain spiritual beings of the rank of the Thrones were excluded from the regular course of their evolutionary process.[16] This difficult destiny caused these excluded Thrones great suffering. The Dynameis then approached them and worked upon them in such a way that these Thrones became able to bear the heavy burden of their destiny. By means of their capacity for movement the Dynameis gave them "strengthening force." This strengthening force can be described as an inner strength which seeks to make the best of even the most difficult situation. "Never to lose courage" is the archetypal meaning of "strengthening force."

Yet there is something else that the Dynameis accomplished in that ancient time. Through their activity our human ancestors received an astral body of their own. But, owing to the irregular cosmic evolution of that time, the human astral body became more or less turbid or darkened. That is why even in ordinary life of the present time our inner soul movements and stirrings are rather chaotic and irregular. Because of its relatively young, passionate, and immature nature, the human astral body often harbors causes for illness. Our health depends to a great extent on our ability to make our inner soul movements regular, orderly, consistent, and purposeful.

In the first verse the divine essence is given to the "I" in the Saturn sphere. In the second verse this essence fills the soul with light in the Jupiter sphere. But in the third verse this light is darkened by the turbidity of our astral body as we enter the Mars sphere. The imperfections in our astral body often will lead us into situations where we are exposed to blows of destiny. To meet these blows of destiny in a healthful way one needs the strengthening force which the Dynameis make available in the Mars sphere, at the behest of the Kyriotetes. However, this strengthening force can only prove effective if it is received by a soul that has prepared itself in a very specific way. The mood of soul that is appropriate here is often described as the "strength of inner tranquility." Only when permeated by the strength of inner tranquility can the human being hope to carry out an ordered set of actions, steering with inner certainty toward a conscious goal. This mood is the soul-soil into which the "strengthening force" must be planted in order to be effective in overcoming the astral imperfections in a healthful way:

(3) On my soul bestow a strength'ning force.

The fourth verse leads us from the Mars sphere to the Sun sphere. What the Sun is in the organism of the macrocosm, the heart is in the human microcosm. In the Sun sphere the Spirits of Form, the Exusiai, rule. In ancient times of the Earth's evolution these exalted beings set to work on human beings. At that time the human ancestors were rather animal-like. The Exusiai implanted into them the "I," that higher principle which enabled human beings to raise themselves definitively above the level of the animal kingdom in the course of time. A similar transformation is achieved during every period of sleep when the divine-spiritual essence, which was given to the human "I" in the Saturn sphere, which then filled the soul with light in the Jupiter sphere, which then was permeated with strengthening force in the Mars sphere, is now allowed to permeate the human heart.

(4)   Strength'ning force too for my heart.

What has been described so far as the activities of the hierarchical spiritual beings as well as the human soul moods that need to be developed inwardly to meet these activities is represented symbolically in Figure 4.

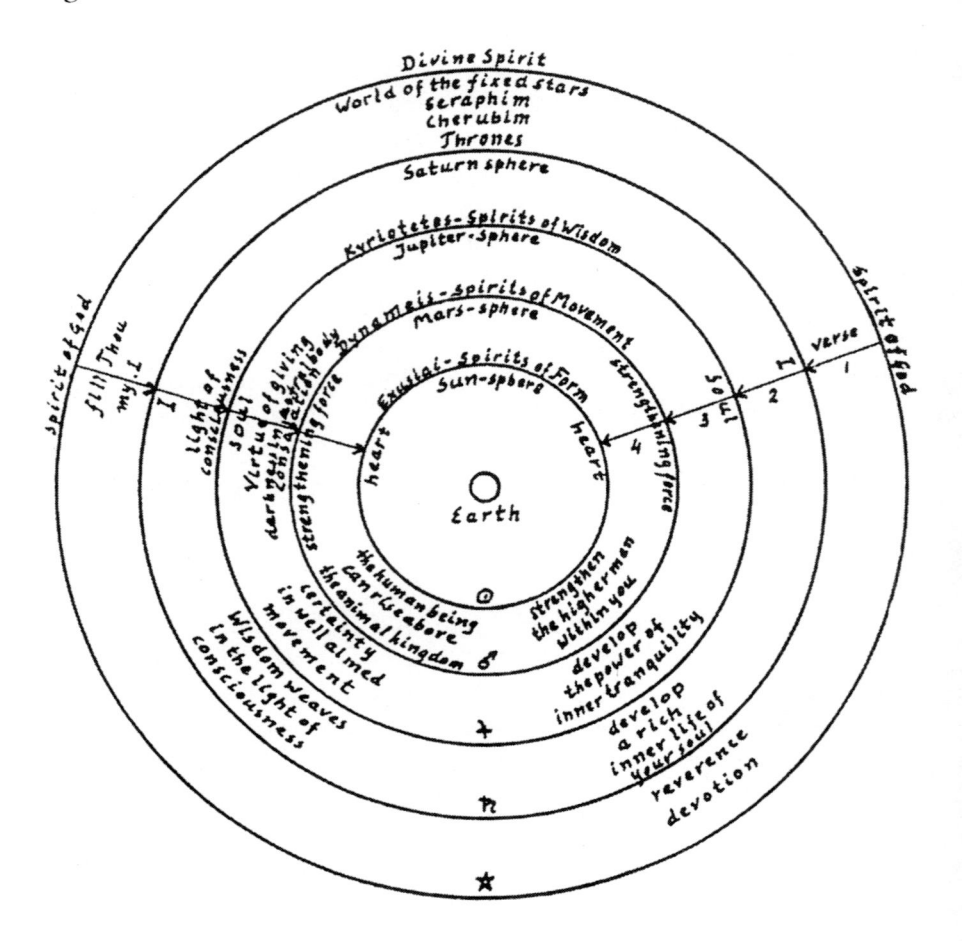

FIGURE 4

Symbolic representation of the cosmic and hierarchical aspects of the first four verses

So far, a process has been described whereby a sphere gradually contracted. Starting from interstellar space it contracted to the Saturn sphere, then to the Jupiter sphere, the Mars sphere, and finally to the Sun sphere. The Sun is the heart of our planetary system. Like the spheres of the outer planets, the Sun sphere has been discussed so far as an including sphere. The mood of this part of the cosmic journey has been one of joy, light, and strength. This mood can be characterized more precisely as a series of inner soul states (see Figure 4) that agree exactly with the feelings which Rudolf Steiner introduces in the same sequential order in chapter one of *How to Know Higher Worlds,* in which the author says that these feelings need to be inculcated in the student of spirit knowledge if they are at all lacking.

As the cosmic journey continues one reaches the excluding Sun sphere before one enters the excluding spheres of the inner planets, Venus and Mercury. A different mood now prevails, a feeling of losing the intimate contact with the spiritual beings of the outer planets and the Sun. In the sub-solar region one is thrown back upon oneself, with the result that a nostalgic mood emerges. Indeed, In the fifth verse one seeks for the spiritual world which one has just left or lost, for this verse is related to the excluding Sun sphere:

(5)   For my heart that seeketh Thee.

In the sixth verse, which is related to the Venus sphere, this mood becomes a deep longing:

(6)   Seeketh Thee with deepest longing.

In the seventh verse, which is related to the Mercury sphere, this longing crystallizes into a longing for health. A healthy human being is a microcosm filled with the macrocosmic Spirit of God:

(7)   Deepest longing for good health.

Figure 5 (below) pictures symbolically the process of the verses five, six, and seven, in a similar manner as the one in Figure 4 for the verses one through four.

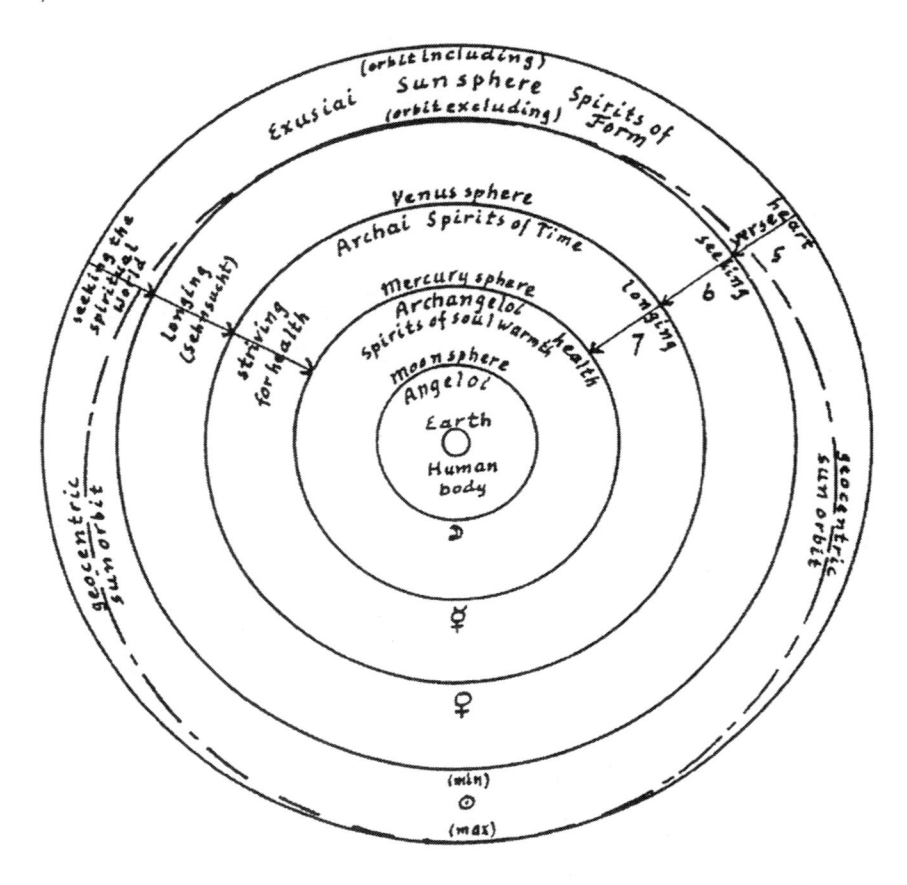

FIGURE 5
Symbolic representation of the cosmic and hierarchical aspects of verses 5, 6, and 7

The Moon sphere is a very complicated organ in the spiritual cosmos. A first feature is that it is the domain of activity of the angels, in particular of our guardian angel. However, there also emanates from the Moon sphere an influence thst permeates the entire spiritual cosmos. This influence may be described as a call, directed especially to all human souls who dwell in the spiritual world after having completed an incarnation on the Earth. In that state the human soul is exposed to a great temptation. It is the temptation to remain forever within the spiritual world, to forego further incarnations. The call that rings forth from the Moon sphere encourages these human souls to devote themselves to the needs of the Earth, and in so doing, to develop further their innate potentials, and to awaken more and more strength for adhering to the good. This call resounds in order to counteract the temptation just mentioned, for when the human soul sojourns in the spiritual world between incarnations, a tremendous strength and courage is needed to accept a new incarnation with all its attendant suffering, including the experience of another death. From the Moon sphere the Angeloi provide the human soul with the necessary strong courage for a life in a body (*Starkmut*). This will-to-live, or trust in life, is an important health factor. Medical practitioners know well that healing often depends decisively on the will-to-live of the patient.

The eighth verse expresses how upon arrival in the Moon sphere the divine-spiritual essence is enriched by the Angeloi with this trust in life:

(8) For good health and trust in life.

This then leads to the incorporation of the results of this cosmic journey into the human body, expressed in the ninth verse:

(9) Trust in life that through my body streams.

What was expressed in the first verse as a divine-spiritual essence that was to fill the human "I," and what in the second verse filled the soul with light, has now descended from its divine origin through the planetary spheres, and has finally arrived in the human body. There it streams through the whole body, permeating all of its members and organs. A cosmic in-breathing has been completed. It would be good to remind oneself from time to time that what streams as a refreshing and regenerating force through the human body after each period of sleep is of divine origin.

Breathing in must be followed by breathing out. The out-breathing is described in the tenth and eleventh verses, and is completed in the twelfth. The out-breathing happens much faster than the in-breathing. It has the character of a retrospect (*Rückschau*). The tenth verse takes us back to the Jupiter sphere where the virtue of giving prevails:

(10) Streams as precious gift divine.

The eleventh verse returns us to the Saturn sphere:

(11) Gift divine from Thee, O Spirit of God.

Finally, the twelfth verse directs our gaze again towards the shining, light-permeated world of the fixed stars, which arches majestically beyond the Saturn sphere, and which we now behold in a mood of devotion, reverence, and gratitude, as the imaginative expression of the Spirit of God:

(12) O Spirit of God — fill my I.

The last four verses, nine through twelve, can also be described from another viewpoint, an earthly or microcosmic point of view. From this viewpoint the ninth verse pertains to the physical body as it receives the enlivening force from the etheric life body:

(9) Trust in life that through my body streams.

The tenth verse then relates this in-streaming trust in life to what the etheric body receives from the prototypes which the divine Spirit has implanted in the astral body:

(10) Streams as precious gift divine.

The eleventh verse relates to what the astral body with its prototypes receives from the divine world of the fixed stars, the abode of the Spirit of God:

(11) Gift divine from Thee, O Spirit of God.

Finally the twelfth verse unites the revitalization of the three lower members of the human being with the human I:

(12) O Spirit of God — fill my I.

While the first nine verses express health as the gift from the hierarchies in the macrocosm, the last four verses express health as the harmony among the four members of the microcosmic human being. The ninth verse is the link that forms a bridge between these two complementary approaches. As the in-breathing is described from the macrocosmic viewpoint, involving all of the hierarchies of spiritual beings and the planetary spheres, it is much longer than the description of the out-breathing, from the microcosmic viewpoint, which involves only the four principal members of the human being.

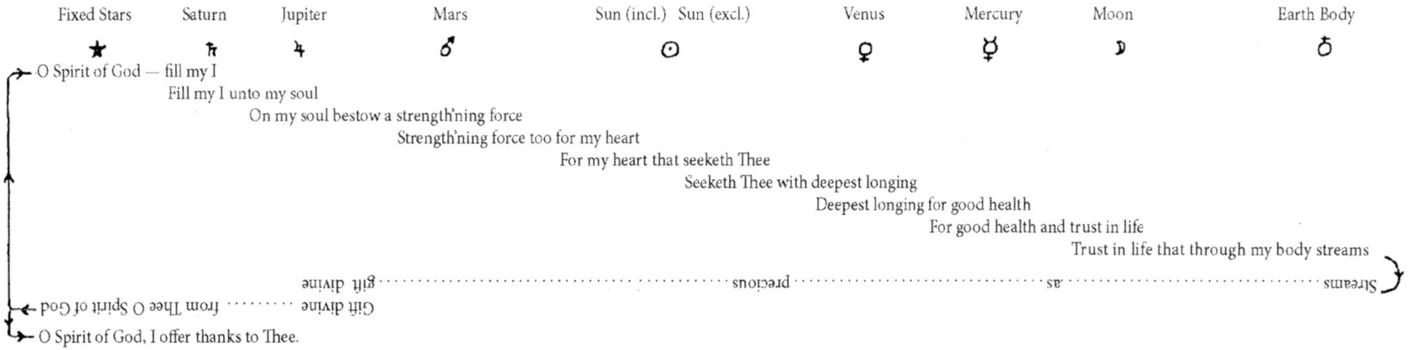

Fixed Stars	Saturn	Jupiter	Mars	Sun (incl.)	Sun (excl.)	Venus	Mercury	Moon	Earth Body
★	♄	♃	♂	☉		♀	☿	☽	⊕

O Spirit of God — fill my I
　Fill my I unto my soul
　　On my soul bestow a strength'ning force
　　　Strength'ning force too for my heart
　　　　For my heart that seeketh Thee
　　　　　Seeketh Thee with deepest longing
　　　　　　Deepest longing for good health
　　　　　　　For good health and trust in life
　　　　　　　　Trust in life that through my body streams

precious .... as .... Streams

Gift divine .... gift divine
　from Thee O Spirit of God
O Spirit of God, I offer thanks to Thee.

FIGURE 6

A survey of the cosmic breathing process inherent in the poem.

Epilogue

The present essay attempts to reveal the cosmic secrets in Rudolf Steiner's mantric poem in a way that may lead to a deeper insight into its relation to human health. To achieve this goal one cannot stay within the limits of what is given literally in the condensed form of the mantra itself. Of necessity a meditative approach has to be allowed, which goes beyond what is given literally, and thereby tries to unveil some part of what may live behind the words and verses as spiritual reality. If such a meditative approach, which goes beyond the literal meaning of each word and verse, is to be in agreement with Rudolf Steiner's intentions, it must be guided by insights from Spiritual Science. These intentions are stated most clearly in Rudolf Steiner's second *Mystery Drama*, "The Soul's Probation,"[17] 1911) by words spoken by Benedictus, the archetypal sun-initiate who may be seen as a representative of Rudolf Steiner:

> I do not wish my words to say alone
> What they convey as covering for concepts.
> They turn the innate forces of the soul
> To the realities of spirit.
> Their meaning is reached only
> When they unlock the power of sight
> In souls surrendered to their force.[17]

Only by going beyond the literal wording in this way, guided by anthroposophical ideas that Rudolf Steiner formulated elsewhere, can one hope to penetrate in a living way into the feeling or mood that corresponds to what is secretly contained in each verse as a cosmic element. Only then can this poem lead one to that spiritual source that continually pours vitality and health into mankind. That is the reason why this poem, if meditated upon in the right way, can strengthen the forces of health in a person. Once this spiritual source is discovered by the method described here, its cosmic secret becomes an open secret. Access to the inner experience of this source is then open to each person. In Figure 6 the essential relationships are pictured once more in a different way. No claim is made that the approach presented here is the only valid one. This poem certainly contains other hidden secrets that wait to be brought to light. However, the discovery of such hidden relationships as are presented here can also give rise to feelings of awe and admiration for the exactness with which Rudolf Steiner clothed spiritual contents in human language.

7

Thoughts about the Foundation Stone

I. The Foundation Stone

THE GENERAL ANTHROPOSOPHICAL SOCIETY was founded at the famous Christmas Conference,[1] which took place in Dornach, Switzerland, from December 24, 1923, to January 1, 1924, with approximately 800 members attending. Here Rudolf Steiner spoke the Foundation Stone and exhorted his listeners to take these verses into their hearts. The Foundation Stone consists of three similarly structured panels of twenty-two lines each and a different fourth panel of twenty-five lines. The verses were not given all at once, but in parts, spread over different days. In addition, on each of seven days Rudolf Steiner wrote on a blackboard certain sets of selected lines, which he referred to as "rhythms." He indicated that meditation on these "rhythms" is essential for penetrating to the inner substance of the Foundation Stone.

There exist more than a dozen different translations of these verses. Consultation with several translations is necessary if one wishes to grasp the fine nuances of meaning in the original, for no single translation can render fully all aspects of these verses. Each translator comes up with a compromise.

The translation at the beginning of this essay attempts to render faithfully into English the meaning of the German original while retaining as closely as possible its pattern of beat and some of its sound quality, and thus preserving its mantric quality in a form suitable for meditation.

II. The Inner Nature, of the Foundation Stone

Born out of fire, through pain and suffering, that magical formula, the Foundation Stone, is destined to guide the souls of seeking human beings, in the present time and in centuries to come, toward solutions of the great riddles of existence, toward overcoming the great scourges of our time—deep loneliness, desperate anxiety, and tragic confusion—by touching the timeless, ever-flowing wellsprings of spirit-life, spirit-love, and spirit-light, behind which the mystery of Christ holds sway.

Ancient Wisdom told that the Dark Age—Kali Yuga—would last till the end of the nineteenth century. The great challenge of the twentieth century was to establish the new, enlightened mysteries, which, unlike the ancient secret mysteries, are open to all who earnestly seek them. Openness and universality are called for in the present time. Openness is the hallmark of the Mystery of Golgotha, the greatest and most universal of all mysteries. Enacted on the physical plane of world historic events, its open secrets await to be illuminated more and more in our time and in times to come.

It was Rudolf Steiner's destiny to meet these challenges. Loftiest cosmic spirit powers, whose central concern is the destiny of mankind, guided Rudolf Steiner to shape the verses of the Foundation Stone as a true spiritual cornerstone, a living seed, for the new mysteries, which recognize the unique and central significance of the Mystery of Golgotha, the Mystery of the Risen Christ.

Note well, the Foundation Stone is a *living* seed. Secretly enfolded therein lies infinite life and wisdom, which spring forth when it is planted in the right soil. Where is this soil that must embrace the seed and bring forth its hidden life? It is the heart, the soul, of the individual human being who has found the way to the new mysteries. How can this seed be kept alive in these arid times and be allowed to germinate, grow, and reveal its hidden treasures? Many a student of anthroposophy has tried to enliven this seed by devoting attention and care to its verses, only to discover after some time that it has become stale. It is no longer life-giving, rather it feels like a foreign object in the soul. If the Foundation Stone, that open mystery, is not approached with the right attitude of soul, it will wither and reveal none of its secret magic. What is the right attitude with which to approach this soul mystery?

Certainly *all* mysteries should be approached with a mood of reverence and wonder, with persistence and clarity of thought, and with openness and sensitivity. But all of this is not enough. In our time one further step of preparation must be taken, one additional virtue must be cultivated by the seeking human being, and this is indeed the most essential virtue.

What is this most essential virtue? In each cultural epoch one eminent virtue is told about by a major legend. For our epoch Rudolf Steiner indicated that this is the legend of Parsifal's search for the Holy Grail. The eminent virtue that Parsifal must develop is: *To ask at the right time the right human question as it springs from the heart*. People today are quite good at asking all sorts of questions: clever, intellectual, irrelevant, even nonsensical questions. But the ability to ask questions that spring from the heart is often lacking. However, in order to be acceptable to the spiritual world, souls of the present epoch must develop the virtue of asking questions that spring from the heart.

What happens when one approaches the Foundation Stone with questions of the heart? It comes alive and grows—and yields growing answers. These answers are not abstract or intellectual. They are life-forces, which awaken and sustain the soul. Thus conversation with the verses can become a living source of inspiration. This is the magic of the Foundation Stone: it can awaken life-giving, life-sustaining soul forces. But if one fails to approach its verses with questions of the heart one will find oneself, as it were, rejected. Thus the Foundation Stone can be experienced as belonging to the mysteries surrounding the Holy Grail.

The inner conversation with the Foundation Stone might well begin by asking: For whom are these verses intended? The answer springs forth immediately: Three of its four panels open with the call "Human Soul!" (*Menschenseele*) and close with the admonition "May human beings hear it." The fourth panel tells of Christ's mission on earth, which is valid for all of mankind. The Foundation Stone addresses itself to "all who have ears to hear it." It is intended for all who are willing to listen to it intimately, to work with it in a living way, with the forces of heart and soul.

Why is the Foundation Stone built of three similar panels and a fourth panel of markedly different tone and structure? This order can be seen as an imprint of the cosmos. Of the twelve signs of the zodiac, four are called principal signs. A simplified view may take these four signs as representing the zodiac. They are:

- Taurus, the Bull, which is related to the human metabolic system: limbs and digestion.

- Leo, the Lion, which is related to the human rhythmical system, centered in heart and lungs.
- Scorpio, the Scorpion, originally called the Eagle, which is related to the human system of nerves and senses, centered in the head.
- Aquarius, the Waterman, more accurately the Etheric Human Form, which is related to the life that permeates and integrates the whole human body.

The four panels of the Foundation Stone clearly relate to the four principal signs of the zodiac: the first panel to the limbs, and thereby to Taurus, the second panel to heart and lungs, and thereby to Leo, the third panel to the head, and thereby to Scorpio, and the fourth panel to Christ as the integrating force of the human body.

How does the Christ-impulse work as the integrating force of the human body? First, it permeates the limbs, resulting in the upright human posture; secondly, it permeates the rhythmic system, resulting in the faculty of speech; thirdly, it permeates the nerve-and-senses system, resulting in our faculty of thinking. Walking, speaking, and thinking, the human being owes to the Christ Spirit, Who imbued mankind with these forces long, long ago, through three etheric sacrificial deeds, the fruits of which reawaken with each small child when it learns to walk, to speak, and to think. Through these sacrificial deeds the forces of the Bull, the Lion, and the Eagle were made subservient to a higher purpose. This goal became fully manifest in the earthly, fourth sacrifice of Christ at the turning point of time, after the baptism by John, a representative image of the Waterman. Thus the fourfold structure of the Foundation Stone expresses the fact that the human body, the Temple of God, functions according to cosmic laws, of which the signs of the zodiac are an etheric image.

Now when one hears the Foundation Stone call thrice "Human Soul," this call resounds from the cosmos as well as from our body, and we may ask: Who is it who calls thus three times? The Foundation Stone answers thus: First note that the Spirit who calls means well with the human being, for He points to three tasks, the practice of which will enable one to "truly live," "truly feel," and "truly think," in short, to become "truly human." Further, observe that the Spirit who calls commands the spirits of all nine hierarchic ranks to perform their tasks in the cosmos in a definite way, namely, so that thereby the foundation is created on which the "truly human" can develop. *Therefore, the One who calls "Human Soul!" is a being who is higher than all nine hierarchies! He is of divine rank.* One may feel awestruck by such a revelation.

The Four Principal Signs of the Zodiac and their Relation to the Human Body.

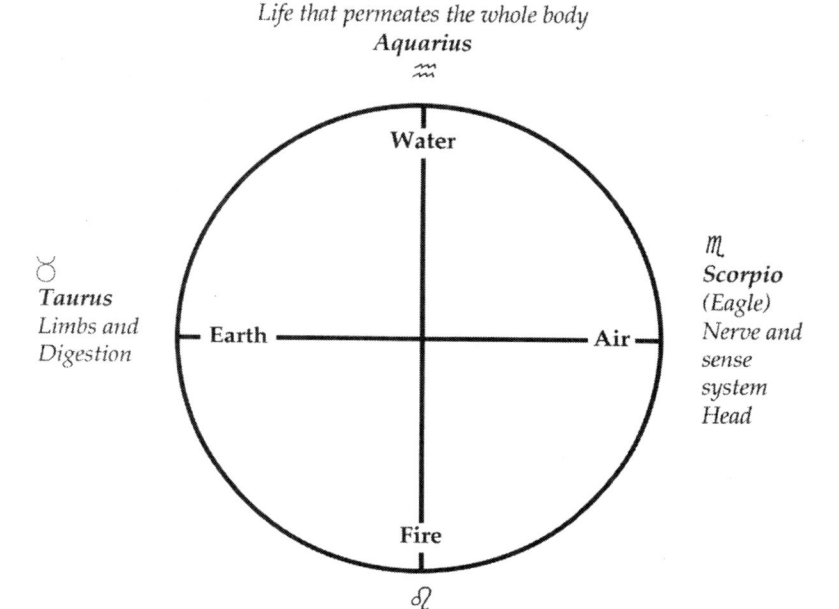

Life that permeates the whole body
Aquarius
♒

Water

♉
Taurus
Limbs and
Digestion

— Earth ——————————— Air —

♏
Scorpio
(Eagle)
Nerve and
sense
system
Head

Fire

♌
Leo
Rhythmic system
Heart and lungs

Meditation on the Foundation Stone is difficult because of its length and its complexity. Rudolf Steiner anticipated this difficulty, for he was a master teacher. He gave seven ways to enter into a relationship with its verses. By focusing on seven simple sets of relationships, a living entrance into the verses can be achieved. He called these entranceways the seven "rhythms." They will be discussed in the next section.

The Foundation Stone is not meant only to be listened to. It asks that one shall *"do"* something. Out of one's own free will one is asked to perform three specific inner activities, to practice three specific soul virtues: spirit recalling, spirit meditating, and spirit envisioning. One is advised to engage in three exercises in order to travel the road toward truly human stature. This is clearly the core of the Foundation Stone.

How can one understand the meaning of spirit-recalling, spirit-meditating, and spirit-envisioning? One can give starting points, seeds of meaning, as it were. They cannot be defined in a conventional way. Rudolf Steiner often emphasized the importance of living thinking in contrast to dead thinking. A dead thought can be understood but not experienced. As soon as it is conceived, it is fully matured. As soon as it is born, it is old. It cannot grow. A living thought, on the other hand, can be experienced. It can be grasped, but only to a certain extent, for the experience of its reality is dependent upon our own maturity. As we grow and mature, so does the living thought within us grow and mature. That is why Rudolf Steiner recommends the use of living characterizations, rather than dead definitions.

The living seeds of meaning that characterize the experiences of spirit-recalling, spirit-meditating, and spirit-envisioning can grow with practice. They must be derived from the Foundation Stone Meditation itself. They will enable us to become better aware of how we live in the element of *time*.

The Foundation Stone refers entirely to the present, the now. But the present can be viewed from several aspects. One aspect is the past insofar as the past makes itself felt in the present through the process of remembering, or recalling. Whenever an event takes place in the past, it will leave a trace somewhere that persists into the present and can then be experienced anew. The first panel of the Foundation Stone Meditation is imbued with this past-oriented aspect of the present. With our ordinary faculty of remembering, we can call into the present many of our experiences of events that happened in the past. The most remote event we can normally recall is a point in early childhood when we first used the word "I," usually about our third year of life. In a similar fashion spirit-recalling brings into our present awareness what we experienced in a much more distant past, in our past incarnations and in our past states of spiritual existence. The most remote event one can recall in this sense is a moment of indescribable grandeur, which can only become conscious if it is approached with greatest devotion. It is the moment when our "I" began to exist as an identifiable entity within the "I of God," the World-Creator, the Father. Through the practice of spirit-recalling, we may gradually gain more and more clarity concerning that timeless process of divine creation, whereby being "arises" out of nonbeing. Neither the English nor the German language has an appropriate word for this process of "arising," of "coming into being." It is neither an evolutionary process nor a mere becoming. It is a creative event, timeless and enduring. Rudolf Steiner coined a new word for it:

"*erwesen.*" In English we would have to say, "coming into being from non-being." This indicates the greatest span of time that can be recovered by spirit-recalling.

How can one *"practice"* spirit-recalling? No definite directive can be given, but one thing is certain: practice implies a regularly recurring effort. It may be helpful to start with a brief daily meditation on the words:

"Your own 'I' comes into being within the 'I of God.'"

Such a meditation can gradually lead to the experience of our own divine origin, neither as an abstract idea nor as a source of pride, but as a wonderful, life-sustaining, life-enhancing force. Actualization of this force is the fruit of spirit-recalling. The meditation points to such a result with the words: "And you will truly live." As one practices spirit-recalling and comes to experience this life-enhancing force, one thereby understands better and better what spirit-recalling really is.

A second aspect of the present has to do with the fact that the present is not merely an isolated point, but rather a moment in a process, in a stream where forward is qualitatively different from backward. Naturally this concept of a moment lends to each moment a quality that depends on the process, or processes, of which that moment is a part.

In contrast to this living idea of time, Newtonian time flows of itself from the infinite past uniformly toward the infinite future. For such a conception of time, each moment has the same quality as any other moment. This mechanical, dead concept of time is not suitable for the description of living entities. For the living world, time is characterized by cyclic processes. The ancients experienced the universe as a living entity, and thus they conceived time in terms of cyclic processes. For them, each moment was qualitatively different, depending on its place in the cosmic cycles, even as each moment of a day is different, depending upon what time of day and what season it is.

Spirit-meditating points to that soul region where cyclic processes, typified by becoming and fading away, play the primary roles. It is the region of equanimity or balance of the soul (*Seelengleichgewicht*). Such a balance is not a static or rigid state of equilibrium. Rather, it involves an ever-recurring alternation of surrender to the world and of retreat into the inner self. Emphasis on the letter "w" in the German text of the verses reinforces this idea of wavelike movement, of swelling and ebbing, of extroversion and introversion. It is a profound mystery that in these rhythmic processes of the present moment the divine spirit of Christ holds sway.

How can one *practice* spirit-meditating? The verses suggest that a good way to start is to dwell regularly on the words:

"Unite your own 'I' with the 'I of the cosmos.'"

Such a meditation can gradually lead to the awareness that we live not alone in the cosmos. We live not only for the sake of being an individual ego, but also for the sake of being a part of the cosmos. Such an experience can produce a profound transformation of our feeling life. Our feelings can expand their scope, become more differentiated, and gain in richness. They become more and more *true* feelings, as expressed in the line, *"And you will truly feel."*

A word of caution is in order here. Spirit-meditating is concerned with the polar relation of our own "I" and its environment, the "I of the cosmos" (*Welten-Ich*). It is a deeply veiled and holy mystery how the human soul can only function properly by undergoing a process of rhythmical balancing, wherein our own "I" and the "I of the cosmos" come together and then recede again. For the process of coming together, the word "uniting" was chosen, since this uniting takes place repeatedly, which implies receding as well as returning. In this context "uniting" can *never* mean losing or dissolving our own "I" in the "I of the cosmos."

What is the "I of the cosmos?" It is related to our own "I" like the shell of a nut to its kernel. Rudolf Steiner uses the term "I of the cosmos" (*Welten-Ich*) as an equivalent for the divine Christ-Spirit or the Son. Spirit-meditating can reveal the nature of the uniting of one's own "I" with the "I of the cosmos." As one practices spirit-meditating in this sense, one can come closer to the life-giving Christ-force, which the cosmos can bestow on the soul, and thereby one's understanding grows of what spirit-meditating really is or can become.

A third aspect of time has to do with the future, insofar as the future casts its image into the present moment. Human consciousness can be directed at *will* to the future by means of our ability to plan, to set goals, and to chart ways of achieving them, that is, by means of envisioning (*erschauen*). This envisioning appears in microcosmic form as the human faculty of setting goals and charting ways to achieve them. However, it has also a macrocosmic form in the eternal divine aims and the divine ways of bringing them about.

What are these divine aims? The verses encourage one to ponder such a question in modesty and devotion, realizing that one can only reach answers of humanly limited validity. Such a divine goal—this may seem surprising at first—is the divine idea of humanity, what human beings may become when all their spiritual potentials of wisdom, love, and strength of goodness shall be fully developed. All angelic efforts are directed toward the realization of this wonderful goal.

Essential to this lofty goal is the creative, spiritual love of each human being. Achieving this quality brings the possibility of free willing, as explained in Rudolf Steiner's *Philosophy of Freedom*. In free willing we act under no compulsion—neither from nature nor from nurture—and introduce new primary causes into the world. This free willing can be achieved, however, only if we have first learned spirit-envisioning, which enables us to foresee the image of a future that is not yet present, and thus we can rightly understand how our intent will fit into the world. Such spirit-envisioning requires the presence of an inner light within us. This inner light should not be taken for granted. It is a divine gift, given to human beings for the purpose of leading mankind to freedom.

How can one practice spirit-envisioning in this sense? The Foundation Stone suggests that one can make a beginning by dwelling regularly on the words:

"Light of cosmic being is granted to your own 'I' for your free willing."

Such a meditation can gradually lead to a profound transformation of the quality of one's thoughts. Their abstract, shadowy, foreign-to-the-world character is transformed into one that is mobile, truth-seeking, freely-directed, and more in harmony with the thoughts of the cosmos (*Weltgedanken*). The Foundation Stone indicates such a result in the line: *"And you will truly think."*

The way in which cosmic thoughts actuate divine aims in cosmic and human evolution is a deep and marvelous mystery. The cosmic thoughts do not force any development, nor do they impinge on human freedom. They provide the inner light, which they draw (*erflehen* = to obtain through ardent supplication) from the spiritual essence of the World (*Weltenwesen*), where it lives and weaves as an emanation of the Holy Spirit, the third aspect of the divine Trinity. Through a wonderful activity this light is passed on to human beings, provided that they seek it, strive toward it, and ask for it (*erbitten* = to obtain by asking.) As one grows into the practice of spirit-envisioning, one can experience ever more fully the mystery of this spirit light and its relationship to our free willing and strength of goodness. Then one comes to understand better and better what spirit-envisioning really ought to become.

When one begins to fathom how each moment in time has a special quality of its own, one can then grasp the idea that certain moments are of outstanding, decisive importance for the realization of the divine aims. These moments are the "turning points of time." Among them there is one that is the most important, the most decisive. It is the one that is the subject of narration in the fourth panel of the Foundation Stone.

Meditation on the Foundation Stone means more than a gain in knowledge or insight. One can also experience its healthful, healing quality, if one succeeds in awakening the life-element that slumbers in its verses. One can now understand why the elementary spirits on the whole earth listen to the words of these verses. When Christ walked on the earth, the elementary spirits knew Who He was long before human beings knew (Luke 4: 33-41,) and they cried it out to man. In our time they hear the message of these verses, which they understand, for elementary spirits are part of the etheric body of the earth, which is radiated through by the Etheric Christ. But now they are silent. They and, indeed, the entire cosmos wait in silent hope that human beings may hear it. Is perhaps the Foundation Stone a path for human beings to the experience of the Etheric Christ?

III. The Significance of the "Rhythms"

During the Christmas Conference of 1923, Rudolf Steiner presented the Foundation Stone in a most remarkable way. On most days of this nine-days-long conference, only certain parts of this meditation were recited. Only on December 25 and January 1, the verses were presented in their entirety. On December 25 the four panels were recited in the order 4-1-2-3, while on January 1 the regular order of 1-2-3-4 was given, the same order used when the verses were published a few weeks later. If one looks closely, there were not less than fourteen differences among the versions given on the various days and the printed version. Some differences are minor, but others are quite significant. Such variations in Rudolf Steiner's presentation of these verses emphasize the fact that he treated them in a living, non-rigid way.

The Foundation Stone Verses

Given by Rudolf Steiner in connection with the Christmas Conference of 1923 in Dornach, Switzerland

1. Human soul!
2. You live in the limbs;
3. Through the world of space they bear you
4. Into seas of spirit-being:

5. Practice *spirit-recalling*

6. In depths of soul,
7. Where in the wielding
8. World-creator-being
9. Your own "I"
10. Comes into being
11. Within the "I of God;"
12. And you will truly *live*
13. In human cosmic being.

14. For there reigns the Father-spirit of the heights
15. In cosmic depths creating existence.
16. Ye Spirits of Strength,
16a. Seraphim, Cherubim, Thrones,
17. Let from the heights ring forth
18. What in the depths finds its echo;
19. This speaks thus:
20. From the divine mankind takes being.

21. Thus hear it the elementary spirits in the East, West, North, South:
22. May human beings hear it!

Human soul!
You live in the beat of heart and lungs;
Through the rhythm of time it leads you
Into the feeling of your own soul-being:

Practice *spirit-meditating*

In equanimity of soul,
Where by the surging
Deeds of world-becoming
Your own "I"
Is united
With the "I of the cosmos;"
And you will truly *feel*
In human weaving of souls.

For there reigns the will of Christ all around us
In cosmic rhythms bestowing grace onto souls.
Ye Spirits of Light,
Kyriotetes, Dynameis, Exusiai,
Let from the East be enkindled
What through the West takes on form;
This speaks thus:
In Christ death becomes life.

Thus hear it the elementary spirits in the East, West, North, South:
May human beings hear it!

Human soul!
You live in the resting head;
From eternal grounds it discloses
The thoughts of the cosmos to you:

Practice *spirit-envisioning*

In stillness of thought,
Where by the eternal aims of gods
Light of cosmic being
To your own "I"
Is granted
For your free willing;
And you will truly *think*
In human spirit-grounds.

For there reign the cosmic thoughts of the Spirit
In cosmic being light imploring.
Ye Spirits of Soul,
Archai, Archangeloi, Angeloi,
Let from the depths be entreated
What in the heights will be answered;
This speaks thus:
In the Spirit's cosmic thoughts the soul awakens.

Thus hear it the elementary spirits in the East, West, North, South:
May human beings hear it!

At the turning point of time
Came the cosmic spirit-light
Into the earthly stream of being.

Night darkness
Had reached its power's end;
Light, bright as day,
Rayed forth in human souls;

Light
That gives warmth
To simple hearts of shepherds;

Light
That enlightens
The wise heads of kings.

Light divine,
Christ-Sun,
Give warmth
to our hearts;
Enlighten
our heads;

That good may become
What from our hearts
We are founding,
What from our heads
We shall guide
With our purposeful willing.

On each of the seven days from December 26 to January 1, Rudolf Steiner wrote on the blackboard certain sets of selected verses which he called "rhythms." The use of the word, "rhythm," in this context has puzzled many anthroposophists, who understand "rhythm" as a regular recurrence of features or patterns. Clearly such a meaning does not fit here. *The American College Dictionary*[2] gives several meanings of the word "rhythm." The one that fits here is mentioned in earlier editions of this dictionary but is not widely known and is deleted in more recent editions: *"a proper relation and interdependence of parts with reference to one another and to an artistic whole."* According to this definition, a "rhythm" can be established by juxtaposing two short parts taken from different places in the verses. The juxtaposition of short parts causes a certain tension to be felt, which impels one to seek for their relationship. In addition, the value of each part within the verses as a whole can be sensed. Thus, each pair of parts which Rudolf Steiner wrote on the blackboard becomes a challenge. We must not rest content with understanding the meaning of each word or phrase. We should try to become aware that in each "rhythm" a double relationship exists: on the one hand, the two chosen parts are related to each other and, on the other hand, each part is related to the Foundation Stone as a whole.

Meditating on these "rhythms" is a free, creative thought-activity. It can awaken questions that may lead to the kind of living conversation with the verses discussed in section II. The beauty of this approach is that one can become actively engaged in a process of living inner growth. And one can come to recognize that these "rhythms," which Rudolf Steiner carefully selected, are the seven principal doorways to the living grasp of the entire Foundation Stone. If the Foundation Stone is experienced as a living organic entity, then the seven "rhythms" are its vital organs.

On each of the seven days mentioned, Rudolf Steiner wrote one new "rhythm" (a selected pair of lines) on the blackboard. The accompanying table at the beginning of this section gives a survey of the "rhythms" in relation to the days on which they were spoken.

The "rhythms" I, II, III, and IV each have three columns. "Rhythm" V is special in that the three practices are written in a special geometrical pattern, suggesting as it were a protective dome for the second part of the "rhythm," which is meant to be the same for the three columns.

"Rhythm" VI occupies a unique place among the "rhythms" in that there is no division of its content into three columns. After this contraction, "rhythm" VII expands again into three separate columns. On the evening of January 1 during the final session of the conference, Rudolf Steiner recited the entire Foundation Stone and then closed with what can be called the "coda:"

Light divine
Christ-Sun
Give warmth to our hearts
Enlighten our heads.

Strictly speaking, this "coda" is not a "rhythm" as it does not consist of two parts.

How can one work meditatively with the "rhythms"? To meditate on the whole Foundation Stone is difficult because of its great length and its complexity. By working with the "rhythms," one can gain much more meaning from the verses than if one merely recites the Foundation Stone daily, outwardly or inwardly. Working with the "rhythms" can lead to a clearer survey of the meditative content. It is a great discovery, made by Dr. F. W. Zeylmans van Emmichoven,[3] that the "rhythms" bear an intimate relation to the days of the week on which they were given. Accordingly, Dr. Zeylmans suggested meditating on the "rhythm" given on Wednesday (December 26, 1923) on every Wednesday, the "rhythm" given on Thursday (December 27) on every Thursday, and so forth, so that in the course of a week one has worked upon all seven "rhythms." If one does this week after week, the question may then arise: Does one not neglect the Foundation Stone as a whole by focusing only on its parts? I have found it helpful to work with the "rhythms" in the morning and to dwell upon the whole Foundation Stone before going to sleep in the evening.

A noteworthy feature of the "rhythms" is that they come in three columns. How does this feature enter into one's meditation? Consider the first "rhythm" as an example of how this can work. The three activities of spirit recalling, spirit meditating, and spirit envisioning are here not represented as tasks, for the word "practice" is not included. Rather, the first "rhythm" seems to ask that one consider what these words themselves mean. We have already commented on how the first activity—spirit-recalling—can lead one back to that early stage of world-evolution when the human "I" came into being within the "I of God."

Wonderful as this realization is, one may feel after a while an incompleteness. The human "I" feels lonely if it can only be aware of itself. It wishes to find something else. This something is given in the second column of this "rhythm." Here, by spirit meditating, the human "I" is united with the "I of the cosmos." How this uniting is to be understood was commented on earlier. As the human "I" becomes aware of the "I of the cosmos" and moves toward union with it, it may be seized by a terrible fear, the fear of losing oneself. As a result the "I" withdraws into its own self, albeit enriched by the momentary contact with the "I of the cosmos." Thus an alternation of approaching and withdrawing can come about. What is the enrichment that the human "I" gains from this process? The third column of the "rhythm" gives the answer to this question. By means of spirit-envisioning the "I" can strive toward inner freedom and achieve it.

This sketchily drawn train of thought is intended to show one possible way that one may proceed from column to column while meditating on the first "rhythm." When this meditation is deepened, one may become aware more specifically of what the "I" gains by the activity performed in each column. The "I" receives spirit-life by coming into being, as indicated in the first column. The force that attracts the human "I" to the "I of the cosmos," as indicated in the second column, can be recognized as spirit love. Through what is contained in the third column, the "I" gains spirit-light. But this light and the freedom that comes with it can become a source of confusion if they are not rightly integrated into the world. The individualized spirit-light wishes to find its connection with the cosmic spirit-light. How this can come about is described in the fourth column.

Each person who would like to take up meditating on the "rhythms" needs to create an individual train of thought when moving from column to column. One should explore various possibilities and hold fast to what seems best, as long as it proves to be alive. Because meditation on a "rhythm" is meant to be a creative and free activity of the mind, many other approaches are possible. The above example is given only as an indication. What matters most is that one forms the habit of regular meditation, and that one does not remain at the level of intellectual thought analysis but rather reaches deeper, so that feelings and the will also become engaged.

The transition from one column of a "rhythm" to the next one is not easy. A different way to work with the three columns of the "rhythms" is to distribute such work over the seasons of the year, so that one works at any one time only with one column of the "rhythms." I find the following way quite effective. Through March, April, and May one works with the "rhythms" of the first column, which relate mostly to the first panel of the Foundation Stone. Through June, July, and August one works with the "rhythms" of the second column, which relate mostly to the second panel. Through September, October, and November one works with the "rhythms" of the third column, which relate mostly to the third panel. Finally, through December, January, and February one works only with the fourth panel of the Foundation Stone and one allows the "rhythms" to rest. A few examples indicating possible ways of how one might work with one column of a "rhythm" follow.

Consider, for example, the case of a Wednesday in April. One would then choose to consider the first column of "rhythm" I:

Spirit-recalling

Your own "I"
Comes into being
Within the "I of God"

This "rhythm" tells in effect what spirit recalling is. By contemplating this "rhythm" we can become aware that we bear within us that spiritual kernel which we call our "I." This "I" is of divine origin. In fact, the "I" could not continue to exist if it were not maintained in existence each and every moment by the Creator, the "I of God." In earlier times the human "I" led a dormant existence, but gradually during the evolution of the world and of humanity it has become more awake. Rudolf Steiner has described the entire evolution of the cosmos and of mankind in chapter four of his basic book *An Outline of Esoteric Science*.[4] This description can be viewed as the result of spirit recalling on a grand scale. Such considerations can give one a great sense of purpose in life, as well as a feeling of gratitude and awe. Many other feelings can arise and enliven the relationship between these parts and the Foundation Stone as a whole.

Likewise, for a Wednesday in June one would consider in a similar way the second column of the first "rhythm:"

Spirit meditating

Your own "I"
Is united
With the "I of the cosmos"

Again the second part of this "rhythm" elucidates the meaning of spirit meditating. Awareness of the union of one's own "I" with the world can be achieved at several levels stage by stage. The highest level reaches the "I of the cosmos." Thus spirit-meditating can guide a person along a path of inner development. Rudolf Steiner describes this path in several works, notably in the fifth chapter of *An Outline of Esoteric Science*. There, union with the "I of the cosmos" is represented as union with the "Greater Guardian of the Threshold," who is then recognized as the Christ-Spirit.[5] Also in his book *How to Know Higher Worlds*[6] this path is described, and near the end we find the sentence: "An indescribable splendor shines forth from the Second Guardian of the Threshold; union with Him looms as a far distant ideal before the soul's vision." These descriptions can be viewed as the result of spirit meditating with the widest possible scope by Rudolf Steiner.

A similar treatment of the third column of the first "rhythm" can be developed by relating it to the sixth chapter of *An Outline of Esoteric Science*, where Rudolf Steiner envisions the future consequences of the past evolution of mankind and the world.

As a different and last example, consider the "rhythm" for a Monday in any month from March to November:

Light divine
Christ-Sun

Thus hear it the elementary spirits in the East, West, North, South.
May human beings hear it!

The elementary spirits make up the etheric body of the earth. They live mostly near the surface of the earth: the gnomes somewhat below the surface, as far down as plant roots and crystals grow; the sylphs up in the atmosphere, as high as birds and insects rise; and the undines in the domain that lies in between. Only the fire-spirits penetrate deeper and also higher. Thus, on a global scale the realm of the elementary spirits is mainly a very thin layer, where up and down has very little significance in comparison with the importance of East, West, North, and South. Into the etheric domain of the earth, the sunlight penetrates. The light of the sun not only illumines; it also carries etheric sound, which the elementary spirits can hear. Goethe describes some of these etheric sounds of the sunlight in his "Prologue" to *Faust:* "The sun *resounds* as in olden times in the choir of fraternal spheres." In the first scene of the second part of *Faust*, the elementary spirits are warned about the thunderous and deafening sound of the rising sun.

Yet another light shines into the world of the elementary spirits. It is the light that shines outward from the Mystery of Golgotha. This light shines as a divine light throughout the etheric body of the earth, the domain of the elementary spirits. It is the light of a different kind of sun. Perhaps the most concrete imagination of this sun and its radiance was envisioned in 1492 A.D. by Matthias Grünewald when he painted the resurrection panel of the altar of the monastery of Isenheim. From this world famous painting one can gain an impression, in a unique and almost magical way, of the etheric sun-like radiance that emanates from the Christ as He rises from the grave. In the etheric realm this Christ-Sun not only illumines. Its light also sounds; it even carries messages which the human heart can hear. The elementary spirits hear this message. Are we human beings hearing it too? What is the message that sounds in this etheric divine light? Through Rudolf Steiner this message has come into expression as a concrete inspiration in the entire Foundation Stone.

May these indications give an impression of how one can work with the "rhythms" of the Foundation Stone, though each person must of course find her or his individual meditative approach to its verses.

8

Contemplations on the Holy Spirit

I

THE WRITER OF THIS ESSAY had concerned himself for some time with questions about the Holy Spirit when, in the Dutch anthroposophical newsletter of May 1963, the following question was printed: "What is the sin against the Holy Spirit and why can this sin not be forgiven?" This is a good question because it touches the deepest core of Anthroposophy. An effort will be made in this, the first in a series of three essays, to collect some material that allows this question to be approached from a variety of angles. These essays do not aspire in any way to provide a complete answer to this question. The few main threads indicated here are meant to stimulate the reader to further independent research. In view of this the text provides sources for many references.

To enter into this question it is first necessary to form a concept of what is really meant by the Holy Spirit. This is not an easy task. When one tries to form as clearly as possible a concept of the three members of the Holy Trinity, namely God the Father, Christ the Son, and the Holy Spirit, then one will soon notice that one has rather little difficulty conceptualizing the first two, while the concept of the Holy Spirit seems to lie relatively farther away. One can already notice here that the relationship of modern man to the three principles of the trinity is very unequal. This inequality of relationship can also come to expression in many other ways.

For example, let us look at how the festivals of the year are experienced. The Christmas and Easter festivals are strongly experienced. Our culture has a well defined relationship to both of these festivals, and these are expressed in many ways, even into the simple detail of celebrating these particular holidays. All of this is much less the case with the festival of Pentecost, the festival of the Holy Spirit. Let us penetrate deeper into the esoteric background of the festivals. For this we have access to a large literary treasure of lectures by Rudolf Steiner. Let us first look at the Christmas festival. In this festival, the central event is the birth of the Jesus child, or more exactly, as we know from Anthroposophy, the birth of the two Jesus children. Further, if one looks at the original concept that lives on in the Greek-Catholic church, then there is also the birth of Christ at the baptism in the Jordan. In the Roman-Western culture this last concept has slipped into the background and is only mentioned in passing on January 6th. In its archetypal form this birth arises in our consciousness and one becomes aware that the human being, coming from a divine spiritual world, is born into the spatial world of the Father-God. From a certain point of view it is therefore correct to say that in the Christmas festival it is mainly the impulse of the Father God that comes to expression. One can read about this in the lecture given in Dornach by Rudolf Steiner on June 4, 1924.

At Easter it is mainly the Christ impulse that is working. Through the overcoming of death and the connection with the earth the Christ has given new meaning to human death, and this is the essence of the Easter festival.

But who knows how to approach Pentecost, the festival of the Holy Spirit, as is done with Christmas or Easter? Have we understood the resurrection into a new life through the Holy Spirit, and have we connected with it in our souls to the same degree as with the other two festivals? The unequal relation to the three members of the Trinity did not originate in modern times. It was already like this in the Middle Ages. If you look at the many beautiful works of religious art from that time, you will find many of them are based on the events of Christmas and many that are based on the suffering, death and resurrection of Christ. But in comparison not many artworks are based on Pentecost, the receiving of the Holy Spirit by the Apostles. This shows how already in the Middle Ages the concept of the Holy Spirit was difficult to grasp.

However, it has not always been like this. In the first centuries after the life of Christ on earth, Christians had a living consciousness of the Holy Spirit, how It works and Its purpose. In the Acts of the Apostles and in the Epistles of Paul, and also in the Gospels, one can find clear descriptions of the Holy Spirit. We will come back to this subject in the third essay. The important point here is that in earlier times a consciousness and a concept existed about the Holy Spirit, which later in the Middle Ages was almost completely lost.

A very tragic occurrence in the year 869 is the cause of this loss. In that year, a decision was made at the Council of Constantinople, which in its effect threw a heavy shadow over the further development of spiritual life by modern humanity that has lasted into our time. Namely, the decision was made that the human being may no longer be considered as having three equal members: body, soul and spirit, but only two principles: body and soul. On many occasions Rudolf Steiner points out how this decision had a detrimental influence on the whole orientation of modern thought life and concepts. And indeed, the longer one contemplates this fact the more one can perceive that our modern life has been distorted in myriad ways by this decision.

One of the results of this decision from 869 is that from then on the concept of the Holy Spirit lost its living content. This is because the human being is a microcosm, created in the image of God. When the human being looks at his body he can form a concept of the creative Father God. When the human being perceives his inner life—his feelings and heart forces—he can discover a path to the Christ in his soul. However, since 869, the human being does not possess a foundation of knowledge within himself sufficient to have a real relationship to the third member of the Trinity, to the Holy Spirit. The Holy Spirit can only be understood when one recognizes that this macrocosmic being is represented microcosmically in the human spirit. In this way the abolishment of the human spirit has also veiled the true gateway to the Holy Spirit. Only through the work of Rudolf Steiner has a change come about that has opened the gate once again. Once a person knows about this doorway it is possible to once again find it in the Bible.

The being of the Holy Spirit is focused on the formation of a free brotherhood of humanity in which every individual has a deep understanding of Christ. If one has developed to the point of envisioning this impulse, and after that with full insight turns away from this impulse of brotherhood to develop one's own existence separate from human evolution, then one commits a "sin against the Holy Spirit." And because full insight is required to commit this sin it cannot be forgiven. There is passage in the New Testament where Paul explains this matter. Paul writes in his epistle to the Hebrews 6:4-6: "For as touching those who were once enlightened and tasted of the heavenly gift, and were made partakers of the Holy Spirit, and tasted the good word of God, and the powers of the age to come, and then fell away, it is impossible to renew them again unto repentance; seeing they crucify to themselves the Son of God afresh, and put him to an open shame."

As an anthroposophist, one can recognize the enlightenment, the tasting of the heavenly gift and the partaking of the Holy Spirit, etc., as stages of a spiritual initiation schooling. And Paul is saying here that those who have inwardly developed themselves, those who have entered into the spiritual world and acknowledged with full consciousness the impulse of the Holy Spirit and then turned away, can no longer come to the Christ.

We are here dealing with the choice between white and black magic. From a certain point of view one can feel how terrible it is that in the end all souls will not be redeemed and not all sins can be forgiven. It is not guaranteed, even after many incarnations, that the good in every person will come to full development in the end. From a higher point of view one can see that it cannot be otherwise than that the possibility has to exist to turn away with full consciousness and freedom from the good in its highest form. In this matter there is no question of individual predestination. It is up to everyone who develops toward freedom, to connect out of freedom with good or evil. We will discuss this question more in the second essay.

Anthroposophy is the modern science of the spirit, including the human spirit and the hierarchical spiritual beings, up to the Holy Spirit. Consequently, students of Anthroposophy from the beginning of their study, for example in the book *Theosophy*, learn as one of the founding principles how to gain insight once again into the threefold human being that consists of body, soul, and spirit. For this reason Rudolf Steiner tirelessly, again and again, brings forward the thought of a threefold human being.

Through the decision by the Council of Constantinople, an esoteric path of development, a path of initiation that leads to a true experience and understanding of the spiritual world, has been eradicated from culture. The path of initiation by the Holy Spirit in a new form that is adjusted to the demands and needs of our modern time lives again in Anthroposophy. Considering this, an error that has been growing wildly for more than a thousand years has been counteracted. Anthroposophy originated in the inspiration of the Holy Spirit itself. One can come to this conclusion by reading Rudolf Steiner's various Pentecost lectures, for example in the English collection *The Festivals and Their Meaning*, specifically the lectures "Ascension and Pentecost." Through Anthroposophy, the Holy Spirit calls for the human spirit to understand, to gain spiritual insight, into the microcosm and macrocosm, having the Mystery of Golgotha as its central point.

It is for this reason that one could wish that through the course of time the festival of Pentecost would become increasingly meaningful in anthroposophical circles. This is because the festival of Pentecost is the festival of the impulse of the Holy Spirit, which is the founding impulse of Anthroposophy itself.

Summarizing, one can say that the concept of the Holy Spirit and its effect has been veiled by the Council's decision in 869. The Holy Spirit can only be approached by schooling a conscious human striving for truth, a truth that is equally true for all people. Recognition of such truth makes the human being free, and if this striving is permeated by an understanding of the Christ impulse, then an impulse of brotherhood will embrace all of humanity. The developmental stream of the Holy Spirit characterized in this essay lies at the foundation of anthroposophical spiritual science. For those who feel connected with Anthroposophy it is therefore very important to increasingly come to a living concept of the Holy Spirit, to celebrate an ever more meaningful Pentecost festival. They can then also work more effectively against inner tendencies of separation and thus be prepared in the future to stand firm against temptations of personal desires which are the result of separating from the context of evolution. In the next essay this context will be discussed further.

II

The last essay described the connection existing between the decision by the Council of Constantinople in 869, whereby the human spirit was "denounced," and the recognition once again of the human spirit by Anthroposophy. Through the Council's decision, the living understanding of the Holy Spirit was veiled. Anthroposophy makes understanding the Holy Spirit accessible once again. In this essay I want to illustrate this with some examples.

The first example is from a lecture given by Rudolf Steiner in Berlin on March 25, 1907, called "The Mystery of the Blood and the Sin Against the Holy Spirit." In this lecture, some aspects of the relationship of Anthroposophy to the Holy Spirit are developed that will be briefly mentioned here. That Anthroposophy is not a religion is emphasized first; it is instead the instrument to learn to understand the different religions and to access their universal kernels of truth. Then the following thought process is developed.

When the human being develops his "spirit self," he undergoes the preparatory stages of an esoteric schooling by purifying and elevating his astral body with his "I." He becomes a seeker of the truth. This development of the astral body into spirit self is called in Christian esotericism "the influence of the Holy Spirit." Through further esoteric schooling the "I" works formatively on the ether body to develop the "life spirit," and this is called "taking the Christ into oneself." Finally, the "I" works on the spiritualization of the physical body through the breathing, and this is called "coming to the Father."

Rudolf Steiner continues to describe how in ancient times the authority and leadership of the great initiates influenced groups of people, which today is taken over by the free and self directing individual. But all individuals are guided more and more by the common spirit of truth, the Holy Spirit, to a brotherhood of humanity. One truth and wisdom becomes the highest authority uniting all as free individuals. And the sin against the Holy Spirit is defined as the sin against the spirit of truth and wisdom. The sinner against this spirit strives for separation and fragmentation instead of the unifying spirit of truth that leads to a future of brotherliness.

What follows is an important passage wherein the question is asked where one can learn about this unifying spirit. The answer that is given is: in true spiritual science. This is because the goal of spiritual science is not the preaching of morals, but the imparting of concrete wisdom leading to brotherliness. Whoever develops himself by taking in Anthroposophy also joins humanity (in this 1907 lecture Rudolf Steiner still speaks of "true Theosophy").

Without restraint, Rudolf Steiner says in this lecture that Anthroposophy is meant as the instrument for the working of the Holy Spirit in the human being and that this working of its own accord leads to brotherliness. That was said in 1907. Most tragic were the developments that occurred 28 years later (1935). And today, after another 28 years (1963), one hardly dares to mention this without heaving a profound sigh.

When in broad strokes you understand the meaning of the Holy Spirit for Anthroposophy, another light can be shed on two passages from the book "How to Attain Knowledge of the Higher Worlds." These passages form the two examples that will be discussed in this essay.

The first passage from this book is found in the chapter called "How is Knowledge of the Higher Worlds Attained: Conditions." In it two directions of development are characterized, of which one is detrimental and the other beneficial for the human being.

The one is described as follows. "Yet if he stops short at the enjoyment he shuts himself up within himself. He will only be something to himself and nothing to the world. However much he may live within himself, however intensely he may cultivate his ego—the world will reject him." This is typically the path of fragmentation. What at one time was All-Spirit threatens to fall apart in egotistical egoities without community and living apart from each other. The modern scientific picture of rushing and colliding molecules in a gas, when transferred to the life of soul, is the picture of fragmentation to which the above mentioned direction of development leads.

The other direction of development is described as follows. "The student of higher knowledge considers enjoyment only as a means of ennobling himself for the world... He does not learn in order to accumulate learning as his own treasure, but in order that he may devote his learning to the service of the world... All knowledge pursued merely for the enrichment of personal learning and the accumulation of personal treasure leads you away from the path; but all knowledge pursued for growth to ripeness within the process of human ennoblement and cosmic development brings you a step forward." This is the path that leads to the service of truth and human brotherhood. It is the anthroposophical esoteric path of schooling as is described further in the above mentioned book.

By studying this passage one can gain insight into this sin against the Holy Spirit, and why it cannot be forgiven. This sin exists because one closes oneself off from that stream of world development out of which all forgiveness flows.

The theme of watching out for unjustified egoism and the associated exclusion and splitting off of the individual from the world-all, and thus the theme of avoiding the sin against the Holy Spirit, permeates the course of the above mentioned book. This theme occurs again at the end of the book in its true appearance and full meaning, namely, in the impressive description of the encounter with the "Greater Guardian of the Threshold." This is what the Guardian says to the student who is making progress:

"You have attained your present degree of perfection thanks to the faculties you were able to develop in the sense-world as long as you were still confined to it. But now a new era is to begin, in which your liberated powers must be applied to further work in the world of the senses. Up till now you have sought only your own release, but now, having yourself become free, you can go forth as a liberator of your fellow human beings. Until today you have striven as an individual, but now seek to coordinate yourself with the whole, so that you may bring into the supersensible world not yourself alone, but all things else existing in the world of the senses."

Thus the Greater Guardian warns us against individual separation and demands brotherliness. He continues to say:

> As a separate freed being, you would fain enter at once the kingdom of the supersensible; yet you would be forced to look down on the still unredeemed beings in the physical world, having separated your destiny from theirs, although you and they are inseparably united.... To separate yourself from your fellows would mean to abuse those very powers which you could not have developed except in their company.... I bar your entrance as long as powers unused in the sense-world still remain in you. And if you refuse to apply your powers in this world, others will come who will not refuse; and a higher supersensible world will receive all the fruits of the sense-world, while you will lose from under your feet the very ground in which you were rooted. The purified world will develop above and beyond you, and you shall be excluded from it. Thus you would tread the black path, while the others from whom you did sever yourself tread the white path.

The sin against the Holy Spirit is clearly expressed in this passage. It is the free decision based on profound acquired insight to follow the black path of self exclusion. Because this decision has been taken in freedom there is, in contrast to other sins, no possibility for forgiveness. As the Greater Guardian says, one has attained freedom and then decided as a free human being to tread the path toward unfreedom. That this is possible is inherent in the essence of freedom as spiritual activity. What leads a person to make this choice is not easy to comprehend from today's viewpoint of unfreedom, but one can admit that such a possibility exists.

Rudolf Steiner adds a further comment:

> It does not follow that, when called upon to decide, anyone will naturally follow the white path. That depends entirely upon whether he is so far purified at the time of his decision that no trace of self-seeking makes this prospect of felicity appear desirable. For the allurements here are the strongest possible; whereas on the other side no special allurements are evident. Here nothing appeals to his egotism. The gift he receives in the higher regions of the supersensible world is nothing that comes to him, but only something that flows from him, that is, love for the world and for his fellows.... No one therefore should expect the occultists of the white path to give him instruction for the development of his own egotistical self. They do not take the slightest interest in the felicity of the individual man.... They never actually refuse anyone, for even the greatest egotist can purify himself; but no one merely seeking an advantage for himself will ever obtain assistance from the white occultists. Even when they do not refuse their help, he, the seeker, deprives himself of the advantage resulting from their assistance.

One sees the discourse of this book closing, as it were, into a complete circle. At the end of the book Rudolf Steiner comes back on a higher level to the same theme that was announced at the beginning. What is first spoken of on a lower level as the advice of a teacher who cloaks in words what the invisible Guardian has to say is at the end in its archetypal form spoken by the Greater Guardian Himself. Who is the Greater Guardian? Rudolf Steiner identifies Him in *Occult Science* as the spirit of Christ.

These three examples, the first from the lecture of 1907 and the other two from the 1904 book *How to Attain Knowledge of the Higher Worlds*, can provide a foundation for a concept about the working of the Holy Spirit and about the nature of the sin against the Holy Spirit. When one thinks through these three examples, it can rapidly become clear how Anthroposophy is intimately permeated with the being and working of the Holy Spirit. That is why the question about the nature of the sin against the Holy Spirit is a particularly important question within the realm of Anthroposophy. It is indeed the one sin about which we have to be most awake. Time and again one finds great examples in the life of Rudolf Steiner of how the connection with and the service to the world is primary. Not everyone can accomplish such great things as Rudolf Steiner, but each from his own place in life can strive in the indicated direction. The forces developed through such striving are of decisive importance for the future. In the following essay we will discuss this aspect of the future.

III

In the first essay the discussion is about why today there is so little understanding of the Holy Spirit. In the second essay the meaning of the Holy Spirit for the human being is described. In the third essay I will try to paint a picture of how the meaning developed over the course of time.

In the pre-Christian mysteries the Holy Spirit was only accessible to the highest initiates. It was known under many names, such as Isis or Sophia. Those who were not highly initiated learned about it in myths and pictures. In the Israelite stream, which prepared the way for the coming of the Christ-Messiah, the picture consciousness had to be replaced by a consciousness directed to the world of the senses. Consequently the Holy Spirit is not mentioned once in the Old Testament. Nevertheless, the New Testament contains indications that the Holy Spirit was known to the highest Israelite initiates. Paul writes in his epistles to the Hebrews, Chapter 9, how the high priest only entered into the holiest place of the temple behind the second curtain once a year. What he experienced there he did not reveal to the community. This experience related to the Holy Spirit. The community was still on the level of group or folk soul consciousness, while the experience of the Holy Spirit requires a humanity-consciousness.

We find a further indication that goes in the same direction in the Acts of Apostles (28:25), were Paul says that the Holy Spirit spoke through the prophet Isaiah, but the people did not understand.

If one understands how to read with anthroposophical knowledge the picture language of the Old Testament, then one can come to perceive a mighty picture that is a sign of the Holy Spirit, and spiritually encompasses the time period from the great Atlantean flood until the baptism of Jesus in the Jordan. You can perceive this when you juxtapose the following two pictures. First, the picture of Noah's ark at the end of the flood, when the dove flies away over the waters without returning. Here, the dove points in an early time to the mystery of the Holy Spirit in the same picture language that applies to the second picture. Second, the picture of the baptism of Jesus of Nazareth submerged in the water of the Jordan, with the Holy Spirit in the form of a dove descending upon him (Luke 3:22), which remains with Him (John 1:32). It can become clear when contemplating the relationship of these two pictures that mystery knowledge of the Holy Spirit in pre-Christian times existed among the Israelites of the Old Testament. And with continued study, one can come to know certain characteristics of this mystery knowledge.

One could make an extensive study of the workings in different cultures of the Holy Spirit in these old times. For our purpose, it is enough to see that the Holy Spirit was known in the old times, not so much by the people, but certainly by the high priests and initiates.

Let us now look at what is written about the Holy Spirit in the New Testament. The places where the Holy Spirit is mentioned can be divided into two groups. The first group is related to the circumstances surrounding the birth and baptism of Jesus, and can be found in the four Gospels. The second group is related to the work of the Apostles from Pentecost on, and is mainly written down in the Acts of Apostles and in the Epistles of Paul and Peter.

With regard to the first group, it is characteristic of all the people being filled with the Holy Spirit that they start to have an understanding of the earthly-cosmic meaning of the coming of Christ on earth, and in many cases, they relate their understanding to others in most exalted words. For example, one can verify this for Maria (Matthew 1:18-21), (Luke 1:35); for Elizabeth (Luke 1:41), Simeon (Luke 2:25-35), and John the Baptist (John 1:32). In addition, it is good to consult Rudolf Steiner's cycles on the gospels. In all these cases the bible text gives subtle indications that concern the purification of the astral body of the people mentioned. This is in accordance with the key that Rudolf Steiner gives (see Essay II), namely that the transformation of the astral body by the "I," which in Anthroposophy is called the "Spirit Self," and in Christian esotericism is called "being filled by the Holy Spirit." In all these cases, the working of the Holy Spirit is essentially the same as was known in the pre-Christian mysteries. With regards to the second group, the most important description of the Holy Spirit is found at the event of Pentecost (Acts 2:1-12). Comprehending Rudolf Steiner's lecture cycle *The Fifth Gospel* is necessary for understanding Pentecost. From this we can learn how after the Last Supper the Apostles were in a strange half-conscious state from which they were awakened at Pentecost by the deeply felt loss because of their Master's departure. It was only at Pentecost that they understood all that had occurred while they were in the above-mentioned state. It is significant that only then did they understand the full meaning of the Mystery of Golgotha. They came to this understanding through the descent of the Holy Spirit. Their "I" is now fully awake and permeates the astral body with forces that stream to them from the Mystery of Golgotha. This is expressed in the fact that they now see fiery tongues in each other's aura. The inspiration of the Holy Spirit makes them speak an exalted language, heralding the earthly-cosmic meaning of Christ to the people of many different nations (The Bible counts up to 19 different nations).

In their speaking, the mystery of the Holy Spirit becomes manifest for the first time. Through the impulse of this mystery the Apostles break from tribal and group ties to come to a brotherhood embracing all people and nations.

How did the tribal and group ties come about in the past? Without doubt, an important factor was that each group had their own language. The different languages formed a unifying bond for the members of each group, but they were a divisive force between the groups. In primeval times all people spoke and understood the same language. This archetypal language was however not at all a language in today's meaning of the word. It worked from soul to soul mainly in the astral world. Later, when man became more earthly, he went through the phase of development mentioned in the Bible as the Babylonian confusion of tongues. Each group developed its own language and could no longer communicate with the other groups directly.

At this first Christian Pentecost festival, a mystery was placed on the earth through the working of the Holy Spirit, which replaced the divisive power of the different languages with a new force connecting all of humanity in brotherhood. This is expressed by the representatives of all 19 nations who were able to understand the Apostles as if they were hearing their own languages. This so called mystery of Glossolalia will be able to fully develop only in the sixth and seventh post-Atlantean epochs, when the impulse of brotherhood will have developed further. It appears for the first time in public at this first Pentecost event.

To remove any doubt about the working of the Holy Spirit, the Acts of the Apostles (10:44) gives another example. A scene is described where, under the influence of the words of Peter, all who listened were filled with the Holy Spirit. And special mention is made of the fact that some are surprised that the gift of the Holy Spirit is equally poured on the Jews (who were circumcised) and the pagans. And here you find again the impulse of brotherhood in overcoming group and blood ties through the gift of the Holy Spirit. It works through the forces of the word and affects brotherliness in humanity, thereby overcoming the old divisive powers. With this, a powerful new impulse started to work among the peoples.

One could make a much more expansive study of this second group regarding the effect of the Holy Spirit at the beginning of our era. However, what is said above touches upon its most essential aspects.

And how does the Holy Spirit work in our time? Where do we find the impulse to a brotherhood of humanity which comes forth from an esoteric understanding of the earthy-cosmic meaning of the Christ? In our time there are many streams that seek the Christ. There are also many streams that strive for truth and rigorous scientific understanding, and many streams searching for the spiritual world in an esoteric manner. At the same time one can truly say that only Anthroposophy can be characterized as embodying all three characteristics together.

It is an esoteric striving for the spiritual world based on a rigorous scientific comprehension of the truth, and this leads to an insight into the central impulse that brings people together, namely, the Christ impulse that leads human evolution.

If you have a clear understanding of the matter, there can never be a conflict between the statement that Anthroposophy wants to serve the Christ impulse and the statement that Anthroposophy is the inspiration of the Holy Spirit. This is because the Holy Spirit is sent by Christ and is the force through which the awakening human insight can be led back to Christ. Nevertheless, one should not confuse the two impulses. The mutual relationship can be exactly determined. One can get a good impression of this relationship by seriously studying the first part of the first lecture of Rudolf Steiner's lecture cycle *Inner Experiences of Evolution* (Berlin, October 31, 1911). This lecture clearly describes the difficulties of penetrating the (Devachanic) spiritual world and two ways of overcoming them. The two ways are characterized as the Christ impulse and the receiving of the Holy Spirit, but only the latter is characterized as the path of anthroposophical spiritual science.

But even if we did not have this description of Rudolf Steiner we can come to the same conclusion with the strength of our own insight once we have truly understood the essence of anthroposophical striving for truth. True Anthroposophy is the working of the Holy Spirit. That is why it was permissible in the second essay to give the examples of the working of the Holy Spirit through the description of the anthroposophical way of schooling.

We now return again to our opening question: What light can be shed, with the knowledge of all the above mentioned connections, on the question of the sin against the Holy Spirit? We can achieve through these connections a certain degree of insight into the consequences of this sin.

It is deeply tragic what future incarnations will hold for souls who turn away from spiritual science. In *Occult Science* Rudolf Steiner dedicates a short chapter to the future development of the earth and the human being. A far future humanity is described that will be divided into two groups: a good group that follows the white path and an evil group that follows the black path. "During that state (the Venus state) a special cosmic body splits off that contains all the beings who have resisted evolution, a "irredeemable moon," so to speak, which now moves toward an evolution, the character of which no expression can be found because it is too dissimilar to anything that man can experience on earth. The evolved humankind, however, advances in a completely spiritualized existence." In this passage, the final objective meaning is given to the unforgivable sin against the Holy Spirit.

The seeds for the future are already sown in our present time. We can be filled with gratitude and trust that at the same time through Anthroposophy the possibility has been given to lead the development of these seeds in the right direction.

9

About Rudolf Steiner's Concept of Four Kinds of Etheric Forces

Summary

It is suggested that nature, even lifeless nature, is governed by four lawful types of order, which are cognized by four types of thought processes. Four types of "etheric formative forces" are manifest in these orders and in these thought processes. These four types of formative forces are equated with Rudolf Steiner's four types of etheric formative forces. Examples of these four types are given. They form a hierarchy in which each type depends on the previous one and the fourth type is intrinsically the last one.

It is further suggested that students be taught natural science in four rounds corresponding to these four types of order, in order to replace the widespread attitude of antipathy against science, as well as the dogmatic submission to an "absolute scientific authority," by a free and productive attitude. Especially the first and the fourth types of laws and relationships should not be omitted, as they help the student in growing towards a sense for freedom and a free relation into the world, and toward a sense for the dignity and uniqueness of the human being as a member of the fourth kingdom of nature, the human kingdom.

Introduction

In the first essay the discussion is about why today there is so little understanding of the Holy Spirit. In the second essay the meaning of the Holy Spirit for the human being is described. In the third essay I will try to paint a picture of how the meaning developed over the course of time.

The present study aims at clarification of this problem. The results should be particularly relevant for science teachers.

Physical Forces and Etheric Formative Forces

When I hold a heavy stone in my hand, I have to exert my muscles to prevent the stone from falling to the ground. We say, I have to exert a force upward. We imply thereby that we prevent the manifestation of the force of gravity, the falling of the stone. I cancel this manifestation by holding the stone. We generalize this experience by stating: *A physical force is an agency whose manifestation I can cancel by exerting my muscles, my will, in a certain way.*

In the above example, I become aware of the force of gravity primarily through my exertion to cancel it, to prevent it from manifesting itself by the falling movement of the stone. Likewise, wherever we would have to exert our will through our muscles to prevent a change in the state of motion or rest of a body (or of a system of bodies) we say that a physical force is present, whose manifestation is cancelled by our effort. Without our effort this force would manifest itself by a change in the state of motion or rest of the body (or the system). In the absence of a physical force the state of motion or rest of a body (or system of bodies) remains unchanged. (We will not enter here into the well known details of defining an inertial reference system with the help of the "fixed" stars.)

From this starting point, scientists have traveled a long way to develop methods of measuring forces quantitatively. But we should remember that the true starting point of it all is the sensation of human muscular exertion, applied so as to cancel, the change in the state of motion or rest of a body (or system of bodies). All physical forces can be described by indicating what muscular exertion would be required to cancel their effect. Methods have even been developed to measure very small forces, too small for our coarse muscular sensation; and very large forces, too large to be canceled by the muscular exertion of one man. Thus one has come to know forces of gravity, pressure, elasticity, electromagnetism, friction, and many other physical forces.

At one time some scientists believed that living entities differed from lifeless objects through the presence of a special *physical* force in living entities, which was held to be absent in the lifeless world. They called it the life force. However, extensive research showed that no phenomena could be found in living organisms manifesting in the movements or rest of particles, other than those known in the lifeless world. Consequently, the idea of a special "life force" was abandoned. It was recognized that physical forces work in living organisms just as in the lifeless world. The difference between living and lifeless objects must be grasped in other ways than through the working of physical forces.

Rudolf Steiner agrees emphatically with this rejection of a special physical force in living organisms. His concept of etheric formative forces is not at all similar to the concept of "life force," described above, and should not be confused with this rightly abandoned concept. Such confusion can easily arise because Steiner's etheric formative forces manifest almost exclusively in living organisms. However, much insight can be gained by studying their manifestations in the lifeless world where manifestations can also be found. Etheric formative forces are not of the nature of a physical "life force." It follows that etheric formative forces are not physical forces at all. It is essential to understand that the qualifier "etheric" or "formative" gives to the word "force" a meaning that lies *outside* the domain of all forces of the physical sciences, in the sense in which the word force is understood there. Then, what is an etheric formative force, and how does it manifest?

In order to arrive at an answer to this question, let us consider an idealized system, consisting of a multitude of spherical grains of sand, which have a variety of colors and are spread out on a frictionless horizontal surface. The system is in "indifferent equilibrium." It takes no physical force to move a grain horizontally or to exchange places with a nearby grain. Now suppose an artist arranges the grains of sand so that a picture emerges, a beautiful landscape. No physical force is needed to accomplish this. Later, someone rearranges the grains randomly. They now show no picture at all. Again no physical force is needed. Yet, now we have *"chaos."*

The agency by which the grains of colored sand are arranged so as to form a definite picture is not a physical force. We shall call it a "formative force." In this example the formative force was due to a human artist. If, however, such an arrangement were to come about without immediate human organizing activity we shall call the organizing agent an "etheric formative force." Here nature herself takes on the role of artist. And we, who behold such a work of art of nature, must develop a sense of artistic perception to recognize it.

Etheric formative forces manifest by creating a certain order or pattern, which is an image of something else. This may be the reason why students of Steiner, whenever they attempted to demonstrate etheric formative forces, developed systems capable of many states of the same (free) energy, with which an image-like result could be obtained. Pfeiffer's copper chloride crystallizations, L. Kolisko's capillary dynamics patterns, and W. Schwenk's falling drop analysis, all have this picture aspect in common. We are here reminded of a statement by Steiner: "To understand nature where she works artistically we cannot suffice with mere logic; we must develop artistic perception."[1]

The First Kind of Etheric Formative Force[2]

From the characterization of etheric formative forces, given so far, it follows that these forces manifest in various kinds of order, without involving physical forces. Here we must inquire how we perceive order.

Let us assume we study some domain of phenomena. What is given at the start is a multitude of sense perceptions. Before these pure sense perceptions are permeated by our organizing thinking mind we face pure chaos.[3] It is important to realize that without this thinking activity we cannot recognize any order. With this activity, we often succeed in discovering an order in the phenomena. Thus discovered, such an order is objectively present in the phenomena, and subjectively[4] present in our understanding mind. We cannot find an order in nature that is not there, as little as we can pour water from a pitcher that has none in it. Thus when we discover order in phenomena, the etheric formative force which expresses itself in this order works both objectively in the phenomena *and* subjectively in our mind. Sometimes, based on past efforts and experience, we discover an order very fast, almost instantaneously, but we should not overlook this organizing activity of our mind that finds order in the perceptual chaos.

We inquire: What is the first, most primitive kind of ordering that our mind can perform in the perceptive chaos of phenomena? It is the recognition or isolation of one or more primary qualities. All further research in a domain of phenomena is based on the recognition of some first basic quality or qualities. Only *after* the existence or presence of these basic qualities is established can their relations be determined.

The ordering agent responsible for this very first step away from chaos we call an etheric formative force of the first kind, and we equate this formative force with what Rudolf Steiner called the warmth ether.

Examples of Etheric Formative Forces of the First Kind — A Classical Example

Let us consider the sum-total of all perceptual impressions of the whole world. To begin with, no order at all is perceptible in this totality. Even the distinction of "existent" and "non-existent" has not yet been introduced, nor the distinction of "earlier" and "later," i.e., the idea of time. We experience complete chaos. For modern man this is a bewildering experience. It is useful to try to experience this chaos, by quieting our mind.

Consider from this viewpoint the Gospel of Saint John. Its author wished to have as a starting point a most primeval ordering principle, which our mind can discern in this chaotic world. This very first ordering principle itself lies of necessity beyond this chaos, beyond time, beyond the distinction of existence and non-existence. When the very first ordering principle works, time begins, and existence becomes discernible from non-existence. Saint John calls this most primeval ordering principle the "Logos," which is Greek for the "Word."

On this basis we can recognize one aspect of meaning in his opening statement: "In the beginning was the Word ... and the Word was divine..." All entities that became bearers of existence (i.e., all "things") could be distinguished by means of It from the non-existent. In that sense, they were "made by It," whereas without It no thing could become existent. In other words, Saint John's starting point is "In the beginning," that is, when time became distinct from timeless chaos, there was a divine principle, the "Word," which imparted existence to all entities that became existent, all that became the world of "things," bearers of the quality of "existence." Nothing could become existent unless existence was imparted to it by the "Word."

The idea of the Logos as first ordering principle was not new with Saint John. In fact it was well known in his time and can be traced back to ancient Greek philosophers, in particular to Heraclitus of Ephesus, that Saint John used this Greek approach because he saw as one of his tasks "to transplant into the world of Hellenic culture a revelation originally given through Judaism."[5]

Thus the opening words of Saint John's gospel can be interpreted as an attempt to penetrate to the most primary, most encompassing ordering principle[6] that enables us to lift all "things" out of cosmic chaos as well as out of perceptual chaos. In the mental process that leads to the recognition of this primeval universal ordering principle, this "divine Word," works an etheric formative force of the first kind, the warmth ether.

We shall now turn to three easier examples, which deal with domains smaller than the whole world and with qualities more easily grasped than existence and non-existence. Nevertheless, each example will illustrate a process of a first step of ordering away from chaos, hence a working of a formative force of the first kind, of the warmth ether.

Crystals

Consider the domain of forms of all naturally occurring solid objects. We face a *chaos* of forms. As a first ordering quality we conceive of forms bounded by planes. Such forms we will call crystal forms. And we notice that in the perceptual world, in the chaos of forms, such crystal forms do indeed occur.

The basic quality "to be bounded by planes" is a manifestation of an etheric formative force of the first kind, which we recognize both in the conceptual world and in the perceptual world. This formative force underlies the idea of a "form bounded by planes" in our mind as well as the forms of "bodies bounded by planes" in the perceptual outer world. I equate this formative force to Rudolf Steiner's warmth ether force.

Chemical Elements

Consider the domain of all chemical substances. We face a *chaos of kinds of substances*. As a first ordering quality we conceive of substances that cannot be decomposed into other chemical substances by means of any chemical or physical process (I exclude radioactive or nuclear decompositions). We distinguish these from all other substances that can be decomposed in the most multifarious ways by chemical or physical treatment. The non-decomposable substances we call (chemical) elements. And we notice that in the perceptual world of substances such elements do indeed occur.

The basic quality of being "non-decomposable" is the manifestation of an etheric force of the first kind, which we recognize both in the conceptual world and in the perceptual world. This formative force underlies the idea of "non-decomposable substance" in our mind as well as the chemical elements in the perceptual world. I equate this formative force again with the warmth ether force.

The Paths of Planets

Consider the domain of all paths of the planets of our solar system. As seen from the earth *these paths appear very irregular and chaotic*. Astronomers tried to find some order in this chaos. As long as one clung to the geocentric view no simple ordering principle could be found. However, when the sun was taken as a center of reference the path of each planet was found to lie in a plane with the sun. The mental process which led astronomers to consider the sun as a center of reference for the description of the paths of planets is again a manifestation of the warmth ether force. This formative force is manifest in the idea of a sun-related planetary path in our mind as well as in the actual planetary paths in the perceptual world.

Conventionally, in each of these three examples certain physical forces are considered to be the causes of the order observed. There is no conflict with what is said here about the underlying etheric forces, just as there is no conflict with the idea that the same phenomena are ruled by the "laws of nature."

The Second Kind of Etheric Formative Force.

The second kind of etheric formative force is manifest in *relations that exist between primal qualities,* both in the perceptual world and in our mind as we come to know these relations conceptually. It follows that this second kind of ordering forces can only manifest when the primal qualities are established by the first kind of ordering forces, the warmth ether forces. I equate the second kind of etheric formative forces with what Rudolf Steiner called the light ether forces. How do these forces manifest themselves in practice? In general, relations between the primary qualities are amenable to measurement. They can be expressed by means of measurable *continuous* variables $x_1, x_2, \ldots x_n$. The relation(s) can usually be brought into the form

$$F(x_1, x_2, \ldots x_n) = c \text{ (a constant)} \quad (1)$$

The variables $x_1, x_2, \ldots x_n$ define an n-dimensional space, in which this equation can be imaged as an (n-1)-dimensional (hyper-)surface of some sort. We take the existence of the measurable continuous variables and their relations of the form (1), as well as the geometric figures which are the images of these equations, as manifestations of the light ether forces.

An especially important class of relations has time (t) as one of the variables, say $x_n = t$. The relations can then often be brought into the form

$$F'(x_1, x_2, \ldots x_n{-}1) = f(t) \quad (2)$$

This equation can be imaged geometrically as a continuously metamorphosing (n-2)-dimensional hypersurface in an (n-1)-dimensional space. Thus the concept of metamorphosis as a continuously changing order in time belongs to the light ether forces.

When Plato said "God geometrizes" he may have wanted to express an aspect of order in the world that can be represented geometrically, and this belongs to the order of the light ether forces.

Examples of Etheric Formative Forces of the Second Kind — A Classic Example

Goethe's idea of metamorphosis belongs to the order of the light ether forces. For it wishes to express—usually in images—continuous variations in time (or a similar variable) of forms which can be described by relations of continuous variables, $(x_1, x_2, \ldots x_n{-}1)$. Though Goethe and Goetheanists usually do not formulate their ideas mathematically, their ideas permit such a formulation, albeit that the number of variables required for such a formulation may be very large.

Consider for example Goethe's idea of the "primeval plant" (*Urpflanze*). Goethe describes this idea as being in a process of continuous transformation in his mind, passing through such plant forms as may be found in nature and through other plant forms, which, though not occurring in nature at this time, are possible, i.e., may be found at some future time.

The transformations of this constantly metamorphosing picture of the primeval plant are not arbitrary. The images must remain within the plant-domain. That means precisely that some function must remain constant, thus expressing the constant plant character.

Admittedly, I am not aware that anyone has tried to specify the undoubtedly very large number of continuous variables $x_1, \ldots x_n$, which taken together could describe each momentary state of the idea of the primeval plant. My point is that the "something" that enables us to decide whether a proposed transformation, applied to one plant form, produces another possible plant form, rather than a form that is no longer a possible plant. This "something" is an etheric formative force of the second kind, i.e., of the light ether. It is a matter of logic that the same formative light ether force must underlie all plant formations in nature.

The First Law of Crystallography

Consider a multitude of crystals of one substance, for example quartz. No two of them have precisely the same form. Yet, they are similar in some way. The similarity may be described by noting that they can all be reduced to the same form, by moving their planes parallel inward or outward without changing their orientation. This can be expressed more simply as: "The angles between corresponding pairs of planes are constant, i.e., the same for crystals of the same substance." This is the famous "law of constant angles," the first law of crystallography. This law expresses a formative force of the light ether.

The First Laws of Chemistry

Consider the mass x_0 of a quantity of any chemical compound. And let the masses of the chemical elements into which it may be decomposed by $x_1 \ldots x_n$. Two fundamental Laws of chemistry relate these measurable continuous variables. The first one is the famous "law of constant proportions:"

$$\frac{x_k}{x_0} = C_k \quad (k = 1, 2, \ldots n) \quad (3)$$

Here C_k is one of n constants, characteristic for the given compound.

The second law is the "law of conservation of matter:"

$$\sum_{n} \frac{x_k}{x_0} = \sum_{n} C_k = 1 \quad (4)$$

These two laws express formative principles which belong to the domain of the light ether forces.

The same mass ratios apply when forming a compound from the elements. Thus, when x_1 gram of Hydrogen and x_2 gram of Oxygen combine to form x_0 gram of water, one has empirically:

$$\frac{x_1}{x_0} = 0.11190 = C_1 \text{ and } \frac{x_2}{x_0} = 0.88810 = C_2 \quad (C_1 + C_2 = 1)$$

The same constants are valid when water is decomposed into hydrogen and oxygen.

Planetary Paths — Kepler's First and Second Laws

As discussed earlier, each planet travels in a plane containing the sun. To describe the actual path of a planet we choose plane polar coordinates. Following the exposition that leads to equation (1) we define x_1 = the distance from the sun to the planet, and x_2 m the angle of the radius from the sun to the planet with the radius from the sun to the perihelion. These measurable continuous variables are related by two empirical laws. The first Law can be expressed in the form (1) thus:

$$x_1(1 + e \cos x_2) = C \text{ (a constant characteristic for each planet).}$$

This formula expresses the geometric fact that the path of the planet has the shape of an ellipse with eccentricity e and with the sun in one of its focal points.[7] This is the famous first law of Kepler.

The second law involves time (t). In terms of equation (2) it can be written in form:

$$\int_0^{x_2} x_1^2 \, dx_2 = k(t-t_0)$$

(k is a constant characteristic for each planet).

This equation expresses the geometric fact that the radius from the sun to the planet sweeps out equal areas in equal times. This is the famous second Law of Kepler. Underlying both laws are again formative principles of the light ether. With these examples I hope to have explained sufficiently what kind of order may be seen as the expression of the light ether forces, both in nature and in our thoughts about nature. We note that all of the examples in this section on formative forces of the second kind rest on the foundation of the formative forces of the first kind. For the formative forces of the first kind provide the existence of all planets, crystals, chemical elements, and planar planetary paths, while the formative forces of the second kind provide information about a more detailed ordering within each of these domains.

The Third Kind of Etheric Formative Forces

Nature makes no jumps in the domain of the formative forces of the second kind, the light ether forces. The opposite is true in the domain of the formative forces of the third kind. Here we are concerned with measurable variables that can take only discrete values, which can be imaged on the domain of integers. The thought processes that lead to the discovery of relations of this kind are manifestations of formative principles of the third kind. They differ in an essential way from manifestations of the formative forces of the second kind. Rudolf Steiner states that it is difficult to find a suitable name for the formative forces of the third kind. He calls them sometimes forces of the chemical ether, the sound or tone ether, the astral ether, the cosmic forming force, the number ether. The designation "number ether" seems to me to be the most universally applicable one.

Systems ordered by the number ether are composed of parts that can be enumerated. This feature gives to the parts a certain degree of independence, of "thing-character." Yet, they are parts of a higher unity, often called the "spectrum," like the organs of an organism.

Examples of Etheric Formative Forces of the Third Kind — A Classical Example.

Pythagorean triangles are defined as right triangles whose ratios of sides can be expressed by integers. Well known examples are the triangles a:b:c =

3:4:5 and a:b:c = 5:12:13. An infinite number of such triangles exists.[8] Pythagoras was particularly sensitive to the manifestations of the number ether. Not only did this lead him to the study of properties of numbers and of the above-mentioned triangles, it also led him to the study of harmonious musical tones by means of the monochord. He found that the ratios of the string lengths of the monochord for harmonious tones could be expressed by integers. He also searched for laws governing the circulation of the planets in terms of integer ratios. This search was much later taken up again, with partial success, by Kepler and others (see below). However, when Pythagoras discovered the existence of right triangles whose ratios of sides a:b:c could NOT be represented by integers, he made the transition from the number ether to the light ether.

The First Law of Crystallography

Consider the angles between various pairs of planes of one crystal. These angles take only definite values, which are ruled by the "law of rational indices." I do not wish to discuss here the precise formulation of this law. What matters is that this law expresses the relations of the angles by means of (small) integers. Thus, the law of rational indices expresses a formative principle of the number ether.

The Second Law of Crystallography

Different chemical compounds may consist of the same elements. For example, both water and hydrogen peroxide consist of hydrogen and oxygen only. The famous "law of multiple proportions" expresses the double ratio of two constants of two such compounds as the ratio of two (small) integers: $C'_k : C'_l / C''_k : C''_l = (p : q)_{kl}$. (The constants C have been defined above and the primes refer to one compound, the double primes to the other compound). Thus, with C' for water and C'' for peroxide we have empirically: $C'_H = 0.11190$ and C'_O or 0.88810, and $C''_H = 0.059266$ and $C''_O = 0.940734$. These constants represent the mass fractions of hydrogen and oxygen in each compound. The double ratio is: $C'_H : C'_O / C''_H : C''_O = 2.00000$.

It is customary to formulate the law of multiple proportions in a different way, with the aid of atom models. Here I wished to formulate it in terms of the directly measurable masses of the various substances. The entire formula chemistry can be built up from these immediately measurable masses (as was done historically). The pedagogical value of following this procedure, rather than the customary one, will be briefly commented on in the last section of this paper.

The Order of the Planets in our Solar System

The space of our solar system is not filled merely with a continuum of gas. Rather, matter is concentrated in planetary bodies, which circulate at definite distances from the sun. Astronomers have felt since ancient times that the (mean) radii (r) of the planetary orbits must form a sequence of lawfully organized numbers, representing an order that pervades the solar system.

Various functions (r(n)) have been proposed to express the mean radii as a function of the ordinal numbers n = 1, 2, 3, ... etc., of the planets.[9] All of these functions indicate that a reasonable fit can be obtained only if one counts for n = 5 one planet in the asteroid belt between Mars (n = 4) and Jupiter (n = 6). This is quite often taken as supportive evidence that the asteroids are the remains of a shattered former planet. But no mechanical explanation is known why the radii are as they are. Textbooks rarely mention this question, perhaps because they wish to focus only on what is understood in a mechanical sense.

With these examples, I hope to have clarified the kind of order that is a manifestation of the etheric formative force of the number ether. Of course, well-known explanations with customary scientific models exist for many of the examples given above. We should recognize that these are not in conflict with the primary recognition of the *kinds* of order described.

The Fourth (Last) Kind of Etheric Formative Forces

Up to this point we have explored three kinds of order in nature, which are grasped with three kinds of conceptual thoughts. We have interpreted these kinds of order as manifestations of the first three kinds of etheric formative forces, namely, the warmth ether, the light ether, and the number ether. From the examples, it is clear that the second kind of order presupposes the first, and the third kind of order presupposes the second. We shall also see that the fourth kind will presuppose the third, but in a different way, for the fourth kind of order will lead to an endpoint, just as the first kind of order is the very first beginning as one emerges from the orderless chaos.

The first three kinds of order cover a certain domain of perceptions in which they are valid. The fourth kind of order applies only to a domain that has shrunk to one single entity. In other words, this fourth kind of order breaks out of the character of more or less general validity of the first three kinds of order. The formative forces that manifest in this fourth kind of order I equate with Rudolf Steiner's life ether forces. These forces form what is unique, what occurs only once, what is individualized, what is unpredictable. What is thus formed is not reproducible. With this kind of order we reach the very end of ordering, and thereby we reach also the limits of conventional science that demands reproducibility, and we transcend these limits. When we survey the four "kingdoms of nature," we find that the mineral kingdom is permeated by a high degree of reproducibility, the plant kingdom already shows some features of individuality, mingled with a great deal of reproducibility. This trend is carried further in the animal kingdom, where the process of individualization has gone further than in the plant kingdom. Finally, in the human kingdom each individual human being has a completely unique "I," which gives to his life an absolutely unique stamp, even though this is superimposed on a physical, etheric, and astral body that are governed mainly by orders of the lower kinds.

In anthroposophic terms, the first kind of order in nature, the warmth ether, is created by the hierarchy of the Thrones; the second kind of order, the light ether, by the hierarchy of the Kyriotetes; the third kind of order, the number ether, by the hierarchy of the Dynameis; and the fourth kind of order, the life ether, by the hierarchy of the Exusiai or Elohim. It would lead beyond the scope of this essay to pursue this line of thought further.

Because our culture and our science climate is strongly permeated with an urge toward reproducible order, one will have to expect much antagonism for any endeavor, such as anthroposophy, which includes in its cognitional horizon the unique, non-reproducible, unpredictable. Yet, the dignity of man depends on his uniqueness.

Examples of Etheric Formative Forces of the Fourth Kind — A Classical Example

In ancient times the concept of time was rooted in the fact that we experience cyclic processes: the cycle of the year, of the day, of our breathing and heart beat, etc. Even in ancient Greek times the revolutions of the stars and planets were described as circles carrying other circles, etc. And it was believed that the affairs of man on the earth were governed by these cosmic cycling processes, and hence were also cyclic in nature. The life outlook that results from such a view of time can be summarized by the saying, "There is nothing new under the sun."

A thoroughly revolutionizing concept of time was introduced about 600 B.C. by Heraclitus, the great initiate and king of Ephesus, who recognized the uniqueness of every moment of time, so that nothing is reproducible in the strict sense of the word. He expressed this in one of his often quoted sayings: "You cannot swim twice in the same wave (or river)." This idea is formed by life ether forces.

Ideal Crystals and Real Crystals

Accurate observations reveal that crystals, as we know them in nature, or as they are made artificially, are not bounded exactly by planes. Examination under the electron microscope shows spiral-shaped terraces. These are the result of faults in the crystal lattice, so called dislocations. Can one produce a crystal without such dislocations? Thermodynamic considerations prove that it is impossible to make such an "ideal crystal." Any "real crystal" is permeated by an array of dislocations, which influence some physical properties of the crystal very strongly, and other properties in the minor or hardly detectable way. These dislocations are located differently in each individual crystal in an unpredictable manner.

If one disregards the sub-microscopic deviations from the plane form of the surface, and measures very precisely the angles between corresponding pairs of planes in several crystals of the same substance, then one finds that the angles are not exactly constant. Discrepancies of the order of magnitude of minutes of arc are observed. Hence both the law of constant angles and the law of rational indices are also only approximately satisfied. Thus, precise observation transcends the model of the "ideal crystal," which would satisfy the basic laws of crystallography exactly. We come to realize that every single crystal carries within itself traces of its growth and of its history like a kind of memory. Workers in the diamond industry have of course known since a long time that each diamond is individually different.

True, the science of crystals is able to explain, and in many cases to control, those phenomena that are caused by dislocations. But there remains a residue of individual properties of each crystal which is neither predictable nor reproducible. Observations and thoughts that pertain to this residue are manifestations of the formative forces of the life ether.

Ideal and Real Chemical Compounds

The law of constant proportions is not exactly satisfied when elements combine to form a compound. According to thermodynamics, a slight excess of one component or another is possible. In the case of compounds of metals (alloys) the deviations can be considerable, but also water, H_2O, has in reality always a slight excess of either hydrogen or oxygen. Nowhere has absolutely precise H_2O ever been seen. Relative to such an "ideal compound" any "real compound" carries all sorts of "impurities" in varying amounts. These influence some of the properties of the real substance, sometimes considerably.

Historically, the basic laws of empirical chemistry, as expressed earlier in this essay, led to finding the characteristic masses of each element that would be the units for chemical reactions, and from there to the hypotheses of atoms and molecules and the concept of valence. The discovery of the law of multiple proportions then led to a refinement and broadening of the concepts of valence and chemical bonding, with their electronic images. When teaching chemistry it is good to follow the same sequence, rather than to start with the present day model. If this is done, it will be easier to understand how the concept of a molecule is broadened by the idea—now current in solid state physics—that a crystal is a macro-molecule that carries with it individual characteristics, connected with its dislocations. Continuing this line of thought, one could consider a living cell as a macromolecule. While the crystal-macromolecule is a rather fixed entity (if we disregard deformations), which is not too difficult to survey, the inner configuration of the cell-macromolecule constantly changes. This is much more difficult to survey conceptually. From here one could take a further step and consider a living being, such as the human body, as a constantly metamorphosing macro-macromolecule, and still further even the whole earth could be considered in this way. It is clear, however, that the concept of a molecule becomes less and less applicable as one deals with larger and larger systems, for it was introduced for small systems.

Eventually one reaches a limit where the concept of a molecule becomes useless for one's understanding of the system considered. From the standpoint of the molecular concept, the behavior of the system becomes more and more unsurveyable and unpredictable the larger the system is. In this sense, such large systems transcend the domain of validity of the molecular concept.

When one reaches the stage where real substances become so complicated that they develop individual characteristics, one transcends in an essential way the domain where the concept of the "ideal chemical substance" is valid. Such "real substances" may even carry with them their history as a kind of (structural) memory. Magnetic hysteresis is an example of such a memory, inelastic hysteresis is another example. Carrying this idea further, it becomes conceivable that two samples of the "same substance" prepared in "exactly the same way" by two different individuals may show individual differences in some respects. Rudolf Steiner pointed repeatedly to this possibility as something that may be expected to be discovered in the future.

Whenever we reach a situation where the concepts of the first three kinds of order are transcended in a way that leads to individualization, unpredictability, uniqueness, we have manifestations of the fourth kind of etheric formative force, the life ether. As noted earlier, the appearance of such manifestations, or even the thought thereof, arouses antagonistic feelings in the minds of those who want to deny the possibility of non-reproducibility (other than on the basis of pure chance) in the world, or at least in what we can know about the world.

The Real Paths of Planets

When one studies celestial mechanics more carefully, one also reaches the limits of applicability of the customary descriptions of planetary orbits and their predictability, for every planetary orbit is exposed to "perturbations." The effects of some of these perturbations can be calculated. These usually result in an orbit that has the shape of a slightly deformed ellipse whose major axis slowly precesses. However, there also exist perturbations that are in principle unpredictable. In most cases these are very small. But it is important to realize that they set a limit to the calculability and predictability of the paths of the planets, especially if one wishes to apply such calculations over large intervals of time.

We can point to various sources of such unpredictable perturbations, for example, the eruptions of protuberances on the sun, irregular visits of bodies flying into our solar systems from outer space, and irregular mass shifts on the earth and on other planets, such as volcanic eruptions. Even each breath changes slightly the course of all planets. Thus the laws of celestial mechanics reach limits of applicability. By these kinds of unpredictable perturbations each revolution of each planet becomes a unique non-repeatable event. This uniqueness feature is again a manifestation of the life ether.

General Remarks

The last three examples show how materialistic models, consistently applied, can reach limits of applicability. Ideas and situations that reveal such limits are manifestations of the life ether. There seems to exist often a kind of complementarity between the orders of the first three ethers and orders of the fourth one. Where orders of the first three kinds become so complicated that they lose their predictive power, one enters often into a new world which can be described simply in terms of properties of the fourth kind, and vice versa. Perhaps it is useful to refer here to an example that Rudolf Steiner often used: the phenomenon of "the slap in the face (*Ohrfeige*)." From the materialistic viewpoint a slap involves an immeasurably complicated analysis of neurological processes, processes of metabolic chemistry, and physical-chemical processes of senses and muscles. Psychologically, it can be described and understood quite simply.

I hope that these examples will suffice to explain the meaning of the four kinds of order, the four kinds of etheric formative forces, and why the fourth one is logically the last kind of order possible in this series.

Educational Aspects of the Four Kinds of Etheric Formative Forces: A Major Problem in Science Education

Conventional science education often results in a negative attitude towards science, which may take the form of a lack of interest in science, an aversion toward science, sometimes bordering on fear, of antipathy against natural science, which is seen as the bringer of deadening, unhealthy, and destructive influences, and of an outlook that denies human dignity and morality.

The opposite attitude is also a danger. Namely, the satisfaction of individual curiosity at the expense of causing suffering in the world, the belief that through science, as conventionally understood, all problems can and will eventually be solved, and the belief in "science" as an absolute authority, that is, the deification of science.

These problems all lie in the domain of human feelings, which have come about as a result of exposure of the human soul to science in a way that does not take account of the fact that science can be either alive or dead in human minds.

The human soul has an innate need to connect itself with the world by developing fruitful insight, access to truth about the world order. If science teaching is seen as a way toward truth about the world then it must become inwardly alive. This implies that the several stages of this way must be attuned to human soul life. Only if this is adhered to will the truths, to which we aspire through our scientific pursuits, make us free.

In the following section, suggestions are given how this may be achieved without engendering the above-mentioned negative feelings. The effectiveness of these suggestions cannot be proved in the usual sense. They are merely based on my lifelong observation of students' and other people's attitudes toward science and science teaching under different conditions.

Suggestions about Science Teaching

Science teaching can proceed in four rounds, and I suggest that this is a good way. In the first round, the student is only presented with aspects of order of the first, qualitative kind. No measurement. No theory. Such qualitative aspects or facts are, for example, straight or curved, warm or cold, fast or slow, moving or stationary, etc. Also leaf and flower and seed and root, stone and crystal, crystal, plant, animal and man, solids, liquids, gasses, and their transformations, friction, fracture, drop formation, cloud formations, etc., etc. An important domain of such qualities, which is often neglected, is concerned with area, rotation and mirroring. If aspects of the first order are presented in the right way, they will evoke feelings of amazement and wonder, which form the essential soul soil upon which scientific knowledge can later grow in such a way that it becomes the student's own insight. If the first round is contaminated with conceptual models, or neglected completely, then a feeling of estrangement from the world of science results, which often grows into a feeling of antipathy against science. Such feelings are very widespread today, and I see lack of appreciation of the proper conditions of the first round as their cause.

In the second round, the students, usually slightly older, will become involved in measurements and other aspects of order of the second kind. This should lead to feelings of trust in the world order, and happiness about one's understanding. In this round it is important to avoid introducing theoretical models, but rather to let the results of measurements and their direct relations speak.

In the third round, one can bring in relations of the third kind. These will then awaken a feeling for the harmony and wisdom of the universe. It adds to the happiness of these feelings if now theoretical models are introduced.

Conventional teaching often over-emphasizes the "problem solving" aspect, which belongs to the second and third round. This engenders a feeling of losing the forest because of the trees. There should be a balance between problem solving on the one hand and creating questions or allowing questions to develop in the student's mind on the other.

Finally, in the fourth round, one should bring in relations of the fourth kind, which lead to an appreciation of the limits of applicability of what has been learned so far. Thereby the student is given the means to avoid (or overcome) dogmatic attitudes of determinism and materialism. The sense for true freedom is awakened and supported.

Not all domains have these four stages; sometimes only two or three are realized in the world. It is then stimulating to speculate how in the future perhaps the four stages might be completed.

If one avoids the fourth round one breeds "true believers in the absolute authority of science." If one brings the viewpoints of the fourth kind, after the first three kinds have been thoroughly absorbed, one will open the way for understanding and dealing effectively with such problems as how freedom is compatible with the lawful order of nature, how the etheric is compatible with the physical, and many other "enigmas." Above all, science and the pursuit of knowledge can then be felt as a dignified human activity, which, in regard to the conventional three kingdoms of nature, minerals, plants, and animals, elevates the human being to a fourth kingdom of nature. In this fourth kingdom, the individualized order of the fourth kind can hold sway.

Notes

(Note: the most recent editions of earlier translations have been added when possible)

1. Mission of Rudolf Steiner

1 Kraljevec was located at that time within the Austrian empire. Presently it is in Croatia.
2 *The Last Address*, given by Rudolf Steiner, Rudolf Steiner Press, London, 1967; also in *Karmic Relationships*, Vol. IV, Rudolf Steiner Press, London, 1997.
3 *The Michael Mystery*, St. George Publications, Spring Valley, NY, 1984.
4 Rudolf Steiner, *The Archangel Michael*, Anthroposophic Press, Hudson, NY, 1994, Appendix.
5 *A Christian Rosenkreutz Anthology*, ed. Paul M. Allen, Rudolf Steiner Publications, Blauvelt, NY, 1974.
6 Rudolf Steiner, *The Secret Stream*, Anthroposophic Press, Great Barrington, MA, 2000.
7 Rudolf Steiner, *The Course of My Life*, trans. O. D. Wannamaker, Anthroposophic Press, NY, 1951, p. 12. (See *Autobiography. Chapters in the Course of My Life*, trans. revised by Rita Stebbing, SteinerBooks, Great Barrington, MA, 2006).
8 In those days, gathering and selling medicinal herbs required a state license based on passing a state board exam.
9 We owe knowledge of the identity of Felix to research by the Rev. Emil Bock, published in German in Rudolf Steiner, *Studien zu seinem Lebensgaitg und Lebenswerk*, Verlag Freies Geistesleben, Stuttgart, 1961. It was Felix Koguzki (born in Vienna on August 1, 1833, and died in Trumau, 1909). Rudolf Steiner memorialized him in 1910 in his first Mystery Play as Felix Balde.
10 When Rudolf Steiner visited Edouard Schuré in the Alsatian village of Barr, he wrote (at Schuré's request) an autobiographical sketch known as the "Barr document." Only through this document do we know about Rudolf Steiner's contact with the "Master." The Barr document can be found in *Rudolf Steiner/Marie Steiner-von Sivers: Briefwechsel und Dokumente 1901-1925* (GA 262), pp. 7-21. In English: *Correspondence and Documents 1901-1925* (CW 262), Anthroposophic Press, Hudson, NY, 1988.
11 *Correspondence and Documents 1901-1925*, Letter of January 9, 1905.

2. Essays on Rudolf Steiner's *Philosophy of Spiritual Activity*

1 *The Riddles of Philosophy*, SteinerBooks, Great Barrington, MA, 2009.
2 The author modified and improved his translations. The verse was changed in 2000 as follows.

At the turning point of time
Came the cosmic spirit-light
Into the earthly stream of being.

Night darkness
Had reached its power's end;
Light, bright as day,
Rayed forth in human souls;

Light
That gives warmth
To simple hearts of shepherds;

Light
That enlightens
The wise heads of kings;

Light divine,
Christ-Sun,

Give warmth to our hearts;
Enlighten our heads,

That good may become
What from our hearts
We are founding,
What from our heads
We shall guide
With our purposeful willing.

3. About Your Relation to Rudolf Steiner

1 Edouard Schuré, *The Great Initiates*, St. George Books, West Nyack, NY, 1961.
2 Rudolf Steiner, *Knowledge of the Higher Worlds and its Attainment*, Anthroposophic Press, Spring Valley, NY, 1983, p. 4. (Also translated as *How to Know Higher Worlds*, Anthroposophic Press, Hudson, NY, 1994).

3   C. S. Lewis, *The Four Loves*, Chapter IV, Harcourt Brace Jovanovich, Inc., NY, 1960.
4   a. W. E. Leonard, *Gilgamesh, A Rendering in Free Rhythms*, The Viking Press, NY, 1934.
    b. N. K. Sanders, *The Epic of Gilgamesh*, Penguin Books Inc., Baltimore, MD, 1972.
    c. John Gardner and John Maier, *Gilgamesh*, Alfred Knopf, NY, 1984.
5   Rudolf Steiner, *The Course of My Life*, Anthroposophic Press, NY, 1951, pp. 64-74, esp. p. 67. (See also *Autobiography*).
6   F.W. Zeylmans van Emmichoven, essay in "Rudolf Steiner, Recollections by Some of his Pupils," *The Golden Blade*, London, 1958 (The translation given in this chapter has been revised by the present author so as to correspond more accurately to the German original.).
7   Rudolf Steiner, *The Last Address, Dornach, 28 September, 1924*, Rudolf Steiner Publishing Co., London, 1967.
8   Rudolf Steiner, see reference 2 above, p. 18.
9   Ibid. p. 115.
10 Ibid p. 9.
11 Ibid. pp. XIII, XIV.
12 Ibid. pp. XIII, XIV.
13 Rudolf Steiner, *The Calendar of the Soul*, trans. Ruth and Hans Pusch, Anthroposophic Press, Spring Valley, NY, 1982, second revised edition 1988.
14 a. Christian Morgenstern, *Gedichte*, R. Piper & Co., Munchen, 1961, p. 267.
    b. M. von Beheim—Schwarzbach, *Christian Morgenstern*, Rowohlt Taschenbuch Verlag, Reinbeck bei Hamburg, 1964, pp. 122, 123.
15 Arnold Freeman and Charles Waterman, eds, Rudolf Steiner, "Recollections by Some of his Pupils," *The Golden Blade*, London, 1958.
16 G. Wachsmuth, *The Life and Work of Rudolf Steiner*, Whittier Books, Inc., NY, 1955, p. 564.
17 Rudolf Steiner, *The Soul's Probation*, Scene Five, Steiner Book Centre, Toronto, 1973, pp. 53-57.
18 What do the terms "spiritual moon sphere" and "spiritual sun sphere" mean? Anthroposophy distinguishes several levels of consciousness. First, there is the waking consciousness of human earthly life. By an inner development a higher form of consciousness can be achieved, a pictorial super-wakefulness with full consciousness of self. This form of consciousness also holds sway for a time after death. It offers some insight into the workings of forces of the spiritual world. It is called the consciousness of the (spiritual) "moon sphere."

It is felt as a spherical space, bounded more or less by the orbit of the moon around the earth.

19 A still higher stage of development, as well as a later phase of life after death, leads to a consciousness that reveals spiritual beings, among whom the human being lives as a spiritual being. Here everything is imbued with a moral quality, an intent of will. This is called the consciousness of the (spiritual) "sun sphere." It is experienced as a more or less spherical "space," extending throughout the solar system, especially the geocentric space containing the orbits of the inner planets. There are still higher forms of consciousness, which lead, however, beyond the pale of the present discussion.

20 Rudolf Steiner, *The Philosophy of Freedom*, Anthroposophic Press, Spring Valley, NY, 1964. (Also translated as *Intuitive Thinking as a Spiritual Path*, Steiner-Books/Anthroposophic Press, Great Barrington, MA, 1995 and *The Philosophy of Spiritual Activity*, SteinerBooks, Great Barrington, MA, 2007).

21 Each of the fairies' gifts is expressed in German by a three-word merger: "Lebenshoffnungstrank;" "Lebensglaubensstarke;" and "Lebensliebesstrahlen," which may be translated approximately as hope, faith, and love. The German language allows such multiple word mergers; in English this cannot be done. To express concepts referring to the spiritual sun sphere, Steiner often uses three-word mergers, while mergers of two words often point to the spiritual moon sphere.

22 The time for one revolution of the vernal equinox with respect to the fixed stars of the zodiac—associated with the precession of the earth axis—was called by the ancients a "Platonic Year," and set at 25,920 years. The rise and decline of a culture was considered to last one-twelfth of this, one "Platonic Month," or 2,160 years.

23 a. Rudolf Steiner, *Briefe*, Volume I, Selbstverlag Marie Steiner, Dornach, 1948, p. 34.
b. Emil Bock, *Rudolf Steiner, Studien zu seinem Lebensgang*, Verlag Freies Geistesleben, Stuttgart, 1961, pp. 37-38.

24 The formulation given here differs slightly from the one given by E. Bock in reference 23. It was given thus by Dr. Walter Johannes Stein in a public lecture in the hall of Pulchri Studio in The Hague, Holland, in the early thirties, at which the writer was present.

25 Rudolf Steiner, *The Foundation Stone*, Rudolf Steiner Press, London, 1996.

26 Rudolf Steiner, *Four Mystery Plays*, Steiner Book Centre, Toronto, 1973.

27 Rudolf Steiner, *The Soul's Awakening*, Scene Five, "The Spirit Realm," Steiner Book Centre, Toronto, 1973, p. 83.

28 Steiner coins here the German word "erstrahlen," for which no English

equivalent exists, by making use of the German prefix "er," which usually indicates an activity which begins, where before there was none, a becoming rather than a state of being. Thus "erstrahlen" means to become radiant, to light up radiantly.

29 Rudolf Steiner, *The Soul's Probation*, Scene One, Steiner Book Centre, Toronto, 1973, p. 21.

30 Rudolf Steiner, *Truth-Wrought Words and other Verses*, Anthroposophic Press, Spring Valley, NY, 1979, pp. 76, 77 (The translation given here is by the present author.).

31 The contrast and opposition between the forces connected with the sun sphere and the moon sphere comes to expression in numerous places in Steiner's work, for example, in the first scene of the first mystery play, where professor Capesius reports about some of the (to him) incomprehensible utterances of the recluse Felix Balde: "He speaks of sun-born beings that dwell within the stones / Of moon-dark demons who constantly disturb their work."

4. Meditation — An Introduction

1 Biographical Material on Rudolf Steiner in English:
   a. R. Steiner, *Autobiography*, SteinerBooks, Great Barrington, MA, 2006.
   b. G. Wachsmuth, *The Life and Work of Rudolf Steiner*, Garber Communications.
   c. F. Rittelmeyer, *Rudolf Steiner Enters my Life*, The Christian Community Press.
   d. "Recollections of Some of Rudolf Steiner's Pupils," *The Golden Blade*, London, 1958.
   e. A. P. Shepherd, *A Scientist of the Invisible*, Hodder & Stoughton, 1954.
   f. A. Steffen, *Meetings with Rudolf Steiner*, Verlag fuer schoene Wissenschaften, Dornach, 1961.
   g. O. D. Wannamaker, *Rudolf Steiner, An Introduction to His Life and Thought*, Anthroposophic Press, Hudson, NY, 1941.
   h. F. McKnight, *Rudolf Steiner and Anthroposophy*, Anthroposophical Society in America, NY, 1967.
   i. Frans Carlgren, *Rudolf Steiner and Anthroposophy*, Goetheanum, Dornach, 1990.

2 Literature on Meditation and Self-Development.
   a. R. Steiner, *How to Know Higher Worlds*, Anthroposophic Press, Great Barrington, MA, 1994.
   b. R. Steiner, *Theosophy*, Chapter. 4, Anthroposophic Press, Hudson, NY, 1994.

    c. R. Steiner, *An Outline of Esoteric Science*, Chapter 5, Anthroposophic Press, Hudson, NY, 1997.
    d. F. Rittelmeyer, *Meditation*, The Christian Community Press, London, 1948.
    e. R. Steiner, "Practical Training in Thought," in *Anthroposophy in Everyday Life,* Anthroposophic Press/SteinerBooks, Great Barrington, MA, 1995.
    f. R. Steiner, *Stages of Higher Knowledge*, SteinerBooks, Great Barrington, MA, 2009.
    g. R. Steiner, *A Way of Self-Knowledge and the Threshold of the Spiritual World*, SteinerBooks, Great Barrington, MA, 2006.
    h. R. Steiner, *The Life of the Soul,* Rudolf Steiner Press, London.
    i. R. Steiner, *The Portal of Initiation*, Garber Communications.
    j. A. Freeman, *Meditation under the Guidance of Rudolf Steiner*, Rudolf Steiner Press, London.
    k. A. Freeman, *What R. Steiner Says Concerning Initiation and Meditation*, Rudolf Steiner Press, London, 1964.

3 R. Steiner, *Guidance in Esoteric Training*, Rudolf Steiner Press, Sussex, UK, 2001.

4 For basic source material for such exercises see ref. 2 a, b, c, e, f, g, j, and R. Steiner, *Verses and Meditations*, Rudolf Steiner Press, London, 1972, and R. Steiner, *The Calendar of the Soul,* Anthroposophic Press, 2009.

5 R. Steiner, *How to Know Higher Worlds*, p. 17, Anthroposophic Press, 1994.

5. Meditation According to Rudolf Steiner

1 Rudolf Steiner, *Knowledge of the Higher Worlds and its Attainment*, Anthroposophic Press, Spring Valley and Hudson, NY, 1983. (See also *How to Know Higher Worlds*).
    p. XIII, "I trust I have here succeeded in emphasizing more strongly that for one seeking spiritual schooling in accord with present spiritual conditions an absolutely direct relation to the objective spiritual world is of far greater importance than a relation to the personality of a teacher.
    p. 9. "It must be emphasized that higher knowledge is not concerned with the veneration of persons but with the veneration of truth and knowledge."

2 Pythagoras, one of the great Greek philosophers, was born on the island of Samos about 580 B.C. and died at Metapontium in Italy about 500 B.C. During the early part of his life he traveled extensively in the Middle East, including Egypt, thereby receiving initiations from several Mystery Schools. Later he founded the famous school in Croton (S. Italy), whose students and

alumni, the "Pythagoreans," adhered to a clean code of ethics and brotherhood. The school developed new ideas and insights mainly in mathematics, astronomy, and the physics of music, all based on the importance attributed to numbers.

3   The letter was written from Munich during a lecture trip through Germany on January 9, 1905, and is published in GA 262, pp. 47-49. The critical sentences follow here in translation: "Not a day passes in which the Masters do not clearly sound the warning: 'Be careful, think of the immaturity of the time... It is your destiny that you must communicate high esoteric teachings!... I can tell you that if the Master had not succeeded in convincing me that notwithstanding all of this (difficulty) Theosophy is needed for our time, I would also *after* 1901 only have written philosophical books and spoken on literary and philosophical themes." (Translation by Ernst Katz).

4   Rudolf Steiner, *Verses and Meditations*, Anthroposophic Press, Hudson and Spring Valley, NY, 1972, pp. 34-35. (The English translation in the text is by the present author.) The German reads:

Warum strebt des Menschen
Suchende Seele
Nach Erkenntnis
Der hoheren Welten?
Weil jeder seeleentsprossene Buick
In die Sinneswelt
Zur sehnsuchtsvollen Frage wird
Nach dem Geistessein.

5   The two premises of Anthroposophy are stated, among other places, in Rudolf Steiner, *An Outline of Occult Science*, Chapter 1, Anthroposophic Press, Spring Valley and Hudson, NY, 1985, as follows: "First, behind the visible there exists an invisible world, concealed at the outset from the senses and the thinking bound up with the senses; and the second, it is possible for man, through the development of capacities slumbering within him, to penetrate into this hidden world." (See also *An Outline of Esoteric Science*).

6   Rudolf Steiner, *Knowledge of the Higher Worlds and its Attainment*, Anthroposophic Press, Spring Valley and Hudson, NY, 1983. (See also *How to Know Higher Worlds*).

7   Rudolf Steiner, *An Outline of Occult Science*, Anthroposophic Press, Spring Valley and Hudson, NY, 1985. (See also *An Outline of Esoteric Science*).

8   Rudolf Steiner, *Theosophy*, Anthroposophic Press, Hudson, NY, 1994.

9   Rudolf Steiner, *Four Mystery Plays*, Steiner Book Center, Toronto, 1973,

(CW 14), trans. Hans and Ruth Pusch. See the current edition, *Four Mystery Dramas,* SteinerBooks, Great Barrington, MA, 2001. The plays form a tetralogy as follows:
"The Portal of Initiation," written in 1910
"The Soul's Probation," written in 1911
"The Guardian of the Threshold," written in 1912
"The Soul's Awakening," written in 1913

Three more plays for following years were never written owing to the start of World War I in June 1914. Of other translations of these plays we mention: *Four Mystery Plays,* Anthroposophic Press, trans. Adam Bittleston; *The Portal of Initiation,* Rudolf Steiner Publications, Blauvelt, NY, 1989.

10 These lessons are available in German as GA 270, Vols. 1-4, and in English to members through the Anthroposophical Society.

11 Rudolf Steiner, *Verses and Meditations,* Anthroposophic Press, Spring Valley and Hudson, NY, 1972.

12 Rudolf Steiner, *Guidance in Esoteric Training* (CW 42/245), Rudolf Steiner Press, London, 1972.

13 Rudolf Steiner, *A Way of Self-Knowledge,* SteinerBooks, Great Barrington, MA, 2006.

14 Rudolf Steiner, *Zur Geschichte and aus den Inhalten der ersten Abteilung der Esoterischen Schule, 1904-1914* (GA 264), and *Rudolf Steiner, Zur Geschichte und aus den Inhalten der erkenntniskultischen Abteilung der Esoterischen Schule, 1904-1914* (GA 265). In English: *From the History and Contents of the First Section of the Esoteric School 1904-1914. Letters, Documents, and Lectures* (CW 264), SteinerBooks, Great Barrington, MA, 2010. *Freemasonry and Ritual Work. The Misraim Service* (CW 265), SteinerBooks, Great Barrington, MA, 2007).

15 Rudolf Steiner, *Die Schopferische Welt der Farbe,* a lecture given in Dornach, July 26, 1914, Philosophisch Anthroposophischer Verlag am Goetheanum, Dornach, 1931, with a color plate. No English translation of this lecture is available.

16 Rudolf Steiner, *Verses and Meditations,* Rudolf Steiner Press, London, 1975, p. 188. *Note:* The archive of the Rudolf Steiner Nachlass in Dornach has two forms of this verse which differ in eight details. Both are in Rudolf Steiner's own handwriting. It is known that he gave this verse to several older members, probably often with slight variations. The title "Prayer during Illness" ("Gebet für Kranke") does not occur in copies of the verse in the archive, and may have been added by the editors of *Verses and Meditations.* From the content of the verse itself it is clear that it is a prayer-meditation to ward off all the illness-causing influences to which all of us

are exposed daily in our civilization. The present translation is based on the second manuscript in the archive, which reads:

O Gottesgeist, erfülle mich,
Erfülle mich in meiner Seele;
Meiner Seele schenke Stärkekraft,
Stärkekraft auch meinem Herzen,
Meinem Herzen das dick sucht,
Sucht durch tiefe Sehnsucht,
Tiefe Sehnsucht nach Gesundheit,
Nach Gesundheit und Starkmut,
Starkmut der durch meine Glieder strömt,
Strömt wie edles Gottgeschenk,
Gottgeschenk von dir, O Gottesgeist,
O Gottesgeist erfülle mich!

O Godly Spirit, abide in me,
Abide in me within my soul,
To my soul grant strengthening force,
Strengthening force too for my heart,
For my heart that seeketh Thee,
Seeketh Thee with deepest longing,
Deepest longing for good health,
For good health and trust in life,
Trust in life which through my body streams,
Streams as a precious gift divine,
Gift divine from Thee, O godly spirit
O godly spirit, abide in me!

(Translation by Ernst Katz)

A study of the open secrets hidden in this verse, by the present author, has appeared in *Mededelingen van de Anthroposofische Vereniging in Nederland*, July/August 1992. [The study is included in this volume as "Cosmic Secrets of Rudolf Steiner's Health Verse."]

17 Rudolf Steiner, *Meditative Betrachtungen und Anleitungen zur Vertiefung der Heilkunst* (GA 316), lecture I of the Easter course, April 21, 1924.
18 Here follows the exact rendering of the question and answer in German (see p. 145 in ref. 17 above). The English translation in the text is by the present author.

Ein Teilnehmer: Was muss ich vom Ich aus tun, wenn ich eine Meditation mache?
Rudolf Steiner: Sie meinen vom Ich aus. Nun, nicht wahr, die Meditation besteht aus folgendem: Als moderner Mensch haben Sie jedem Satz gegenüber das Gefühl, Sie müssen ihn verstehen. Das ist eine ausgesprochene Tatigkeit des Ich in der gegenwartigen Inkarnation. Alles dasjenige, was Sie intellektuell tun, ist eine ausgesprochene Betatigung des Ich. Der Intellekt ist in der gegenwartigen Inkarnation, und alles übrige ist vom Ich zugedeckt, wirkt höchstens traumhaft hinauf und ist unbewusst. Dagegen heisst nun meditieren: ausschalten dieses intellektuelle Streben, und den Meditationsinhalt zunachst so nehmen, wie er gegeben ist, rein, ich möchte sagen, zunachst dem Wortlaut nach. So dass, wenn Sie intellektuell an den Meditationsinhalt herangehen, Sie, bevor Sie den Meditationsinhalt in sich aufnehemen, Ihr Ich in Bewegung bringen, denn Sie denken nach uber den Meditationsinhalt, Sie haben ihn ausser sich. Wenn Sie den Meditationsinhalt, einfach wie er gegeben ist, in Ihrem Bewusstsein anwesend sein lassen, gar nicht nachdenken, sondern im Bewusstsein anwesend sein lassen, dann arbeitet Ihnen nicht Ihr Ich aus der gegenwartigen Inkarnation, sondern das aus der vergangenen. Sie halten Stille den Intellekt; Sie versetzen sich einfach in den Wortinhalt, den Sie innerlich, nicht äusserlich, hören, als Wortinhalt hören, in das versetzen Sie sich, und indem Sie sich in das versetzen, arbeitet im Meditationsinhalt Ihr innerer Mensch, der nicht derjenige ist der gegenwartigen Inkarnation. Dadurch aber wird der Meditationsinhalt nicht zu etwas, was Sie verstehen sollen, sondern das real in Ihnen wirkt, und so real in Ihnen arbeitet dass Sie zuletzt gewahr werden, jetzt habe ich etwas erlebt, was ich früher nicht erleben konnte. Nehmen Sie einen einfachen Meditationsinhalt, den ich oftmals gegeben habe: "Weisheit lebt im Licht." Nun, nicht wahr, wenn man darüber nachdenkt kann man darüber furchtbar viel Gescheites, aber ebensoviel furchtbar Törichtes herausbekommen. Er ist da, um innerlich gehört zu werden: "Weisheit lebt im Licht." Da passt in Ihnen auf, wenn Sie ihn so innerlich hören, dasjenige, was da ist, nicht aus der gegenwärtigen Inkarnation, sondern dasjenige was Sie sich mitgebracht haben aus früheren Erdenleben. Und das denkt und das empfindet, und es leuchtet auf nach einiger Zeit in Ihnen etwas, was Sie früher nicht gewusst haben, was Sie auch nicht aus Ihrem eigenen Intellekt heraus denken können. Sie sind innerlich viel weiter als Ihr Intellekt ist. Der enthält nur einen kleinen Ausschnitt dessen, was da ist.

19 Ernst Katz, *Meditation, an Introduction*, Anthroposophic Press, Spring Valley and Hudson, NY, 1975. Xerox copies obtainable from the Rudolf Steiner Institute of the Great Lakes Area, 1923 Geddes Avenue, Ann Arbor, MI 48014.

20 This point was emphasized by John Alexandra in his lecture: "Spiritual Development in the Midst of the Modern World," on February 19, 1993. See the preface to this article.
21 Rudolf Steiner, *Knowledge of the Higher Worlds and its Attainment*, Anthroposophic Press, Spring Valley and Hudson, NY, 1983, p. 20, 21: "Should anyone really have no more time at his disposal, five minutes a day will suffice. It all depends on the manner in which these five minutes are spent." (See also *How to Know Higher Worlds*).
22 Ibid. ref. 9.
23 The concept of "Situation Meditation" is implicit in many places in Rudolf Steiner's work where meditation is described in such a way that words are being heard, not spoken, by the meditant; heard inwardly, not outwardly. Explicit mention of the concept and its application in particular settings can be found in reference 10, especially in lessons number 11 to 19.
24 Rudolf Steiner, *The Foundation Stone*, Rudolf Steiner Press, London, 1996.
 The Christmas Conference for the Founding of the General Anthroposophical Society 1923/1924 (CW 260), Anthroposophic Press, Hudson, NY, 1990.
 "Commentaries to the Foundation Stone Verse: F. W. Zeylmans van Emmichoven," *The Foundation Stone*, Rudolf Steiner Press, London, 1963.
 Arvia MacKaye Ege, *The Experience of the Christmas Foundation Meeting 1923*, Adonis Press, Hillsdale, NY, 1981.
 H. E. Weisshaar, *The Foundation Stone of the General Anthroposophical Society*, Rudolf Steiner Libraries & Publishing Co, Los Angeles, CA, 1951.
 Jorgen Smit, *Spiritual Development, Meditation in Daily Life*, Floris Books, Edinburgh, UK, 1991.
 Sergei Prokofieff, *Rudolf Steiner and the Founding of the New Mysteries*, Chapter 6, Temple Lodge/Rudolf Steiner Press, London, 1986.
 Ernst Katz, "About the Foundation Stone Verse," *Newsletter of the Anthroposophical Society in America*, Christmas, 1990.
 A large number of references dealing with various aspects of the verse could be added.
25 Rudolf Steiner, *Knowledge of the Higher Worlds and its Attainment*, Chapter 10, Anthroposophic Press, Spring Valley and Hudson, NY, 1983, pp. 253-259. (See also *How to Know Higher Worlds*). Rudolf Steiner, *An Outline of Occult Science,* Chapter 5, Anthroposophic Press, Spring Valley and Hudson, NY, 1985, pp. 341-345; 1983, Chapter 10, pp. 253-259. (See also *An Outline of Esoteric Science*).
26 The Gospel of Saint Luke, 24;13-32.
27 Rudolf Steiner, *Man and the World of Stars* (CW 219), lecture of December

3, 1922, "Man's Relation to the World of the Star," Anthroposophic Press, Spring Valley, NY, 1982, 1963, p. 38, 39.
28 See reference 20 above, in which the lecturer, John Alexandra, hinted very forcefully at the dangerous possibility that our civilization may drift further and further into an Ahrimanic future.
29 Rudolf Steiner, *Karmic Relationships,* Vol II (CW 236), lecture of May 9, 1924, Rudolf Steiner Press, London, 1990.
30 Rudolf Steiner, *World History in the Light of Anthroposophy* (CW 233), lecture of January 1, 1924, Rudolf Steiner Press, 1977.
31 Rudolf Steiner, *Truth Wrought Words and other Verses,* Anthroposophic Press, Spring Valley, NY, 1979. The English translation in the text is by the present author. German: *Wahrspruchworte, Richtspruchworte* (GA 40), 1978, pp. 74–77:

Ich möchte jeden Menschen
Aus des Kosmos' Geist entzünden,
Das er Flamme werde
Und feurig seines Wesens
Wesen entfalte.

Die Andern, sie möchten
Aus des Kosmos' Wasser nehmen,
Was die Flammen verlöscht
Und wässrig alles Wesen
Im Innern lähmt.

O Freude, wenn die Menschenflamme
Lodert, auch da, wo sie ruht!
O Bitternis, wenn das Menschending
Gebunden wird, da wo es regsam sein möchte.

32 Dr. Guenther Wachsmuth, Ph.D. was a young associate of Rudolf Steiner, who accompanied him through many years on many of his travels, and in 1923 became a member of the governing council (*Vorstand*) of the General Anthroposophical Society.

6. Cosmic Secrets in Rudolf Steiner's Health Verses

1 *Knowledge of the Higher Worlds and its Attainment,* Anthroposophical Press, New York, 1975, p. 116. (See also *How to Know Higher Worlds*).
2 Several formulations of this poem exist. The archives of the Rudolf Steiner Nachlassverwaltung in Dornach possess two manuscripts of this poem in Rudolf Steiner's own handwriting, which differ slightly from each other

in eight places. Moreover, some older members of the Anthroposophical Society possess variants with further slight differences. Rudolf Steiner had probably given these verses to several members, though not in identical form. The present essay is based on the second manuscript in the archives. Permission to use this manuscript is gratefully acknowledged. The translation presented in this essay was made by its author. The book *Verses and Meditations,* Anthroposophic Publishing Co., London, 1972, p. 188, uses a different German version, adds a title which was not given to it by Rudolf Steiner, omits translation of line 9 completely, and violates the structure of the poem in several places. Moreover, the steady trochaic rhythm of the German is lost. I have tried to avoid these pitfalls in the present work. The German version which I used is as follows:

O Gottesgeist, erfulle mich
Erfulle mich in meiner Seele,
Meiner Seele schenke Starkekraft,
Starkekraft auch meinem Herzen,
Meinem Herzen das dich sucht,
Sucht durch tiefe Sehnsucht,
Tiefe Sehnsucht nach Gesundheit,
Nach Gesundheit and Starkmut,
Starkmut der durch meine Glieder strömt,
Strömt wie edles Gottgeschenk,
Gottgeschenk von dir, o Gottesgeist,
O Gottesgeist, erfulle mich!

3   *Theosophy,* Anthroposophic Press, New York, 1971, p. 167.
4   *Theosophy,* Anthroposophic Press, New York, 1971, p. 158.
5   *Esoteric Lessons for the First Class Vol. I* (CW 270-1), Anthroposophical Society in Great Britain, Rudolf Steiner House, London, 1994, p. 57.
6   *The Spiritual Hierarchies: Their Reflection in the Physical World, Zodiac, Planets, Cosmos* (CW 110), Anthroposophic Press, New York, 1983, p. 74 ff. See also *Life between Death and Rebirth* (CW 140), 1975, p. 64 ff.
7   The members of the Supreme Court of Ancient Athens used to hold their meetings on the Areopagus, a holy mountain site northwest of the city, for which reason they were called Areopagites. When Saint Paul came to Athens in the first century he befriended one of the most respected Areopagites named Dionysius, with the result that Dionysius became the first Christian bishop of Athens. For centuries it was believed that Dionysius the Areopagite had written several books, one of which contains a treatise

that expounds the doctrine of the hierarchies. However, modern scholarship has proved that this treatise was written by a Dionysius in the fifth or sixth century. Of the life of this Dionysius virtually nothing is known. The literature refers to this author as the "pseudo-Dionysius." I assume that the doctrine about the hierarchies originated with the true Dionysius and was handed down from one generation to the next by oral tradition, by persons who, in each successive generation, assumed the name Dionysius. The practice of assuming the name of the founder of a doctrine was not uncommon in ancient esoteric groups. Finally the time came when the cherished wisdom was written down. In this case that happened in the fifth or sixth century by a person who assumed the name Dionysius, and whose identity is unknown. He attributed the authorship of his book to Dionysius the Areopagite. Regardless of who the true originator of this doctrine was, it has had a deep and lasting influence on Christian thought.

8 Rudolf Steiner coined the names "Spirits of Strength," "Spirits of Light," and "Spirits of Soul" for the three hierarchies. He used them only once, namely, in the publication of the "Foundation Stone Mantra" in the first issue of the members' supplement of the weekly *Das Goetheanum* of January 13, 1924 (Vol. I, No. 1). See *The Christmas Conference for the Founding of the General Anthroposophical Society 1923/1924*, p. 286; also plates XXI to XXIII and pp. 289-296, Anthroposophic Press, Hudson, NY, 1990.

9 These names, as well as most in the last column, are found in Rudolf Steiner's basic book *An Outline of Occult Science* (CW 13), Chapter IV, "Cosmic and Human Evolution." (See also *An Outline of Esoteric Science*).

10 The present author suggests that these names can provide further insight into the nature of these spiritual beings.

11 *The Spiritual Hierarchies: Their Reflection in the Physical World, Zodiac, Planets, Cosmos*, lecture of April 15, 1909, Anthroposophic Press, New York, 1983. See also Pauly, *Real Encyclopaedie der Classischen Altertumswissenschaft*, 1963, A-I, Drokenmuller Verlag, Stuttgart, Vol. 24 (27th half-volume), pp. 289-299.

12 *Wonders of the World, Ordeals of the Soul, Revelations of the Spirit* (CW 129), Rudolf Steiner Press, London, 1983, p. 78.

13 *The Inner Realities of Evolution* (CW 132), Anthroposophic Press, New York, 1953, p. 9. (See also *Inner Experiences of Evolution*, SteinerBooks, 2009).

14 *Knowledge of the Higher Worlds and its Attainment*, Anthroposophical Press, New York, 1975, p. 14. (See also *How to Know Higher Worlds*).

15 *The Inner Realities of Evolution*, Anthroposophic Press, New York, 1953, p. 27.

16 *The Inner Realities of Evolution*, Anthroposophic Press, New York, 1953, p. 61.

17 *The Soul's Probation*, Steiner Book Centre, Toronto, 1973, p. 21.

7. Thoughts about the Foundation Stone

1. Rudolf Steiner, *The Christmas Conference for the Foundation of the General Anthroposophical Society 1923/1924*. Anthroposophic Press, Hudson, NY, 1990.
2. *The American College Dictionary*, Random House, New York, 1964 edition.
3. F. W. Zeylmans van Emmichoven, *The Foundation Stone*, Temple Lodge/Rudolf Steiner Press, London, 2002.
4. Rudolf Steiner, *An Outline of Esoteric Science*, Anthroposophic Press, Hudson, NY, 1997.
5. Ibid. p. 374.
6. Rudolf Steiner, *How to Know Higher Worlds*, Anthroposophic Press, Hudson, NY, 1994, p. 204/5.

8. Contemplations on the Holy Spirit

No notes.

9. About Rudolf Steiner's Concept of Four Kinds of Etheric Forces

1. R. Steiner, "Was wollte das Goetheanum und was soil die Anthroposophie?," a lecture given in Basel, April 9, 1923, in GA 84, 1961, p. 40.
2. The conceptualizations in this section derive from Rudolf Steiner's *Philosophy of Spiritual Activity* and from his *Truth and Knowledge*, Rudolf Steiner Publications, West Nyack, NY, 1963.
3. R. Steiner, "Truth and Science" in *The Philosophy of Spiritual Activity*, Rudolf Steiner Publications, West Nyack, NY, 1963, p. 343: "For the world content as given is completely undefined. No part of it of its own accord can provide the occasion for setting it up as the starting point for bringing order into chaos."
4. Following a meaning given in *Webster's New World Dictionary*, Simon & Schuster, NY, "subjective" means here: "of or having to do with the perception or conception of a thing by the mind as opposed to its reality independent of the mind."
5. *Encyclopedia Britannica*, 1929 edition, Vol. 14, p. 335.
6. Abstractly, one may object here that "ordering" should be distinguished from "creating." However, at the stage of primal chaos where existence and non-existence are not yet distinct, the first ordering is of necessity identical with a calling into existence, that is, with creating. In other words, at this

primal stage ordering and creating are identical. Only thereafter can they be distinguished.

7   The semi-axes of the ellipse are $a = C(1-e^2)$ and $b = C(1-e^2)^{3/2}$.

8   Proof: Let p be any even integer and q any odd integer having no common factor with p. Then the identity $(p^2 + q^2)^2 = (p^2 - q^2) + (2pq)^2$ indicates the existence of a Pythagorean triangle with side ratios $a:b:c = |p^2 - q^2| : 2pq : (p^2 + q^2)$

The three integers on the right have no common factor. In this way an infinite series of Pythagorean triangles can be generated. For p=2, q=1 this yields a:b:c = 3:4:5, and for p=2, q=3, one has a:b:c = 5:12:13, etc.

9   One example of such a function is the well-known rule of Bode-Titus (ca. 1760), which relates the semi-major axes of the orbits to the ordinal number by means of a formula with three constants. The agreement with reality is shown in the table. The relation fails for Neptune and Pluto (which had not yet been discovered at the time).

"$(a(n)/a_{earth} - c)$" = p^n/q. For c = 0.2, p = 1.9 and q = 9 we have for $a(n)/a_{earth}$:

	n=1	n=2	n=3	n=4	n=5	n=6	n=7	n=8	n=9	n=10
	Mercury	Venus	Earth	Mars	Asteroids	Jupiter	Saturn	Uranus	Neptune	Pluto
Actual	0.39	0.72	1.0	1.52	-	5.20	9.54	19.2	30.1	39.5
Bode-Titus	0.41	0.60	0.96	1.65	2.95	5.43	10.15	19.1	36.2	68.4